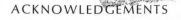

ACKNOWLEDGEMENTS

All the people in this book are real. In some cases I have changed peoples' names to protect their identity but many appear as themselves so I would like to thank everyone who, in one form or other, is mentioned here. Especial thanks to Dr Roger Woolger and William Bloom who have allowed me not only to quote their words but also to make substantial use of material from their books.

More personally I would like to thank Michael Morris, Sarah Leigh, Tony Edwards and Christy Mack for their encouragement. I owe particular thanks to my editors Rosemary Davidson and Marian McCarthy, and to the huge enthusiasm, imagination and energy of everyone at Bloomsbury. They are a truly extraordinary company.

Finally, I would like to thank my daughter Mez whose patience with me is eternal and miraculous.

To Robert
With thanks for your inspiration

CONTENTS

Prologue

I am blessed with wanton curiosity. I want to find out how to be absurdly happy every day. You know those people who always radiate cheerful optimism whatever is going on in their lives? Nauseating, aren't they? I want to become one of those.

I'm not talking about the ones who look cheerful but if you spend more than ten seconds with them you develop a suspicion that they are really intensely depressed. Nor the ones who are 'contented' (my ex-husband is a very 'contented' man). I'd choose despair over contentment every time. I want to find out how to live life completely, abundantly, joyfully, stupidly. This is my quest. Enlightenment.

I'm not doing too well so far.

I was the result of an affair in Paris. My father, apparently, was a Spanish diplomat and now you know as much about him as I do. I like to think Spanish blood gives me an air of exotic mystery. He gave me skin that tans easily in the sun and life itself, for which I thank him. But if you were cast to play his role in the film of my life your career wouldn't be going too well.

My mother was working as a bilingual secretary and, when he refused to marry her, she took off to America to ensure I could be the holder of a US passport and brought me back to England when I was six months old. I think her own mother was a little surprised as she hadn't mentioned my existence. She took my father's name and, although I have no legal right to it, it's been mine all my life. Makes me sound interesting, though, doesn't it?

But this isn't going to be one of those books where you get the entire story of the author's childhood. This is the condensed version. I lived at my grandmother's house and my mother was a weekend visitor. Grandmothers traditionally give you everything you want and mine was a great traditionalist. She let me know that the world spins, with me at its central axis, and that anything I want can be mine. By the time my mother took over when I was five I was already ruined. No one had ever said 'no' to me. It was an excellent start.

I was already promisingly noisy so my mother sent me to an academy of performing arts. You know those ghastly stage-school children? I was one of those. Grinning on TV, singing and dancing in theatres but totally hopeless with addition or subtraction. By the time I was a teenager the school was ninety-eight per cent female and even in those days the boys who wanted to study ballet dancing were not the kind the girls wanted to date. Outside school, I pitched tents and sang inspiring songs with the Girl Guides. I had also once seen a diagram of a penis in a biology class. I'd never actually talked to anyone who owned one.

But I was invincible, which was a good thing because when I was eighteen my mother died and when I was nineteen my grandmother wafted up after her. My relatives seem to have an inconsiderate preference for the next world. Mother, grand-mother, grandfather, aunts, uncles – even the father that I'd never met. When I finally traced him I found that he'd absconded to the higher spiritual spheres too. And my brothers and sisters were not even polite enough to have been born in the first place. It's very reassuring having spirits as family but they've never done much washing-up.

Of course I soon met a man and, with the huge experience of a nineteen-year-old, let him move into my house. I don't think he liked me much and I'm not sure I liked him, but somehow we didn't notice that at the time. He was a good-looking, sexy twenty-eight-year-old but he smoked a pipe, wore slippers and watched the cricket and I suddenly felt that I'd retired eighty years too soon. And he was certainly out of his depth with me. I couldn't cook, I couldn't do housework and, most wretched of all, I was interested in everything.

I started work as as actress. The summer was spent at the Edinburgh Festival appearing in serious drama at obscure venues. At Christmas I would appear in pantomimes; I can boast having played The Bean in *Jack and the Beanstalk* and Sharon in *Aladdin*. Some years I even had the occasional day of work between summer and Christmas. But in the intervening months I was required to become contented.

The man at home just wanted an easy life, to watch test matches undisturbed, and I was always wanting to do something. I would read a book and shout out, 'Wow! Listen to this!' I had – yet again – discovered an idea that changed everything. 'Mmm?' he would mumble, feigning interest and trying to tear his face away from England being thrashed by the West Indies. I would say: 'Herman Hesse says: 'Happiness is a how, not a what; a talent, not an object. Isn't that fascinating?' He would stare at me, wondering why I talked so much and whether I had any plans to make a meal sometime. I wasn't known for doing things like 'lunch' and 'dinner' – I put fruit in my mouth when I was hungry. He came from Yorkshire and expected something hot and dead on a plate at regular intervals.

I could never plan a day ahead and was usually rushing around like Tigger on ecstasy with some crazy scheme to help someone who didn't need helping. I had filled the house with lodgers to bring in money. These innocent souls usually came from far corners of the earth to find that I was to inflict language lessons on them and drag them off to sundry social events. The house was always in a state of chaos. I had it in my mind that people with tidy houses had too little to do and I remember most of my time was taken up trying to persuade the man in the slippers to do things against his wishes and to explore ideas he had no interest in. In all honesty I was trying to change him, but of course I didn't call it that. I think I might have called it 'getting him out of a rut' or even, although he was nine years my senior, 'helping him'.

You would think he would have had the sense to have left me. But he overrated his ability to cope. He married me. He had hoped, I think, that I might settle down a bit and develop a desire to do ironing, but it didn't work. It took him another five years before he found someone with whom he could enjoy simple contentment. He left me with a daughter aged two-and-a-half. Things were not going to plan.

I helped out at the local playgroup and taught my daughter and the other toddlers to sing and be noisy. I loved her to pieces, so much so that I wasn't interested in ninety-eight per cent of the acting roles I was offered. One day my agent gave up – 'I'm sorry, Isabel, but you are just not marketable any more. You either want a thirteen-part period drama series for the BBC or nothing.' I'd have settled for the thirteen-part series but instead she offered nothing. 'You're impossible to find enough work for. I'm taking you off the books.'

So I was now a single parent, with no family, no money and no job, who stayed at home in the evenings. I was twenty-six. When my daughter started school I mooched around the house feeling utterly miserable. I knew I had to do something so I started sleeping as a full-time occupation. I was horribly stuck. People told me that change was inevitable. They lied. Things stayed the same. Months (or was it years?) went by.

I suppose I must have done the washing, as one does. And chatted to the postman, the milkman and the next-door neighbour. I mowed the lawn. I fed the cat. I even dusted. Lodgers moved in and moved out. I had finally become one of those people with a tidy house.

I didn't have the courage to go back to acting with no agent and I couldn't do anything else. Years of stage school meant I was only qualified to tap dance. So I waited – I'm not sure what for. The days flew from the calendar rudely mocking me. 'Another day is gone'; 'Another day is gone.' I'd glare at it and ask 'So?' Nothing was changing. Aside from Divine intervention, which I was not banking on, I looked doomed to be drawing my pension soon.

Then Divine intervention came. A smiling, self-aware friend from drama school popped back into my life to inform me that I was going nowhere and that I needed to go on a course to sort my life out. Her career was going irritatingly well. She said I was 'stagnating'.

'You are one hundred per cent responsible for what happens in your life.' She smiled one of those I-use-Macleans type smiles. I did not make her a cup of decaffeinated coffee. I did not go on her course. I ignored her.

She bought me a tea towel with an irritating logo: 'Choose your rut carefully – you may be in it a long time'. She knew that instead of leaving the dishes on the drainer I had time to dry them. Still I ignored her. I thought that maybe going to university and acquiring a degree might be a good idea. Three years later I was better qualified and still stuck.

'You have the life you want because you created it,' Fiona continued, having paused only briefly during the three years to allow me to sit an exam. 'Come and do a seminar, it will help you to get your life back on track.'

A seminar about life? My resistance was huge. It was obviously a cult.

'The training isn't religious,' she insisted. I was running out of reasons not to go. University had been an interesting diversion, but hadn't helped. But the seminar was run by Americans. Clearly any set of ideas that comes out of California is deeply suspect. I didn't have to know what they were.

'Condemnation before examination?' She quipped. 'I thought better of you. And anyway, what do you have to lose?'

I couldn't think of anything. She was exhaustingly insistent.

'Isabel, take the Insight Seminar. If you don't like it you can always leave.'

So she won. Maybe they would have just one or two things to say that would be useful. I'd listen for those and ignore the rest. I was determined that I wasn't going to have some smiling American man with a blackboard telling me how to live my life. I had a degree now, after all. I could outwit these guys.

But the person who led my first ever seminar was a woman. And she didn't have a blackboard.

Phase One: Out of the Comfort Zone

They give you a label with your name written in large capitals and insist that you wear it. This had an unnerving effect because a total stranger walked up to me and said, 'So, you're Isabel?' And I was able to reply with complete assurance, 'Yes, and you are Tom.' Self-revelation is a wonderful thing.

I had arrived in a north London hotel to be shown into a large conference room with hideous carpet and hideous curtains. The overall effect was, well, hideous. I wondered what on earth I was about to be subjected to. There were about a hundred people of every conceivable age, size and class; elderly matriarchs and hippy-looking twenty-somethings, 'City gents' in suits, and suspicious bedraggled types who looked as though they could be relied on for a local source of something interesting. The good, the bad and the ugly – and they all wore name-badges. I'd heard that John Cleese, Janet Reger, Terence Stamp and Bernard Levin had taken the course, but the week I chose seemed to be conspicuously lacking in celebrities. Shame. I'd have been happy sitting next to Terence Stamp.

Rows of velour-padded chairs stood in front of a platform with a table and a dazzling display of flowers. Large boxes of pastel-coloured tissues had been placed on every flat surface and people stood round the back of the room smiling, rather smugly I thought, as if to say 'Ha ha, we know why these tissues are here.' Perhaps I could just leave now and think up something creative to say to Fiona?

On an overhead projector were the words 'Participate in Your Experience and Experience Your Participation'. I had another quick look round to confirm my suspicion that I was with a bunch of lonely sad people with no lives, and then I started to chat merrily to the victim on the chair next to mine. What exactly could they mean by the words on the screen? They wanted us to 'participate' as fully as possible and 'experience' the fact that we were doing that. That seemed fair enough to me. I didn't expect much from these Californian dudes but I was going to pay attention. I decided that if they had only one useful thing to say that could help me get my life together then I was going to make sure I didn't miss it.

A stunning, slim and sophisticated American woman in a silk suit entered. 'Welcome to Insight Seminars.' She smiled. Already I disliked her. 'So, have you had a look around?' she asked. 'You know they told you it was rude to stare? Well, we invite you to stare. Have a look at all the other people in here. They are a weird bunch, aren't they?' I was a step ahead, I'd already decided that. 'As you look around . . .' she smilingly continued, 'notice what decisions you are making about people . . . which ones look interesting and which ones don't . . .' I hadn't noticed any interesting ones. 'And then you might wonder what they might be thinking while they look at you.' Mmm. I was different from them anyway. I was only here to keep Fiona happy.

'So, let's see how many of you are here just to get some friend off your back.' Was this woman psychic? Everyone in the room raised their hand, including me. Laughter. At least they had a sense of humour. 'Now, let's look at some guidelines for the seminar.' A cute Indian in a suit stepped forward and changed the overhead-projector sheet. 'Use everything for your learning, upliftment and growth.' She had us repeat it like small children as a method of getting the information into our heads. Were we retarded as well as hopeless? Obviously. But I liked the first instruction, it made perfect sense to me. Then the second guideline: 'Look after yourself so you can look after others.' This seemed to be the wrong way round. I was sure I'd heard 'Love others as you love yourself'? Perhaps it was more logical to look after yourself first and then you are not too exhausted to look after those around you. Maybe this was more practical or maybe it was heretical or misguided or maybe it didn't make a huge amount of difference. In a rare moment of wisdom I decided not to get to my feet to debate the point.

She moved on to entertain us with stories about the exercises and games that were to make up our 'experiential learning' over the next couple of days. Then they gave us a chance to check out the other 'cult members', the smiling people who were standing around the edge of the room and not the victims on the chairs. One by one they came to a microphone: 'My name's Martin and I run a software company'; 'My name's Val and I'm a pianist'; 'My name's Paul and I'm a riding instructor'; 'My name's Emma and I'm a photographer'; 'My name's Steven and I'm a solicitor'. It wasn't Hollywood, but they all seemed fairly normal. Maybe they'd all been well brainwashed.

'People sometimes think we are here to brainwash you,' continued the psychic American. 'We are just here to present some ideas to you that we hope will be effective for your life. If you like them, use them, if you don't, fair enough.' It had to be more sinister than this. 'Other people think we are some kind of sinister cult.' Yes, yes! 'Cults usually have a religious leader who wants you to follow them,' she grinned. 'As you see, I'm taking this seminar – and I'm saying now, please don't follow me because I'm going back to America next week and my house is full enough. What with my husband, the children and the dog we are clean out of space.' I had to admit she didn't look like a cult leader. No orange gown or sandals anywhere in sight. She stood no chance of having me as a disciple.

The point of the 'use everything for your growth' command turned out to be that we could observe how we dealt with whatever they threw at us. She gave us some rules for the seminar and all those (not me, of course) who had a problem with rules were up on their feet complaining before she'd even had a chance to finish what she was saying. Due to a pledge of secrecy, I am unable to reveal all the rules to you but I can hint that drug addicts and alcoholics were probably looking round for the door. It didn't take long to realise that this was all part of the 'process' – our Achilles' heels were already beginning to hurt a little. We soon saw who had a problem with rules, lateness, money, talking through microphones, their parents, men, wo-men, or just other human beings. Those who had a problem with other human beings were to realise it before the first evening was over.

We had the first 'process'. Four sentences appeared on the wall from the overhead projector:

I'm willing to be open with you
I'm not willing to be open with you
I'm not sure if I'm willing to be open with you
I don't wish to say if I'm willing to be open with you

The exercise was to walk around the room and as we met a new person say one of the sentences to them. This was easy. I decided I was happy to be open with everyone and anyway I wouldn't want to hurt someone's feelings by saying that I didn't want to be open with them. So I just walked around the room, smiled at people and repeated 'I'm willing to be open with you' without really thinking about what I was doing.

Then she said, 'Please stop. Close your eyes. Now, when you continue this exercise I want you to consider whether there is a deeper level of honesty that you could go to . . . And continue.' I walked on and met some more faces. I found myself saying, 'I'm not sure if I'm willing to be open with you.' Then a man approached who looked very keen. I noted my sense of panic and decided to honour it – 'I'm not willing to be open with you,' I said. He looked crestfallen. 'I'm willing to be open with you.' He bravely tried not to look dejected. Then a strident-looking woman walked up to me. 'I'm not willing to be open with you,' she said. I thought, 'Well, she has a problem.' I contemplated my reply. 'I don't wish to say if I'm willing or not,' I said. But was that what I really felt or just a reaction? The sweetness of revenge? Then the exercise ended. I was glad. It hadn't been as easy as I'd thought.

We sat down and there was an opportunity for anyone who wanted to say anything about this experience to take the microphone. Hands shot up. 'I hated it when anyone said that they weren't willing to be open with me,' said a young girl of about twenty-five. She looked upset. I could see why the tissues might be needed later. She went on, 'I think I'm an open person and I like to be there for people so when people said that they couldn't be open with me I felt really hurt.'

'So you are mostly willing to be open with people?' The sophisticated American metamorphosed into a personification of empathy and understanding.

'Yes.'

'So if someone is not willing to be open with you, who is that about?'

'It's about them, I suppose.'

'Are you responsible for them?'

'No. Oh. Thank you.'

She sat down. We clapped to acknowledge her bravery. This talking-through-the-microphone thing they called 'sharing' – although why it couldn't be called 'speaking' I couldn't understand.

Another hand waved in the air.

'I felt guilty because when people said they were willing to be open with me I said the opposite. But it wasn't how I felt about them. At this moment in my life I'm not willing to be open with anyone.'

There was more to this than met the eye. I was already working out where this fitted into my life. The last 'boyfriend' who had sped through my life since Slipperman had left had only wanted friendship. He would ring every day, take me out for dinner and then put me on the train home. He would never come back and spend the night. Perhaps there was not something wrong with me after all? Perhaps it had also been something to do with him? Perhaps I was not the most undesirable woman in London?

The week progressed. It was all very clever. The 'sharing' thing was saying anything you wanted to, from 'My cat was sick this morning' to 'I'm planning to murder my lover'. No one was forced to speak but, as a group, we were all encouraged to 'share' at some point. The smiling American told us that public speaking is the third greatest fear for women after death and childbirth. For men apparently childbirth is the greatest fear, only then followed by death and public speaking. Of course, it's not a real statistic and she grinned broadly while telling us to make sure we didn't take her too seriously, but it did make the point to those who were feeling that they would rather die than take the microphone. I was feeling smug again. Childbirth I'd done already, and I'm resigned to the fact that all of us will die. But public speaking I love. Any chance to be the centre of attention and I'm there.

I wanted to 'share' about a real problem. Members of the opposite sex can always be relied on to provide those, don't you find? I did have one tiny problem with a man I was fond of who was married and lived on a different continent. He had dropped by once when I was stuck at home and stayed for seven days, just long enough for me to become totally infatuated with him before he took a taxi to a plane and flew away. I knew that projecting a load of unrealistic ideas on to someone unavailable who I never saw, and allowing him to do the same with me, wasn't exactly serving me. So I decided to stand up and talk about it. See what wise advice the lady with all the answers had. 'So you are obsessed with a married man?' she asked. 'Obsessed?! I didn't say "obsessed",' I grimaced, 'I just said that I think about him a lot.' But the point was made. It was true. It was time I left this particular 'dysfunction' alone and at least got myself a dysfunction that was single. No matter that he was the best-looking, hunky, appealing, tall and talented Hollywood film-set designer that I'd ever set my eyes on. No matter that when I met him I finally discovered the meaning of the phrase 'lust at first sight'. No matter that he phoned me regularly to tell me how much he loved me (and how much he loved his wife, he usually mentioned). He would have to go. I would have to be free. A photograph-and-letter-burning ceremony was called for.

Then they started on the 'comfort zone'. (Pay attention now!) She drew a stick figure on a flip chart to represent us. Then she drew a circle round it. 'This represents all the things that we are comfortable doing or being and outside the circle represents our expansion.' Er, yes? 'So you each have a different comfort zone and you each have a place where you start to feel uncomfortable at the thought of taking a risk.' My neighbour had reached hers already, I thought. She'd been trying to pluck up the courage to take the microphone for days and hadn't yet said a word. 'So every time you get to the edge of the comfort zone and start to feel uncomfortable – take a risk.' I wasn't just having to give up my happily dysfunctional habits, I was going to have to grow too? Slowly I stopped being cynical and started to waver between fear and excitement. My comfort zone had become smaller and smaller until I was a single parent who stayed at home. I had developed a habit of rarely going beyond the house.

Quite literally. How could I start to stretch out of this stuck zone and exercise courage? A few small things I'd like to do popped into my head: move house, get a new job, get a new relationship. That would do to start with.

The teaching was alarmingly clear but always with humour. One evening she told us a story. 'All through high school it had been my dream to see Europe', she began. 'I saved and saved and finally the big day came when I could begin my trip. London was the first stop and I was so excited. I flew to London and travelled to my hotel. But when I arrived at the hotel I found that my wallet had been taken from my bag. It had everything in it – passport, money for the whole trip, traveller's cheques, insurance, flight tickets and travel details, everything. I sat on the floor of my hotel and cried. I had to cancel the trip I had been looking forward to for so long.' She stopped and smiled. 'Don't I get any sympathy? Everyone say "Ahhhh".'

We obliged: 'Ahhhh.'

'That's a victim story. We all have them. I'd like you to take a partner and tell them one of yours.'

I turned to face an attractive blonde in a linen suit and a large amount of Chanel No 5. Her name-label informed me that her mother had chosen the name Charlotte-Anne. She looked at me encouragingly. I began. 'I took in a lodger as a favour to a friend last year. He was an actor who was working in a show in the West End. My friend was the director and was desperate to find a place for this actor to stay. I said I could put him up for the three weeks, no problem. I was really nice to him, but when this guy left he hired a van, stole everything he wanted from my house and disappeared. I went to the theatre to complain and they told me in no uncertain terms that they wouldn't do anything. My friend the director just said, "Oh dear, sorry". How's that?'

Charlotte-Anne told hers. 'I was walking down a street in

broad daylight last week and I had a gold watch that was worth £10,000 snatched off my wrist. Two guys just jumped on me, knocked me over and stole it. It was my late father's watch. I was devastated.' I sympathised appropriately. Then the American spoke.

'So, we are exploring the idea of being a little more accountable. I now want to add a couple of details about my story that I didn't tell you before. First of all, I knew it was stupid to carry all the money and all the vital documents in my wallet. But I ignored the warning voice inside my head that said, "Don't be dumb and put all this in the same place". Now, that warning is what we call a red flag.' She drew a red flag on a flip chart. 'I had a backpack and I thought when I was packing that it was probably a bad idea to put the wallet in the little pocket on the back that anyone could steal from. I could have put it round my waist or in the deeper part of the bag that couldn't be opened. That was my second red flag. I ignored it. When I got to the London Underground I saw about ten notices that said 'Beware of pickpockets' and I thought that maybe I should take my wallet out of the back pocket. I didn't.' A row of red flags were appearing. 'Finally, I noticed that the train was very crowded and I felt a number of people jostle me and bump up against me. The thought even crossed my mind "It would be really easy for someone to take my wallet in here".' Four red flags. 'You know what? When I got to the hotel and found my wallet had gone I was amazed.' We laughed. 'Now I'd like you to tell your stories again and add the details that you left out the first time.' We shuffled in our seats.

I began. 'I should tell you that my friend the director didn't actually ask me to put this actor up. I offered. And the director did tell me he had been thrown out of his previous room. I suppose that could have been seen as what she's calling a red flag?' My partner agreed that anyone not colour-blind could have spotted that one. 'And when I offered he actually advised against it, saying that he didn't know the actor too well and wasn't sure he was trustworthy. The truth I suppose is that I wanted to impress the director and help him out. When the guy moved in he didn't give me the rent he had offered and made one excuse after another, so I guess I should have done something immediately.' She was holding three fingers up by this time. 'I knew it was dumb to give him his own keys, but I did it anyway.' Four fingers. 'And when I went away for the weekend at the very time the show ended I thought, "If I go away this weekend he could do a runner and take anything of mine." Then when he did I was stunned. I suppose I could have been a little more accountable?' Amazingly she agreed. Her story seemed different though.

'Surely you were just attacked in broad daylight?'

'Yes. But there are a couple of details I didn't add.'

'There are?' This was fascinating.

'Firstly, of course I knew I shouldn't be wearing a watch that was so valuable both financially and emotionally. My mother had warned me that morning that it was very visible in the outfit I had on and actually asked, "Do you really want to take that?" So I suppose she waved a red flag at me. And I had already felt uncomfortable showing it so visibly so I'd ignored the voice in my own head.' She paused. 'I didn't mention that it was a very dangerous and deprived area of London that I was in when I was attacked, did I?'

'No', I smiled, 'you didn't mention that.'

'And when I said "broad daylight", it was actually dusk. I did see these two men standing doing nothing and looking at me. I thought they looked unsafe so I turned into a sweet-shop. While I was in there I said to myself, "Don't go down that road, turn back". But then I ignored this advice and told myself I was just being paranoid. I even thought about the watch . . . but I walked down the road anyway.' I had lost count of the red flags by now. 'It's interesting now that I think about it. I did sense the danger.' I thanked the watch-less Chanel-smelling Charlotte-Anne for being my partner.

The American started to explain. 'We are not saying that if you get run over it is your fault. This isn't about blaming ourselves. But we are saying that we can all have greater accountability and stop playing the victim in our lives so much. And we are saying that we need to be responsible for the way we respond to what happens to us. We are asking you to look at your 'response-ability'. She wrote the words on her flip chart just to make sure we all got the point.

I thought about my life. It was not my fault that my family had all died. It was no doubt half my fault that my marriage had ended and completely my fault that my agent had put my details in her recycling bin. However, I suppose the way that I responded to all this was up to me. Was I able to respond in a way that looked for opportunities for 'learning, upliftment and growth'? They were obviously quite clever, the mad Californians who had created this seminar.

Then they moved on to show us how we related to our fellow humans. I don't know how you feel about other people, but I used to think that the vast majority were a pretty hopeless bunch. Then there would be the odd one who I'd decide that I liked hugely and wanted to keep for ever. Mother Teresa says that we should look for 'the image of Christ' in a person and love that unique representation of the Divine. This is all very well in theory. But there are people who manage to obscure the image of God almost totally. The last place I expected to be given a lesson in how to look with Mother Teresa's eyes was in a hotel room in Belsize Park.

The exercise was simple. Everybody was to mingle around the room and this time we looked in each other's eyes and said, quite simply, 'The inner beauty I see in you is . . .' and then tell them the qualities that it was possible to discern just by looking at them. It was surprisingly easy. An overweight man with a spotty nose and an extreme case of BO stands in front of me. But instead of allowing myself to think, 'Why don't you get some exercise and wash more often?' I say to him, 'The inner beauty I see in you is . . .' and then I look at him. He is obviously spilling over with a desire to love and be loved. I can tell that he is loyal and hard-working and there is a sensitivity, a deep kindness. So I tell him all this, using the words they have given me. When I say, 'and I see that you have a deep desire to love and be loved' his eyes fill with tears. He has been told how to reply. They give the answer because the standard response would normally be, 'If you knew me better you wouldn't say all those nice things'. As if somehow our knowledge of our shortcomings cancels out our goodness. So, to ensure that we hear the good things, he is just to say 'I know'.

I moved around the room. People would say, 'The inner beauty I see in you is your huge energy, your zest for life, your love, your compassion' and I'd say 'I know' as if it was the most natural thing in the world. Outside a seminar room I would normally say 'thank you' if someone paid me a compliment. But even that can mean 'Thanks for your opinion but I don't agree'. To say 'I know' after someone speaks to you of your goodness is to say that everything they say is true and that you already understand that about yourself. After thirty or more people choosing to say they saw me as honest and warm I had to admit that maybe what they saw in me was really there. After a marriage which had become a study of my failings it was a relief to hear all these good things. I felt my honesty and warmth grow a little as a result of having been noticed and acknowledged.

The exercise had a second part. After speaking of the 'inner beauty' we then had to add 'and the way I experience you hiding that is . . .' Under normal circumstances these comments would count as negative but they didn't feel like that here. I walked up to a stiff-looking woman in formal business clothes. 'The inner beauty I see in you is your childlike quality and playfulness and the way I experience you hiding that is by keeping people at a distance and using your natural authority as a shield.' The woman looked surprised. The reply to give here had also been taught to us: 'Thank you for caring enough to share that with me'. The wording was obviously carefully considered. This second reply meant that my perceptions may or may not have been accurate. They may have been entirely my own projections but the listener heard them and thanked me for making them. If the information was accurate then it may be useful to her. But she did not in her answer have to tell me whether she thought I was right or not.

Then it was my turn. She looked at me carefully. 'The inner beauty I see in you is your caring and vulnerability,' she began. So far, so good. 'And the way I experience you hiding it is with a superiority and a level of arrogance that, although it is based on a genuine self-confidence, pushes many people away from you.' I stood and looked at her. I was speechless until I remembered what to say. 'Oh. Thank you for caring enough to share that with me.' I walked on to the next person, who said, 'The inner beauty I see in you is your softness and the way I experience you hiding it is with your confidence'. This, I think, is what is known as a 'rapid learning curve'! So people see me as arrogant? They couldn't see the vulnerability? Well, it seemed that they could, but that it was in spite of the way I appeared. They hadn't even been deafened by my incessant chatter. They had seen all this just by looking at me. This was something I'd not been aware of in my interactions with others.

Looking for inner beauty in people is a trick I practise in everyday life. With obnoxious petty authoritarians, for example. Occasionally I'll catch myself thinking 'This person is breathing too much air' and look at them again and think, 'The inner beauty I see in you is, er, that you just want to be loved and it's clear you don't know how to get that'. Then I'm nice to them, no matter how small-minded their behaviour.

They change instantly and become human beings. It's a good trick.

As the week went by people relaxed and began to talk about what was really important to them. It was very moving and the tissues began to get used up. 'Since my husband died, I've found that I just don't want to be alive any more.' 'My boyfriend is consistently unfaithful and I know I'm letting it destroy me. I should leave him.' 'I hate my father. I've always hated him but now he's an old man and I want to forgive him. I don't know how.' People began to talk about things they would normally only reveal to a lover or a well-qualified therapist. The advantage here is that no one is alone in the therapist's room. Each story mirrored the experience of others in the group. The American facilitator was highly trained with a seemingly miraculous ability to understand all problems, get to the core of them and then ask questions of the participant so that they found their own way forward. I felt privileged to watch her work.

A woman stood up to say she was unlovable. The facilitator asked the room, 'Does anyone feel closer to Joan now?' Nearly everyone raised their hands. Joan looked round the room timidly at a hundred pairs of eyes telling her that she was very loveable. It struck me that one of the main dangers of a therapy room is the patient thinking that their suffering is unique. In a room like this, no such delusion was possible. We all felt like a family after two days, all our struggles were so similar. I didn't know what these people did for a job but I knew how they felt about their lives. It was unreal, as I'd probably lose touch with most of them, but it was still heartening to see the level of support people had for each other.

They had lots of good games for us all to play. Another of my favourites was 'Ask for what you want'. So many people get frustrated in their work and relationships because they expect people to know what they want. We get annoyed when our fellow human beings are not psychic and don't understand us. They had a beautiful way to show us this. Half the room closed their eyes. The other half chose a partner. I opened my eyes and saw a smiling older woman sitting in front of me. I had to ask her for something I wanted.

'I'd like you to tell me about your life and I'd like to listen.'

'It would be a pleasure,' she said, and started on her story. I sat and listened, delighted by her candour. Then I closed my eyes again and when I opened them a tall, attractive, muscular footballer-type stood in front of me.

'I'd like a back massage,' I said.

'Sure' he smiled and pushed his thumbs into my grateful muscles. Five minutes' bliss. I liked this exercise. I thought I'd experiment with it. The next face in front of me wore a suit; he looked like a banker.

'I'd like you to give me fifty pounds,' I said. Unfortunately the instruction had also been given, 'You can say no or you can negotiate if you are not happy with what someone asks of you'. So he just said, 'No, I'm not prepared to do that. But here is ten.' And he took ten pounds out of his wallet and gave it to me. He never even asked what I wanted it for. This was a phrase I could make use of in my life. 'Ask for what you want.' Yes, an excellent idea.

They had more games to show you how good you are at risk-taking, or how you resist receiving support from others, or to remind you what the concept 'play' was all about. On Saturday night they put on dance music and we played kids' games and had a party. It's sad to watch a City-business-type who doesn't know how to play with his children because he has forgotten how to play himself. And watching someone rediscover their playfulness is like watching a miracle. Like that scene in *Hook* where the businessman Robin Williams remembers he is really Peter Pan and learns how to pretend again. Some shy souls who would never normally go to parties but who had agreed to complete the course stood and struggled a bit. Then you saw them give in and start to dance as if to say, 'I suppose if I really have to learn how to enjoy myself . . . I'd better do it.' Later on they would look as if they had climbed Everest. Victory was theirs as they 'stepped outside their comfort zone'. Better still, they had danced outside it.

Now, I don't mean everyone. Obviously there were some who stood around the edges, arms folded and eyes fixed to the carpet. No one was going to force them to have fun. But by this time I hoped they had at least realised that their suffering was self-inflicted. A woman in a wheelchair danced as if to bring home the point to everyone. She was having a great time. I threw myself around like a crazed nightclub dancer. It was very worrying. I was on Fiona's course and I was having fun.

By the last two days the resistance was gone and everyone was ready to learn whatever they could. One of the times that brought out the tears and the joy was the moment when they asked us to look at our feelings about our parents. It's amazing how many adults are still holding on to resentment about how someone else messed them up. They had a phrase: 'Everyone does the best they can with the knowledge and understanding and awareness that they have at the time.' The first time they put that on the wall a rather overweight businessman who was extremely red in the face shouted, 'Rubbish. My mother didn't love me the best she could.' People had such rage against their parents. I stood up.

'I'd like to say that it's true for me. Speaking as a mother, whatever long-term psychological damage I may or may not be inflicting on my daughter, I'd like to say that with the knowledge, awareness and understanding I have, I'm doing my best. Even if I'm laying a basis for a very well-qualified psychoanalyst to make a fortune in years to come, I'm not doing it on purpose. So will I be worthy of her compassion and forgiveness? I hope so.'

A woman stood up and said that she had been locked in a cupboard as a young child but she acknowledged that her mother had been a severely damaged woman coping the only way she knew how. She told us about hours spent locked in a tiny space shouting, 'Mummy, Mummy'. She wept. We all did.

People who had hated their own relatives for years made peace with them. Forgiveness stopped being a noble concept and became an experience. I thought about the people in my life who I resented. Had my ex-husband done the best he could with the knowledge and awareness and understanding that he'd had at the time he left me? Yes. And it had been brave of him to leave and to seek out a life for himself where he could be happier. I realised I had just had a good thought about my ex-husband. This seminar was miraculous. Either that or they had not only washed my brain, they had bleached it. Very worrying.

On the last day, when they had managed to cover practically every aspect of life in five days, the smiling American lady (who we were all in love with by now but still didn't want to follow home) said, 'You are going to write a letter to your best friend.' Those standing around the room who I was now prepared to refer to as 'volunteers' or 'assistants' gave out paper and pens. I hesitated, who was I to write to? Couldn't write to the gorgeous Adonis who I'd considered as my leading confidant until a week ago. Then the answer came, complete with Californian accent. 'And that, of course, is yourself.'

Uhh? Myself? Write a letter to myself? A penny dropped. This strange idea that you hear about 'learning to love yourself' in this 'New Age' actually had some basis in reality? I was to write a letter of appreciation to myself? I'd come here to do what the lady said. So, no matter how ridiculous this would have felt a week ago, I began. 'Dear Isabel, I'm just writing to let you know that I think you are a pretty OK sort of person. In fact there are a lot of things about you that I really admire. Your energy, your love of life and of people. Your gentle kindness. You really are an inspiring person to know. I understand you and all your good intentions, you just need keeping an eye on. And I want you to know that I'll never leave you (ha ha).'

I drew hearts and smiley faces on the envelope and handed it back to an assistant, now giving out pastel tissues to those who were so touched by the beauty of their own words that they had been moved to tears. As the course ended I had a hundred new friends, all amazing people. Either they had changed from the hopeless losers I'd met on day one or I had. But it was over. I could go home and go back to my old way of seeing people. I didn't want to consider the possibility of being nice to everyone all the time. Far too exhausting. It was bad enough that I was going to have to admit to Fiona that I'd enjoyed the course. Even that I wished it hadn't taken her three years to overcome my prejudices.

I rang her and through gritted teeth managed to say, 'I learned a lot but there was no guy that I wanted to go out with.' I had to complain about something. 'I see,' she said. It was mean of me not to tell her that I'd been very impressed but she was still happy. At least I'd stayed in the room all week. Now she could only wait and see if I'd apply any of what I'd learned.

When the letter I'd written to myself arrived in the post a few weeks later I felt warm all over as I read it. It wasn't just the nice things it said or the memory of the people in the room, but also the realisation that this course had introduced me to myself. I had been converted to what's called 'self-awareness'. I'd had such a good time I definitely wanted more of what I'd learned from these dudes, even if they were from California.

I smiled and wondered whether I was now brainwashed into a cult. Was this some weird and false religion, to be thinking about myself instead of thinking about others? I heard from nowhere the words of Christ, 'The kingdom of God is within you'. And I thought that, in some way which I had yet to fathom, all this did fit together.

Phase Two: T'ai Chi
and Optional Moral Decline

You're probably thinking these courses don't make any difference, aren't you? That people go off and do weird seminars and their lives stay exactly the same? Yup, they do. But just sometimes the poor sad people with no lives get so inspired they actually change something. I did.

I sold the rambling mansion my mother had bought and which I'd lived in for twenty years too long and bought a shoebox in Battersea. Insight had put me on the Battersea Park Road. I decided that if I wasn't going to work as an actress then TV production was a possible solution, and I persisted with this plan until I got myself a job as a researcher on a series about food. It was a start. I told the American Adonis that I'd end up like Miss Haversham and lust after him to the grave if he didn't stop phoning me and I added with a bravery that amazed me, 'So will you please stop phoning me?' I was so nauseatingly positive I even went to the dentist. That was enough change for anyone. I figured another long period of stagnation was called for. It was summertime and I anticipated the joys of becoming a total slob on a debauched holiday in France with my daughter, whose shoe-size was now the same as my own.

But the thing about this 'growing as a person' business is that you never know when an opportunity to learn something is going to turn up uninvited. As far as I can see, the only solution is to keep away from anyone who is going to encourage you to think about anything. If you feel any curiosity coming on, watch some cricket immediately. If you follow a desire to be completely joyful and love others fully there is no knowing where it might lead or when a learning opportunity may strike. Don't say I didn't warn you.

So there I was, feeling very smug and pleased with myself. My Froggy friends and their children, my daughter and I chugged through the Pyrenees in an old camper van and the sun was shining. I was dreaming of baguettes, too much cheese and ridiculous amounts of red wine – a week that I could regret on my return to Battersea.

We arrived at the perfect *gîte*. The mountains ascended on one side, the valley fell away on the other. There was just unspoiled beauty, ancient trees and a picture-postcard fat old man on a bicycle wobbling along and smiling at us. The kind of place that you never want to leave. But as we walked in we knew instantly that something was very wrong. The other guests were worryingly 'evolved' looking. Most were speaking German and wearing comfortable clothes and Birkenstocks. Everyone became excited when they heard us speaking French and the jovial Germans welcomed us warmly to the course. Course? What course? I didn't come here to be improved – just lead me to the wine cellar.

Then I saw a man in white – a gorgeously assured, lithe, beautiful and sensitive presence. He approached us and I answered 'yes' before I knew the question. Whatever course he was running he could put my name down. He fixed his eyes upon me and smiled enticingly. 'We 'ave a small problem [read with 'eavy French accent]; you may like to 'elp us. I am running a multi-lingual t'ai chi course zis week. We teach ze course in German and sen in French. Some of ze French speakers 'ave not come 'ere. We can offer you ze course *gratuitement*, as it ees already paid for. Would you like to join us?' The daughter sighed, but seemed very keen for her mother to sign up.

Would you say no to a free t'ai chi course? Did I want to relate my body to this journey of mine? Not really. I was quite happy reading the odd spiritual book and building up cellulite. The phrase 'mind, body, spirit' had always alarmed me. Do I really have to be fit to become enlightened?

Ze Frenchman suggested that 'ze bodi is veri important' and before I knew what was happening I had signed a piece of paper with German writing on. So somehow, at 6 a.m. the following morning (remember this was a holiday) I found myself in a queue for the lukewarm showers in order to get to the early-morning meditation session at 6.30. Someone else was actually singing. Aren't people who are cheerful in the morning just too much? '*La vie est belle!*' he sang. I discovered I'd left my soap in London.

Have you ever tried sitting still on the floor for half an hour? Forget the lotus position, or any cross-legged position, the sitting-on-a-special-stool position or the kneeling-with-bum-on-cushion position – here I am at 'not yet forty' and I'll be blowed if I can find any position that my body does not take as some perverse kind of practical joke after ten minutes.

I'm supposed to be thinking of the incoming breath. Becoming aware of the air passing in and out of my nostrils. I'm actually thinking, Ow! My back [leg, knee, bum or whatever] hurts. I realise that my body is a wreck and totally outside my area of love or concern. My muscles are so tight I can't even touch my toes and I have neither strength nor flexibility. Worse still, I have never had any intention of improving the situation. I must surely be suffering from premature ageing as no one else in the room seems to have a problem with sitting still for this long. I glance round the room. Serene faces of calm rest in total tranquillity. The master seems to be sitting in his cross-legged bliss several inches above the floor. And is that a ring of light around him?

What seemed like five hours later the half-hour meditation ended and the master descended to the floor. Then he leaped up again like a gazelle and we started 'waking the body' – jumping, hopping and slapping ourselves all over. He was over fifty and had seemingly boundless energy. My energy levels were in shock and I just felt an overwhelming desire to go back to bed. Then he began to dance and everyone in the room started to throw themselves around as if they were in a nightclub. I glanced at my watch. It was not yet 7.30 a.m.

Finally breakfast. Ah! The joys of food in France. What do they do to their bread? I swear French bread never tastes as good in England, even from a French bakery. And the coffee, it can't be just the drinking-it-out-of-a-bowl thing that makes it taste so good. Jam with big lumps of *framboise* in to spread on the bread and squishy plums that have just been picked.

Then the day officially began. All readers who know anything about t'ai chi had better stop reading at this point and skip to the next chapter. I was struggling to understand what was going on in German translated into French. So there was a whole lot of the course I missed altogether. A bit like life. For those of you who know even less than I do – let me educate you.

According to traditional Chinese medicine 'chi', which we could call our 'life-force', flows around the body along specific channels. Almost all wise Chinese men over the age of sixty have spent years studying how it does this and the clever ones have also learned how to put needles in your body where your energy has got blocked up. Anyway, the practice of t'ai chi helps the energy go round your body in the way it should. The 'tai' bit sort of means 'the way', I think. Or maybe that's 'tao'.

I had always thought of t'ai chi as lots of Chinese men standing in a park in Shanghai in the morning doing their workouts. Not exactly Jane Fonda, but an infinitely more graceful form of exercise, with proven benefits like lowering your blood pressure.

After breakfast every day we practised the funny positions till lunchtime. Take one step forward putting seventy per cent of your weight on to the front leg, lift the back leg slightly without shifting the weight. Hold up your arms above your head as if supporting two small clouds and concentrate on relaxation. Ha ha. Stand on one leg like an ostrich and try not to get annoyed with yourself on discovering that you are the only one in the room who can't hold the position without wobbling.

It is rather magical. None of the steps are tiring in themselves. In a sequence of movements that lasts about twenty minutes you are rarely even required to shift one leg high off the ground. It's much more gentle than yoga in that respect. When I last did a yoga class at my local gym I couldn't move for a couple of days afterwards, but this was all easy. Of course, I didn't know any of the movements and I was forced to copy others while looking as if I knew what I was doing. After a morning of this, instead of feeling tired I felt wonderful and had more energy than before I started. Somehow this was exercise and meditation rolled into one. I live my life at two speeds – 'full steam ahead' or 'stop'. Here I was learning to slow down. The very slowness of the movements, and the concentration required to perfect them, concentrates the mind and stills the energy in the body simultaneously.

But there was also more to it than this. Seeing is not believing where t'ai chi is concerned. Our master was about to show us that this 'chi' they speak of doesn't just go round our bodies, it is also in the ground and the sky. It is in everything.

The ancient pensioners are not just moving – they are playing with invisible energy that they can feel both inside their own bodies and outside. We just think it isn't there because we can't see it. I'm losing you? OK, it's like this. If you stand close to someone – 'in their space' so to speak – there is an energy that is not just to do with body-heat. It's more than that. An electricity you can only sense, a light you can't quite see but know is there, an aliveness you can't explain but are quite certain of.

To demonstrate this an expedition had been planned. We were not to speak – our only audible instruction all day was to '*guardez le silence*' – and we were to be blindfolded. A few people kept their eyes open to guide us to follow the master's non-verbal directions. I took a blindfold gladly. I think his intention was to tune up our intuition and our sensitivity so that we could really be aware of the aliveness of nature, the 'chi' in everything.

Parents take note! Forget Alton Towers. Just blindfold your kids and then take them out into nature. It was such simple fun. I stood in a wood unable to see it. Never was there such a magical fairyland. Those of us blessed with sight have taken little notice of our other gifts. Had I ever touched the dry earth before? Had I ever smelled the musty damp moss? What was the wonder of textures that I had never before experienced? A spiky twig. A cold round stone. A crinkle of bark. Crawling around the wood on my knees I gingerly reached out to see what my fingers would find next. Endless variety. The Frenchman passed me a log which appeared to have ears growing out of it. I stroked them, fascinated with the smooth fluffiness, unable to understand what I was holding.

Around us were the sounds of wood in summertime. I stopped the chatter inside my head to listen to the aliveness. Perhaps the birds do sing in Battersea, but I swear I've never heard them. What riches we have on this earth, and it seemed my ears only worked with my eyes closed. Then I became aware of the sound of a tiny waterfall. I moved slowly closer, lifting my hands to drink the icy splashing, and then just sat to listen to the gentleness. That was it. No more life lessons for me. I had arrived.

Then the next lesson. Remove the blindfold. Sight! Try being in nature for three hours with closed eyes and then simply open them. Was this another reality? I was still holding a branch from which grew fluffy toadstools in the shape of ears. I looked at them with a child's delight and from the corner of my eye I saw a laughing Frenchman. I looked around me. Had I ever seen trees before? Had someone repainted the flowers? The sky was the colour it used to be during childhood summers. And wonders were everywhere. Cows.

He led us to a river. He waded across. The current was strong and the water deep and we watched him concentrate to avoid losing his footing. The chubby Germans in silly shorts waded in after him but I had come prepared and produced a swimming costume. I threw myself in the water with joy and waded across with my bag held high before turning around and splashing about in the icy cold water. When I started to go numb I climbed out and jumped up and down, unable to decide whether I was exhilarated or courting pneumonia. I was the only one who had brought a costume and the others looked at me with envy. The Frenchman was laughing at me again, enjoying my appreciation of his day out.

He led us to a field and sat down, leaving us to amuse ourselves. I hadn't been able to communicate with the Germans because we had been trying to use words. Now, with words taken away, it was easy. We played chase and spun each other around, we gave piggyback rides. Some even practised t'ai chi moves. It was easy to see how children of many countries can all play together. We could enjoy ourselves even though we were grown-ups.

Before we left he invited us to play over in our minds the pictures of the day. An ancient bungalow with a low roof that sagged in the middle. A rusty gate that creaked as it swung open. A chained Alsatian, barking endlessly. We were invited to consider what we would like to record on the journey home to give us images for our dreams later that night. It was cheaper and easier than having to carry a video recorder. I looked around and saw the water breaking into strips of light as it danced over the rocks in the river. Yes, that was an image that I'd like to film. Further downstream was an old car-tyre. I'd cut that. I didn't need a documentary with realism.

Finally he led us home. A glorious day of silence. No inane politeness in French, German or any other tongue of man. Just the birds talking to us and the softly spoken teacher. We walked home, we broke bread and ate, we climbed into our beds and slept like children.

Occasionally during the week I'd spot my daughter doubled over with mirth at the sight of her mother trying to perfect the movement 'wave hands like clouds'. One day we became animals and to this day she can still do a passingly good imitation not of a bear but of her mother attempting to lumber and growl. I saw her for a whole five minutes on one of the days, I think. Or maybe I exaggerate. Three minutes. The women friends I'd come with joined the course but the men did not. So in the evenings we all met and sat outside in traditional French fashion to make up for the goodness of the day by drinking large amounts of wine. To my surprise the master did not disappear to meditate but drank more wine than any of us. I love the French. We'd stagger off to bed for a couple of hours sleep before the morning shower-queue.

I bet you think I'm going to say that the cross-legged meditation became dreamy and I no longer wanted coffee? The meditation got worse and only the coffee got better. But another miracle happened later. By now I was ready to follow the Frenchman to the ends of the world and give my body, my life, my soul and anything else he could think of.

On the last morning we had all followed him to a clearing in the forest. We were about to start work with a partner so I edged my way towards him thinking, 'I can impress him. I trained as I dancer. I'll be brilliant.' He turned towards me and placed his two feet squarely on the soil. 'Try and knock mee overe,' he said. 'It's about energi and *equilibre*, and zen you play.' Sure. Two hours later, a laughing teacher and an exhausted English girl. 'You 'ave to know your centre.' Then he waves his arms as if gathering potions from the ground. He whips them up as if making an invisible shape. He plays with the air. He passes it from hand to hand and then he passes it to me. A ball that isn't there. Only I can feel it. No really, I swear to you, I did feel a ball of energy and I didn't imagine it. I felt the air touch my fingers as keenly as I feel the keyboard touch them now.

As we played with that invisible ball, the heavens opened and the rain poured down. People scurried along the path for home but I dawdled. I wanted to see if the master would notice. He missed nothing and when everyone else was out of sight he started to walk with me. The warm rain fell on us in straight lines. I was looking like a wet-T-shirt calendar girl and he was enjoying the effect. He was so attractive. When did a Frenchman ever let a small matter like a torrential downpour get in the way of a little romance? Mmm: use everything for your learning, upliftment, growth and opportunity?

He put down his bag and pulled me towards him to kiss me. And I suppose, to be fair to myself, I did hesitate for about 0.5 of a second before kissing him back. We stood in the pouring rain and kissed like passionate teenagers. Passionate French teenagers. Then we squelched back to the *gîte*. He took a photo of me looking like a drowned rat. My daughter appeared and informed me, 'Mother, that T-shirt is completely see-through, you know.' I avoided saying, 'Yes, dear, that's why he's taking the photo.' Instead I played the obedient daughter. 'All right, don't worry, I'll go and change it.'

In the evenings we all told jokes. The translators worked overtime and the well-educated people laughed twice. One of the Frenchmen had an accordion and a seemingly endless repertoire of songs and dances. On the last evening a German gentleman of about sixty walked up to me like Yul Brynner in *The King and I* and bowed. 'Vaaltz?' he enquired. I managed a deep curtsey as a reply. I knew that ten years at stage school would come in useful some day. And then he threw me around the room for two hours. There is something magical about a waltz. Men in real life may be hopeless at taking the lead but just occasionally, on the dance floor, it's possible to find one who knows what to do. And all I had to do was follow. It was sheer bliss.

Meanwhile I was staring dreamily at the Frenchman and the almost tangible don't-even-think-about-it barrier that seemed to have appeared around him. He certainly didn't kiss all the women in the rain. Surely he must be madly in love with me? I started to fantasise wildly about the options available. Maybe I could appear at his door in the dead of night and, without words, he would beckon me towards him for a night of steamy bliss. Or maybe he would shake his head and say '*Mais non!*' and I'd feel dreadfully humiliated and ridiculously stupid the following day. I could always go and see what happened – after all, body contact and sleep was also a possibility.

Where was the commitment to high ideals that I'd liked to imagine I held? I didn't know anything about him. He may have been married, he may have been living with someone, he may have had a long-term partner. I hadn't asked. He hadn't asked. Why did it seem so unimportant? I imagined he was totally free to do as he pleased. Maybe he found himself a new lover on every course he took? His eyes met mine across the table and I tried desperately to discern what he was saying. My knees felt a little weak and I couldn't remember the French phrase for 'butterflies in the stomach'. I shrugged at him trying delicately to indicate confusion. 'I sayed wuld you like *encore du vin rouge?*' He filled my glass. This must surely be some code for 'Would you like to sleep with me tonight?' Yes, he was obviously crazy about me. Perhaps he was planning to appear at the window, like Gérard Depardieu didn't do in *Cyrano de Bergerac*, to seduce me against my better judgement.

I'd had other boyfriends and sexual partners since Slipperman had shuffled off but no one whom I would have described as a 'lover'. This seemed like a special opportunity for moral decline. I started to justify my fantasies. Whatever 'love' is, I had a lot of it for this man. I enjoyed all his work, the way he looked, the way he moved, and his conversation delighted me. The challenge was to enjoy all this and to not become attached. He had enjoyed my presence all week but he hadn't 'attached' himself to me (French verb form – reflexive). But was this accomplished form of 'non-attachment' simply a way of enjoying the presence of women but not wanting to complicate his life?

Now it's highly possible you are thinking that I was worrying for no reason as he was a Frenchman. But would approaching him be right? Would it be wise? Did it matter? I was learning about being in the present moment, after all. Could I just enjoy being with him and then walk away? I had never done the 'one-night stand' thing in my life. Was it me? Who was I? Where was I?

I seemed to be standing outside to provide nourishment for the mosquitos. Everyone else had gone to bed. Had I been hypnotised by the the heady smell of French cigarettes and the singing of the crickets in the night? Or could I blame the empty bottles of red wine and my desire to contribute to the profits of the local vineyards? I couldn't think of any further justifications. I decided to interpret his smile as an invitation.

There was joy in creeping up the creaky *escalier*. My heart pounded wildly as I knocked, very quietly, on the door. No reply. Perhaps he was out looking for me. I heard footsteps behind me and jumped wildly to one side in an effort to look as if I just happened to be strolling through this part of the *gîte* in the middle of the night. The waltzing German grinned at me. 'Er . . . have you seen my daughter?' I asked, assuming the concerned-parent-of-missing-child role.

'*Nein*.'

'Oh, er, *danke. Guten nacht*, then,' I mumbled with my impressive language skills. He shuffled off in green pyjamas. I don't think he even wondered what I was doing there. He probably wouldn't have noticed if I'd been naked.

No sound from the Frenchman's room. I tapped again. My heart lurched from fear to excitement. He obviously wasn't waiting for me or dabbing after shave behind his ears. Still no reply. Damn it. It's never like this in films. Isn't this supposed to be a romantic moment? I pouted. Not that anyone could see but it made me feel better. Then I remembered that I was an only child and used to having my way.

I seized the handle. It turned. That was it, he had obviously left the door unlocked for me. I pushed it open with a creaking noise that should have woken the *gîte*. Except it didn't. Nor did it wake the Frenchman. A loud snoring noise issued forth from the bed in the corner. A head hung down at a rather unattractive angle and the moonlight revealed hairs growing out of nostrils. He grunted and rolled over. Panic swept over me. What on earth was I doing in the bedroom of a sleeping stranger?

Two milliseconds later I was back in my room two floors away. A tide of annoyance, anger, regret, joy, self-pity, humiliation, happiness and relief flooded over me. I lay in bed and examined my feelings one by one. There was a song in a film with great clothes, classy cars and gunshots. 'You must remember this, A kiss is just a kiss . . .' I sang merrily to myself in the middle of the night. I was a cliché. I had fallen for the teacher and had narrowly avoided making a complete fool of myself.

The following day I had to say goodbye. I stood in a line and was hugged and pecked on the cheek just like everyone else. It seemed to me that he lingered for a minute because he was fond of me, but who knows? I may have imagined it. Damn it, why couldn't I take him home with me in my suitcase? I'm sure there must be a need for master t'ai chi teachers on Battersea Park Road. And there was a space in my bed. Stamp, pout, stamp, pout. I went on stamping and pouting till I wore myself out. Then I just grinned. One of the ideas that I had learned that week was a bit of classical Buddhism: that clinging and attachment is futile. It's inevitable from the moment we meet someone we love that we will be separated, if not sooner then later. I longed to talk to him, to say 'Guess what I did last night?' But there was no way I was going to attempt it. Certainly not with a C in O level French.

And what would he have made of it anyway? He could have been married for all I knew. Should I feel guilty? Surely accepting a kiss is one thing but turning up uninvited in the room of a man I barely knew was definitely another. I decided to spare myself the lecture.

He had given us the earth and the sky as going-home presents and I was thankful to him. I'd managed to walk around all these years as if the world was just a painted set. And I knew now that in my relationships I wanted to give freedom. I didn't want to tie anyone down and I didn't want to be tied down myself. I wanted to love unconditionally with no demands and no expectations.

Short talk coming up: non-attachment is a good lesson. It helps us to appreciate time spent with those we love. If you happen to be married to someone who watches too much TV, take comfort. And if you are in a wonderful relationship go and kiss him or her right now, because all things shall pass. It is said that to lead our lives as if they will go on forever is the most common human vanity. Short talk over.

I had planned to continue learning t'ai chi. I was at last able to do the first thirty seconds of those weird and wonderful movements. I wanted to learn more. I wanted to learn to meditate and rest inside my own body. I wanted to have boundless physical energy that was perfectly tuned to each moment. I wanted to become a master and be able to throw men twice my weight to the floor without the least effort. Then the plane landed.

I came back from my holiday in France without an extra ounce of cellulite. And with a pinch of German to add to my sprinkling of French. I'd bought enough red Bordeaux to wonder whether I should really go through the 'nothing to declare' channel trying to look spiritual.

I was going to need the wine. I had been offered a job making a television series about fashion. I was going to have to dress up in stylish clothes and call everyone 'darling' and 'sweetie'. Work too hard, have no time to think, go to the pub at the end of the day, wake up with a hangover, drink too much coffee, and dream of Frenchmen and Americans. It would be back to normal life.

Phase Three: Nun so Wise

Even the advertisement for the local t'ai chi class put me off. The church hall on a Friday night with teacher Doug Smith somehow lacked the romance of the mountains. At the end of the first week working for Channel Four I was exhausted and it was raining, so I didn't go. So much for good intentions. Friday nights I collapsed at the pub with everybody else. A series later and I was highly stressed and in a bad way. Months of real life *Absolutely Fabulous* had begun to take their toll. I knew the difference between CK and DK. I felt as if I had spent six months walking the Road to Enlightenment in the wrong direction. Making TV programmes is good for the bank balance but if you want to be happy, relaxed and at peace with yourself then I don't recommend a career in the media. A radical recovery zone was needed.

'Why not go on a retreat?' suggested a highbrow Christian friend. This chap, a film writer, had an extraordinary habit of sneaking away from his wife and family every now and again and spending the weekend with monks. Yes, I know, hanging out with bald guys in long frocks 'in an attractive black cotton worn just above the ankle' sounds perverse. He assured me it isn't.

But in my case he advised a weekend with nuns so that I could concentrate on my spiritual life instead of being able to indulge in fantasies of seducing the best-looking monk in the monastery. I was sure I needed to work a sex life into my spiritual life. But not this weekend, it seemed. Shucks. So – to a nunnery with me.

I clambered on to a train to Oxford to contemplate the place of religion in my life. My mother had been a committed atheist and I could have become one myself except I had walked into a church once. It was in the days when I was an actress and still living in sin with Slipperman. I had thought that I would sit and enjoy the peace in the church for a while but on the way out there was a video screen promising a history of the building. Always open to culture, I pressed the play button and was informed 'We are 1,000 people here in the morning and 1,000 in the evening'. A church with people?

Here was an opportunity to have something important to talk about with the man at home. Surely, I reasoned with myself, questions like 'Does God exist?' and 'Is there life after death?' have to be more interesting than Viv Richards' batting average? I had never been to church but they might have something to say about the nature of reality that I hadn't considered. Maybe there was a God.

I had rushed home in a state of excitement, having failed, as usual, to consider that the man at home was more interested in a shopping-bag full of food than a head full of enthusiasm. 'Is there anything for dinner?' he asked hopefully as I arrived. 'Er, no, but we simply must go to church this Sunday!' He looked at me. 'I don't believe in God and I'm not religious,' he said reasonably. 'No, I know, neither do I. I just thought it would be really fascinating . . .'

The following Sunday there we were listening to a charming, good-looking and talented speaker delivering a sermon which was amusing and, more scary still, relevant to life. There was something about this Christ character that was very inviting. I was captivated. Here were articulate, intelligent people interested in ideas, life and truth. Slipperman was worried about me.

Was I becoming 'religious'? Could he handle this latest phase of my lunacy?

I decided to go back. There had to be an argument for apathetic atheism. I remember raising an objection about creation and evolution, seizing, I thought, an area where any form of Christian teaching was obviously misguided. 'Are you referring to Homo Sapiens or Australopithecus man?' asked the smiling vicar who turned out to have a degree in anthropology. I realised I would have to study. Have you ever tried to disprove Christianity? Good luck if you ever do and may God bless all your efforts. I accidentally read C.S. Lewis. Big mistake. Six months I struggled and the more I pitted my mind against the interminably friendly and horribly well-educated Christians the more ground I lost. In the end it was hopeless. I had to admit that there probably is a God.

Of course, all you cynics out there will remind me that I was outnumbered. But I had at last found something with which I hoped to shake the man at home from his 'contentment'. He would have to agree that, to misquote the Bard, 'there are more things in heaven and earth than I had dreamed of in my philosophy'. So, like all good evangelicals – which is what I had unwittingly become – I invited God into my life, admitting that I'd made a pretty hopeless job of it till then, and that if He would like to take over then things could only get better.

They did. The world changed around me. The stars shone in the sky instead of just hanging around up there. The sea was majestic and not just wet. This 'love' thing was all around me and smiling in the faces of strangers. This was where my Road had really begun. That had been the beginning and nothing has ever been the same since.

But I soon found there was a catch. I had been converted in a church where they believed in following exactly what the Bible says – according to how they understand it. They understand it to say 'Don't have sex outside marriage'. I was puzzled. Nowhere could I find Christ saying, 'I have come in order to tell you not to have sex with your boyfriend'. Not in any version of the Bible I looked in. But one would have thought that he had said exclusively that based on the number of sermons about 'relationships'. However, I was hooked and I was all for high ideals. I wanted to do this 'following Christ' thing with my whole heart, soul and, if necessary, body. This meant doing it their way. No one could accuse them of not changing lives. I went home one day and said: 'I've accepted a job with a touring theatre company so I'm going to be away for a couple of months and then I would like us to either get married or split up.' This, I'm ashamed to admit, is where my raving lunatic fundamentalist idealism had brought me, to giving the man who loved me a 'no more sex unless you marry me' ultimatum. Finally I had Slipperman's attention.

Ha. I suppose I didn't really explain to you why he married me, did I? Interesting what storytellers are tempted to leave out. But as I looked back and mused, while the train to Oxford lurched along and the tea slopped over the side of the polystyrene cup, I found I didn't regret any of it.

My evangelical eagerness lasted about two years. Then I decided the evangelicals were too much, even for me, so I moved to my local C of E with the traditional empty pews. I loved the sweet elderly vicar and the good people of his flock. I stayed for an eternity. We all struggled to live our lives as best we knew how. But slowly and surely, like all good members of the Church of England, I had finally stopped going at all. It wasn't that I had stopped believing – but what exactly did I now believe? And how had I ended up on my way to a convent?

I don't know what you'd expect in visiting a nunnery. Not a lot of laughs, that's for sure. I expected a lot of miserable old ladies with worthy things to say in a 'bless you, my child' tone of voice. I wasn't sure I wanted too much of that. I'd rung and they'd asked me what kind of weekend I wanted. I'd chosen a 'two-day, silent, guided retreat'.

That meant I'd meet with a nun for half an hour each morning and after lunch and the rest of the time would be spent in silence. I'd enjoyed the silence in France and I had a sneaking suspicion that any real spirituality or actual experience of what we call God had to include silence and stillness. But I'd never met a nun before. I couldn't imagine what we could possibly have in common or find to talk about. I panicked briefly and then remembered the old Insight ideas about comfort zones and using everything for my learning and growth. I'd packed a book and I hoped for a relaxing weekend. I could ignore the tap-tap of rosary beads and the suppressed sexuality and, if all else failed, I could just sleep a lot.

I walked from the train to the taxi filled with apprehension and as I arrived at the Anglican Community of St Mary the Virgin I was already convinced I had gone too far. Then suddenly a smiling redhead, who appeared to be in fancy dress, tapped on the window.

'Hi, I'm Sister Emma – was your journey OK?' she beamed. Sweeping up my bag in a flurry of black and white, she whisked me in and rapidly explained: 'Dinner is silent and you're a little late. I hope you don't find it strange that we don't talk during meals but just follow along and Sister Alison will come and have a chat with you after supper.' There must have been a mistake – everyone knows that smiling redheads in their twenties don't join convents. I was wondering how I could rescue her. She seemed so nice, so normal. I would clearly have to persuade her to leave with me on Sunday.

I followed her through a large wooden door and down a corridor. The doors all had labels: 'The Laundry', 'The Library', 'Sister Helen's Office'. It was alarmingly quiet but the heating seemed to be working. Then we went into the refectory and I realised I was going to have to rent a mini-bus to rescue half the convent. There were some elderly and stooped types, like nuns are supposed to be, but the rest were all so young. And there were novices (even I knew that a white veil meant a novice), six of them, all young, pretty and without facial hair.

I sat down gingerly. The food was vegetarian and the silent meal meant I could notice what I was putting in my mouth. I'd been told on the phone that the vegetables were all organic as they grew them in the convent garden with no pesticides. They had been perfectly prepared and I wondered how this was possible when there was no cordon bleu chef visible and there were over a hundred people all eating together. Eating slowly without talking. It was a strange new experience – I had time to taste the food. I wasn't rushing out of the door to an appointment or watching some TV documentary that I felt obliged to have an opinion on. When they served the apple crumble and custard it was so exquisite that I was already beginning to question whether God was calling me to stay here forever. I could just hear the conversation: 'Yes Mother, I feel I was called to join you. It was during the apple crumble and custard.'

The meal ended. We all sat and waited for the ones with no teeth to catch up. Then there was a prayer of thanks and a young blonde Sister beckoned me out of the door.

'This is Sister Alison,' said the blonde, indicating a nun with a face of infinite wisdom and patience.

'Welcome,' said the face. 'Would you like to design your own programme for the weekend or would you rather have one suggested?' I plumped for the suggested version. Quite apart from the fact that I didn't have a clue what to suggest for myself, I certainly wasn't here to think about anything. 'In that case I suggest you have a hot bath and an early night and we'll meet after breakfast. If you need anything ask the guest sister on your wing. Goodnight.' And off she went. I looked at my watch. It was 9 p.m. I went to sleep at 9.30 p.m., for what must have been the first time in twenty years. I must have been exhausted and not even realised it.

When I woke, the clock said 6 a.m. but I felt surprisingly chirpy. I floated down to chapel for the morning service to find a hundred nuns who looked as if they had been awake for hours. What an ethereal sound they made. Have you ever tried to sing at six in the morning? Everyone knows it just isn't possible. Which proves that these people were in fact angels. What a beautiful place it was. Morning sunlight shining through the stained glass of the chapel above the altar. Freshly cut flowers everywhere. Wooden pews shiny from years of being polished and a wonderfully subtle smell of incense from nowhere at all.

Gentle faces recited words of poetry written by a Jewish king more than two thousand years ago.

> As a hart longs for flowing streams,
> So longs my soul for thee, O God.

I sat back in my chair, humbled by the beauty of it all. Why would I want to rescue the redhead? Where would I want to take her? To work at an 'important' TV company in Oxford Street?

Then there was breakfast – silent – with home-made yoghurt and honey from the hives in the grounds. Then afterwards the meeting with Sister Alison. I sat in a tiny room furnished with a low table and two chairs. She smiled and waited for me to speak.

'I was wondering whether God really exists, or whether He/ She is just a useful concept?' I ventured, determined to be honest. I had an irrational and perverse feeling, left over from my evangelical phase, that God was more than a subjective opinion, but I thought I'd give her how I felt on the bad days. I reckoned she had heard it all before.

She smiled. 'Take this book and try this exercise. We'll meet at two and you can let me know how you get on. Don't forget to have a coffee break and, if you have too much time, take a walk in the garden. But don't talk to anyone, just spend the time with your own thoughts. The real journey, Isabel, is with yourself.' Fine. This was a pushover. One little 'exercise' and a walk in the garden – I could do this.

'Imagine someone has made a statue of you', said the book. 'You are invited to go and see it before it is unveiled. So go into the room and pull off the dust sheet. What do you think? Notice everything about it.'

How crazy do you think I am now? Walking round a room in a convent pulling imaginary sheets off non-existent statues. 'How does it look?' the book insisted. I imagined a pose my ex-husband used to make when mocking me. Head thrust forward, eyes squinting in the sun, lips pursed, being pushy about something. 'What do you like about it?' I decided it was made of a warm stone that was good to touch and the clothes I was wearing looked good, for a statue. 'Now speak to the statue.'

'What do you look like that for?' I asked accusingly. 'This is how I looked when you made me', said the statue. 'What are you in such a state about? Why don't you lighten up a bit?' I wondered as I walked around admiring the choice of plinth. Then I glanced down at the book. 'Now become the statue,' it said smugly. I staggered on to my beautifully created pedestal but it didn't feel very comfortable. I had stepped into my normal state of physical tension and I seemed to be fretting about nothing specific. This was not what t'ai chi had taught me. Suddenly I needed a shoulder massage and my jaw seemed to be clenched hard enough to keep my dentist in business for years. I didn't like this exercise. This was a version of myself as others must experience me. 'Good grief, I'm glad I don't live with this person,' I thought.

'Now imagine Christ walking into the room to see the statue and see what happens.' This was easier. The statue melted to its knees, no longer made of stone but brought to life by the gaze of pure love. 'And what does Christ say?' Christ says my name – 'Isabel'.

You've got to hand it to these nuns. I'd done stuff I'd have called 'prayer' before but this was way out there. OK, I may have a good imagination, but this nun had me kneeling on the floor of my room with a man who had died 2000 years ago and here I was having a conversation with him. And enjoying his presence. Only of course he wasn't there.

'Do you trust me?' He asked. 'Yes.' I replied, quick as a flash and instantly noticed the lie. 'Do you trust me?' He asked with still more love. 'No, I don't trust you at all, do I?' Closer to the truth perhaps? 'Do you trust me, Isabel?' He asked again. Ah, to spend time with complete patience and complete understanding. 'Well, a little,' I replied and sat silent.

'Continue the conversation as long as you need to,' interjected the book. So I knelt on the floor of my room, chatting to this man who wasn't there, talking with him about my life, all the things I saw as wrong with it, what I'd like to be different, what I was happy about, what I was sad about. And the weird thing was that he knew it all already but seemed to enjoy listening – as if he took even more pleasure in my company than I took in his. And he wasn't angry about anything, or impatient, the way I am with myself, he was just Love.

Eventually I glanced back to the book. 'Allow Christ to leave the room now.' I watched as he winked and closed the door behind him quietly. 'Now step out of the statue and become yourself again,' instructed the book. I went to sit on the rather hard single-bed. I felt more at peace with myself than I had felt for as long as I could remember. I felt calm and confident. It no longer mattered what happened when I got back to Battersea. With this serenity and trust I could handle anything. I floated into the convent garden to enjoy the smiling flowers.

'But it wasn't really Christ,' I complained to Sister Alison at my next session. 'That was me putting words in his mouth. Isn't that dubious in some way?'

'That's why I'm here: to check. What did he say?'

It seems that if I had imagined Christ telling me to put my head in a gas oven she may have told me that perhaps I would benefit from a little professional therapy. But as I told her about my morning she just smiled. 'So it was a bit like when Christ asked Peter three times, "Do you love me?"' I honestly hadn't thought of that; I couldn't even remember the passage. But yes, it was like that. 'And how was the exercise? Did you enjoy it?' I had to admit that it had been extraordinary. 'Good,' she said.

On Saturday afternoon she had me read some stories from the life of Christ and asked me what I felt about them. This was very bizarre. As an evangelical I had been taught to distrust my feelings on the grounds that they are unreliable and of dubious merit as guides. Yet here was a nun, someone who I would have thought wasn't likely to be aware that she had feelings, asking me (a former actress!) to discover mine. The impertinence of the woman. I read the life of Christ from the Gospel of St Matthew and I cried. He was such an exciting man, such a brave one. I had been much happier just examining the story in an intellectual way as an interesting piece of history. But what did I feel? Feelings? Huh. Who needs feelings?

Sunday morning I went to their service and tried to be cerebral about it. I didn't really want to feel that there were any connections between my meeting with a man who wasn't there, the story I'd read about the life of a Jewish carpenter and the bread and wine they offered in the service. Much easier to come up with a few trivial complaints about the form of service. Maybe I was missing the very heart of the weekend or maybe I wasn't. But I knew one thing: I loved it there. I was enjoying it all; I even liked the silent lunches.

I arrived to ask Sister Alison for details of the Sunday afternoon session with trepidation. I was overwhelmed and I didn't want to feel anything new or think anything either. God must have told her.

'I think it would be good for you to go on a walk. Would you like that? Do you like walking?'

'Oh, very much,' I lied, unable to remember the last time I had walked further than the distance from my front door to the bus stop.

'Take one of the "long walk suggested routes" that you'll find among the lounge maps. It's all written out. You've only to pick one up.'

Great. Nothing spiritual about this, thank goodness. Just a walk designed for nuns. I set off after lunch, instructions in hand. 'Walk through Wantage and take Manor Road until you reach The Ridgeway.' Off I strolled through the village, looking at the people, thinking, 'They'd never believe it if they knew where I've just come from.' I walked up the road, and up the road, and up the road, and up the road, until I reached the horizon. 'Er, excuse me,' I broke my silence to a local, 'is this The Ridgeway?' 'Oh, no, that's up that hill over yonder'. (No, I swear to you, I am not making this up, he did say 'yonder'.) I set off to the next horizon. An hour later I saw a sign: 'The Ridgeway'. I looked at the nuns' notes. 'When you get to The Ridgeway turn right and walk along until you get to the village of Letcombe Regis.' I turned and strained my eyes. Village? There was no village. Was this village on the coast? Could I have confused right with left?

I studied the map, turned right and started to walk. Then I remembered to look at the world and be aware of walking. Yes – 'Participate in your experience and experience your participation'. In order to get value for money, concepts that I'd been taught at Insight could be applied to long walks. Pennies were beginning to drop. This was an experience of the fact that I was alive.

What was that amazing sound? A bird far far above me. Singing a song that could only be described as pure joy. If joy can have a sound, this was it. I remembered sound. I remembered the playground forests in France and that nature was alive. I remembered that long ago I had decided that there probably was a God who had created all this. I even remembered that the kingdom of God was in me too. It was exciting. It did all fit together.

I stopped the only passerby I met that afternoon. He and his dog smiled at the city-dweller. 'It's a lark. Isn't it amazing?' Yes, it was amazing, and as I write this sitting on a rainy night on the Battersea Park Road I can still remember the purity of that song. If you've never heard a lark, go walk The Ridgeway in Oxfordshire in summertime.

But to get back to my walk. It was long. When a nun says a long walk, she means a *long* walk. It was 7 p.m. when I walked back through the convent door to the veiled and smiling faces. I had left at 2 p.m. I felt fantastic. Blood had flowed to parts of my body that had quite forgotten what oxygen does for the cells. I listened once again to the nuns' ethereal song and had to tear myself away. If only I could hold on to their stillness. The serene tenderness that I was walking away from.

Never again would I see nuns as messed up and inadequate beings. Me? Yes, maybe. But the nuns? No. They were graceful and gracious, vibrant and joyful. They had taught me how to be just by being. And, with the exception of Alison and the smiling redhead, they hadn't said a word.

Phase Four: The Ram Discovered

So, am I making any progress? Is there any growth in me as a person? Does any of this learning stick, or change me? Am I just more egotistical or am I any kinder, quieter, happier or in any way a more 'aware' female? If I've made any changes in myself for the better, then certainly no one has commented. The problem is that despite dancing joyfully at Insight, walking down cul-de-sacs with sage-like Frenchmen and a heavenly weekend at the convent, in-between times I go on being as grumpy as ever. I still go on being me. And are new people I meet ever impressed by the similarity between myself and a vision of serenity? Nope.

Maybe I'd make a serene impression if I didn't meet people at parties. But how else do you meet new people? I hate parties. I hate the fact that everyone always stares at you and then asks, 'What do you do?' as if we humans are incapable of talking to each other unless we have a label and know which conversational category to put each other into. Why does everyone always want to know what I do? Why can't they just be so stunned by the amazing entity standing before them that they want to bask in my presence? Here I am putting all this effort into what I am and all they want to know is what I do. It is very irritating.

Because I hate this question I, of course, always make more interesting conversation. So I can't imagine why, at the last party

I went to, this man said to me, 'I'm an astrologer.' Maybe he was just desperate to reveal his life-purpose to me. Or maybe I'd had a little too much to drink and forgot that I never ask this question.

In fact, now that I come to think about it, that was almost definitely the case because I remember that this job struck me as hysterically funny. 'An astronomer?' I shouted merrily. 'Or is it astrologer? I can never remember which is which. Patrick Moore or Mystic Meg?'

He winced. 'Mystic Meg.' 'Really? You're not serious? You mean you manage to convince people that their life-choices are affected by which way the moon was moving when they were born? That is the most ridiculous thing I've ever heard. What's more,' my voice echoed across the room, 'it ignores the fact we have free will in our lives! Any reasonable person knows that we forge our own destiny and the planets have nothing to do with it. I ask you! How absurd! And you look like an intelligent man. People pay you for this?'

The smartly suited gentleman with short dark hair and delicate features was by this time looking around helplessly for someone painfully introverted to talk to.

'Yes, I'm booked up six months in advance, actually.'

I re-filled my glass with an excellent 1990 Saint Émilion red Bordeaux.

'Six months in advance! Well, that just goes to show how many gullible people there are around. It's all nonsense – telling the future with signs of the zodiac. Tosh! What star sign am I then? Bet you can't tell me that . . . go on then . . . More wine? What star sign am I then?'

He smiled benignly. 'At a guess, I'd say Aries.'

I stared at him through my fading focus. I had to struggle to think a little. None of the other guests knew my star sign. He was just lucky.

'Listen,' he said, steadying my arm, 'do you know anything at all about readings? You can come and have one done if you like.

You don't have to believe in it.' I suppose he was a nice person. How sickening.

So when I'd got over the hangover and remembered to ring the host to say thank you I enquired about this dubious guest. 'Oh, Richard? He's been reading people's charts for about twenty years. He's very well known in the field. He read mine. It was amazing, you should definitely go if he's offered to let you jump the queue. You never know, you might learn something!'

And that is how I ended up going to 'have my chart read'. It was just too tempting and curiosity got the better of me. So, demonstrating my developing lack of discernment, I rang up this astrologer. I was informed that I needed to supply him with certain significant dates in my life. Did I know my date and time of birth, for instance? Date, no problem, as long as no one tries to work out my age. I am always happy to reveal the date to anyone who is innumerate. But the time?

As luck would have it, the birth certificate was surprisingly specific – 1.13. But then a problem. Did it read a.m. or p.m.? An illegible scribble was about to affect my entire life-path. Bother the doctor who wrote this certificate. Didn't he realise that whether I ever marry again or become a millionaire could be determined by this information?

I rang the astrologer, whom I'd nicknamed Merlin in an attempt to prove I wasn't taking this seriously. 'Does it matter whether it's a.m. or p.m.? I can't read the doctor's handwriting.' Yes, it seemed that my life was going to be quite different. Mother's personality, career success, it was all changed if my moon was rising. 'It looks like you might be a p.m. reading to me, so I'll start working on that one,' said Merlin, 'but if you can check, that would be useful – and bring other significant dates with you.'

Panic set in. I could get the wrong life. The wrong future. My destiny stolen by calligraphy. I stared at the birth certificate and noticed at the bottom 'Chestnut Hill Hospital, Philadelphia'.

Good grief. Maybe, in a store room, somewhere in a hospital that may not have been closed down, was the answer to the mystery of my fate.

Two phonecalls later and a sugar-plum friendly Pennsylvania accent was saying, 'My name's Mary-Lou and I have your birth record right here. There are two little footprints. You had the cutest little feet.' What a weird feeling. Then my voice, being transported by phone into a building across the Atlantic where it had not been heard for . . . quite some years, saying frantically, 'Well, er, thank you. But, er, the time of day, do you have the time at which I was born? A lot could depend on it, you see . . .'

'Oh yes, honey, it's written several times in the record – it was 1.13 a.m. Sure I'm sure, honey – a.m. Eastern Standard Time.' I take back everything bad that I've ever said about BT. They had just changed my life. I rang Merlin, who had been preparing my destiny in anticipation of our meeting. He would have to start over. I had become somebody else. Instead of Uranus, Saturn was now rising.

I pressed the brass doorbell nervously. There was something weirdly scary about going to see this man, death certificate of mother and birth certificate of daughter in hand. Only of course Aries rams don't suffer fools gladly. And anyway, there are definitely no personality traits specific to each sign. Why does this evolving, changing and growing thing have to be such hard work?

I entered a bright and spacious room and was blinded by the appliance of science. A large computer screen was displaying a rather pretty geometric pattern in full colour that apparently told Merlin all he needed to know about me. 'I'll just be one minute,' he said, while lasering me out a print of the pattern and collecting a cassette to record the next hour.

I examined his shelves with scepticism. Lots of books on astrology which I suppose was some comfort. Even if it was a nonsense discipline, at least he'd read up on it. The next shelf displayed more books on astrology, and the next and the next. I counted them. He appeared to have 136. How quaint that so many should have been written. I pulled one out from a shelf and glanced at the introduction:

> Astrology has stimulated the minds of profound thinkers and scientists for thousands of years, yet is still condemned as nonsense by those who have not studied it. Sir Isaac Newton replied to the astronomer Halley, when the latter scorned his interest in astrology, 'Sir, I have studied it, you have not.'

Good grief. Put that book back on the shelf straight away. Do I have to have an open mind towards everything? Merlin sees me looking agitated. 'Isn't all this deeply un-Christian?' I ask. He smiles at me with a look of long-suffering tolerance. 'Are you familiar with the Gospel of St Matthew?'

'Yes, I studied it when I was an evangelical,' I asserted proudly.

'So you'll know Matthew, Chapter Two, Verse Two, then?'

'Er, no, must be something to do with the Birth?'

'Yes, In fact I have the *New English Bible* version from memory – it is: 'Astrologers from the East arrived in Jerusalem, asking, "Where is the child who is to be born King of the Jews? We have observed the rising of his star . . ." Now, if astrology is un-Christian why did the Three Wise Men play such a well-recorded role at the birth of Christ?'

Silence. I'm sure there is an answer to this question. I didn't know it.

'Do you want to have your reading or not? Here's your laser print. Come and sit here so I can test the sound levels for the microphone.'

Then he was off, busy explaining to me why I am the way I am. 'Your sun is in Aries, your moon is in Sagittarius and you have Capricorn ascending. In fact, you have five planets in fire, three in earth, one in air and one in water, so you are basically a fire-earth personality elementally.' He may as well have been doing the reading in ancient Aramaic. 'Er?' I articulated.

'Certain energy drives and qualities are determined at the moment of your birth.' I'm not sure he'd ever done a reading for someone so astrologically uneducated. 'If you imagine someone standing looking out at the position of the stars while you were busy being born, the constellation Sagittarius was behind the moon at the time so we say that your moon was in Sagittarius.'

'I thought the planets all went round the sun?' I ventured, quite sure that there was something I knew.

'Yes, but this is a geocentric discipline so the planets are viewed from their position on earth. You really don't need to understand all this anyway. It is what the planets tell us about you that is important.' And he launched into my character analysis.

'In terms of getting things done, this is the steamroller of the zodiac. A double fire means that you are good at spotting trends and are akin to what is going on in the collective unconscious. You have a great ability to conceive and conceptualise and Aries love challenges. Also . . .' I was beginning to like this. I could sit all day and listen to him telling me how brilliant I am. So this is why people pay him. He went on – 'Not only are you inspiring but also, with you Capricorn ascendant, you always do what you say you are going to do.'

This was all very wonderful but I was beginning to feel that he was going to tell me something for my greater enlightenment.

'However,' that inevitable word, 'there is a heavy imbalance. You have double abundance alongside double deprivation. You have all this masculine energy in your chart. All the things that a woman traditionally looks for in a man . . . [he struggles to be tactful] you've already got them. Or that is what you present to the world.'

This man was getting too clever for words. Was he getting all this from his computer screen or from meeting me? But he kept pointing very specifically at various little signs on my chart.

'You have a need to control what is happening around you or else things may not get done. And you are very good at it but you are not so good at letting things evolve in a spontaneous way. You always want to be pushing things forward. Maybe this is what you did in your last relationship?'

OK, this was enough. Either he had a crystal ball somewhere or he had spent hours on the phone to my friends finding out about me. Maybe it was all a conspiracy that they were hatching to get their own back for my evangelical days? Tell Merlin all about me and tell me nothing, and then sit round in the pub afterwards thinking this frightfully funny.

He went on. 'You have a double polarity here which means that you will tend to polarise things a lot. It's the lack of Libran balance. Have you considered nurturing your feminine side a little?'

'What, you mean standing around looking beautiful, wearing pastel colours and waiting for a man to ride up on his white horse?'

Defensive? Me?

'It's interesting that you see it like that. What about all the wonderful, beautiful, worthy and sexy things about being female?'

'Don't you have to buy those according to size-preference in Harley Street?' I asked, thinking myself very amusing.

'But in your jokes you dismiss the feminine in yourself. The power in your chart is genuine but it also shows that underneath you are paddling furiously and you need to give expression to the part of you which is shy.'

I pouted. 'If all this is in my chart doesn't it mean I'm stuck like this anyway and any attempt at improvement is a lost cause?'

'No, not at all. The chart shows what you already have, which then tells you what you need to work on. Some people believe that it shows what you have learned in past lives, which then gives you a guide as to what you need to concentrate on in this one. You can't lose what you already have. It's just a question of balance so that then you can have it all.'

'So I have to learn to love cooking?'

'Now, you remember that I said you have a tendency to polarise?'

Focus on nurturing my inner feminity. Huh. I thought people went to astrologers so that they could be told they were going to meet a tall, dark, handsome stranger who was going to do that.

'Any tall, dark, handsome strangers in the near future?' I asked, trying to turn the subject away from me.

'Yes, actually. When Uranus comes to Venus it usually does bring strangers. But don't go after them. Let them come to you. Look at what you've been doing so far that hasn't worked for you.'

What, like always having been the one to ask the men in my life out? Like writing loads of ridiculously long letters to the last man I fell for and ignoring the fact that he wasn't writing back? Like following him round Europe just for the pleasure of his presence? Like failing to notice that he spent most of the time he was with me sleeping? Hopeless? Me?

'What should I be looking for? Any tips?' I was beginning to enjoy this again now.

'As you have a lot of psychic power you need someone who operates on a similar level of power and intensity. The woman's moon and the man's sun work well so a Sagittarius man would be good fun for you. You don't want a man who is too passive or he'd drive you crazy. You want a man who is certain of his masculinity. He needs to be spiritually strong and have the capacity to contain emotionally and you need a man with a lot of visibility and who operates on a big stage.'

'The only unmarried man on the planet just went off with my

archetypally female blonde friend,' I whined pathetically. 'Where am I supposed to go to meet men who operate on a big stage?'

'It's not about going out to look. You do the inner work and then they just show up.'

'I don't think I have one single girlfriend who believes that any more.'

'Could be why they are single.' He grinned smugly. 'Just go home and do the work. There are plenty of tall dark strangers around for you in the years to come. The main thing this chart shows is that you need to nurture your feminine side. There is a workshop, 'Awakening the Goddess', that would be a great place to start. I believe it's totally transformative, but it is women only so I've not done it myself. Here's your tape, here's your chart, I've got to dash now.'

Then, as if by magic, he was gone and I was outside in the street. My feminine and masculine sides agreed to walk to a coffee shop. 'I'd like a new dress,' my feminine side requested politely, 'and to be allowed to go to the Goddess workshop.' 'Oh, good grief,' replied my masculine side. 'So does this mean you're going to cook me a meal occasionally?' She smiled and fluttered her eyelashes, 'Oh yes, dear, whatever you'd like.'

So now I'm a dual personality. As if it wasn't bad enough trying to evolve as one person, now I have two of me to contend with. My feminine side wants to go and buy new earrings and my masculine side thinks I should be at home sending a CV to another television company. My feminine side argues that she doesn't like making television programmes anyway and would rather spend time with her daughter. My masculine side says that it is all very well but he has a mortgage to pay. Huh. Now I don't even need a relationship. I can have domestic arguments all by myself. And when my masculine side would rather be out achieving something, he has to suffer the indignity of going to a Goddess workshop.

Phase Five: Manifesting the Inner Goddesses

It was true what the astrologer had told me. I did feel that I was somehow lacking as a woman. That I wasn't feminine enough. But I had no idea what I meant by that or how to change it. Maybe there was some mystique to being a woman that had somehow escaped me. This would explain why the last man I had fallen in love with – a truly remarkable man – had left me and gone off with a blonde. She was petite, she needed looking after, she managed to radiate confident smiles while hinting at vulnerability inside – and she once said to me, 'I can have any man I want' and then she proved it. This incident had left me with the very foundations of my belief in myself as a woman wrecked. I felt, ugly, awkward and masculine. I was horribly aware that my figure was not as society demanded it should be. I was not pretty enough or sexy enough to attract the man I wanted to love. There was obviously something wrong with my femininity.

Maybe this woman who ran Goddess workshops would be able to help me. Maybe I could discover what I was lacking so that next time I met a man I was attracted to he would walk straight up to me and say 'I'm yours' or something. Or at the least maybe I could think about the fact I am a woman instead of a kind of conglomerate: disciplinarian, breadwinner, cook, shelf putter-upper, odd job man, understanding earth father, confused type that runs the house. Now I know I'm not sounding very feminist but from my point of view – not having had a father and all that – I've never had to fight for equality. Thank God other, braver, women before me have done that. But, as Merlin said: 'What about all the wonderful, beautiful, worthy and sexy things about being female?' I knew nothing of these things. Perhaps the goddesses could teach me. The leaflet promised 'A unique experience of yourself as a woman and your feminine power'. It was that or unblocking the sink.

I did not have a good time preparing for the weekend. The leaflet had asked for 'a dress that makes you feel like a goddess' and I didn't have anything at all appropriate. The domestic row I had anticipated was in full swing. Ms Inner Feminine was mooching around the house because she hadn't been bought a new dress specially. 'I haven't got anything pretty to wear.' Mr Inner Masculine was ignoring her. I asked him what his choice would be for the 'music which reflects an inner longing', another requirement for the workshop. He suggested 'Money Makes the World go Round' from *Cabaret*. Or Madonna singing 'Material Girl'.

It was a ridiculous state of affairs.

Meanwhile I was going to have to come up with some solutions. The old dress with the flowers would have to do and some CD would have to be found. I was confused. Music to suggest a longing? 'Longing? *Longing*!' Surely I was supposed to have given that up on the path to enlightenment? I thought the Buddha was supposed to be free of wants and attachment?

I thought I was just supposed to be appreciating life? Longing for things, people, wonderful, passionate sex is all deeply dysfunctional, isn't it? I could hardly take 'Someone to Watch Over Me', with a lyric like 'I'm a little lamb who's lost in the wood . . .' What about 'I'm a little ram who's up to no good'? And opera was definitely out – 'songs for co-dependence', one of my self-actualised friends calls all the great arias. (Sigh.) So no love songs. How about a cassette of birdsong from the

Amazonian rain forest to suggest my longing to be a very long way from Battersea Park Road in October?

Then Mr Inner Masculine rescued me. 'Take something classical.' (Practical as always.) 'How about a Bach cello concerto? It's definitely the sound of some kind of longing.'

'Yes, for Alan Rickman in *Truly, Madly, Deeply*,' chirped Ms Feminine.

I figured I would have to try and be integrated and ignore them both. I walked out of the house to get on a number 19 bus to Highbury and Islington. An unlikely location for a meeting of goddesses.

My heart sank when I arrived. Not that I should have expected anything different from an all-female workshop, but there were no men there. This was worse than the Insight Seminar. There I had decided they were all weird. But this was far further outside my comfort zone. This was a huge mistake. I was the only one with long hair and the only one not wearing trousers. I started to panic. I know I'd asked the universe to find me a relationship but hormones and some old fashioned genetic preference were still insisting that I like men.

'There is something powerful that happens when women sit together,' said the lead goddess. She was a stunningly beautiful woman over fifty. I'd rarely seen a more self-actualised-looking woman. We approached a circle of cushions on the floor. I did not want to be sitting in a circle of women. I didn't want anything powerful to happen. Suddenly I disliked all women intensely.

Then the 'sharing' started. 'I've always had a problem with men,' said one pair of trousers. 'I feel like a man in the body of a woman,' said a second. 'Since doing this workshop the first time,' said a third, 'I feel my sexuality has taken a whole new direction.'

I don't think I've ever been so scared in my whole life. Ms Feminine was wishing she was at the pub with a group of football hooligans leering and wolf-whistling. Then suddenly they were all looking at me.

'And you, Isabel . . .' said the chief goddess soothingly, 'what has brought you here?'

'I, er . . . I, er . . .'

'Yes, it is difficult to talk sometimes, isn't it?'

Never before this moment.

'I have been told that my masculine side is stronger than my feminine side so I'm here, er, to think about what being female is all about.'

'Yes, yes. I see.' She nodded sympathetically.

The woman next to me burst into tears. I was surprised that she could have been so touched by my few brief words. Perhaps she was amazed by how evolved I was? But no, it turned out that she was depressed. 'I feel I'm always a bud and that I shall never flower.' She began to weep copiously. Mr Masculine felt deeply unsympathetic.

There was another hour to sit and be moved. They talked on, one at a time, about how wrong their lives were. My sympathy was running low and the look of loving concern on my face was beginning to feel painful. If I was lucky I could get to the pub before closing time.

To my surprise a tall and elegant goddess joined me for a drink. She turned out to be rather interesting to listen to: 'For me, being female has always been to do with what I thought I should be in order to be acceptable and pleasing to a male. But being a woman, that is something different. As you'll find out this weekend.'

'But aren't all these women . . .?'

She threw back her head of very short hair.

'No, they are not. All the women I know there have husbands and rather beautiful male lovers. I may be wrong. I don't know all of them. But why do you make assumptions? And anyway, even if some of them are gay . . .'

How could she be so outspoken?

'Don't you think you could learn from them too?'

'Yes, of course. It's just that I . . . like men.'

Oh dear. Things were going from bad to worse. Now I felt homophobic. It was all a strange reversal of another bizarre situation that had occurred the previous Christmas. I was living in a tiny flat in Manhattan and I'd sent Christmas cards home informing friends that I was living very happily with a woman. I received the season's greetings by return congratulating me for 'coming out'. When I had to write back telling them that sharing the room with a woman was quite innocent and I was at the same time enjoying a predictable and old fashioned relationship with a man, everyone was very upset. My vicar and his wife were devastated. They had hoped to have their first real 'out' lesbian in the community. I was a huge disappointment to them.

This was the second time, therefore, that I had experienced my lack of sexual broadmindedness as rather a limitation.

Saturday morning I arrived with a smile and a tracksuit. I recited, like a mantra, the now well-used Insight teaching – 'Use everything for your learning, upliftment and growth. Use everything . . .'

The morning went well with some great exercises. The usual: listening skills, expressing anger, nothing I hadn't done before. I was much more comfortable. I knew all this and I was feeling pleasantly superior again. It's so good to be in a place where you know that you know better than everyone around you.

At lunch I asked more questions about being a woman. 'It's about timelessness, absolute receptiveness. A woman absorbs everything and learns from it.'

'Yes, but this is all very theoretical,' I said in a masculine kind of way. 'How do you change the way you are?'

'I simply observe every time I make excuses for behaviour that is not really what I want to do. I watch every avoidance technique and ask myself, "What am I left with if I don't do the avoidance?"'

Ouch. So I really shouldn't ring that man that I know isn't interested in me just so that I can avoid sitting feeling sorry for myself. Or the one who is interested in me but who I'm not really attracted to just so I can enjoy the attention? Blast these weekend workshops. And couldn't the lead goddess stop being quite so supportive-looking? Even over lunch?

When we returned to our room we were informed that one of the women wanted to 'clear the energy in the room'.

'Negativity has been left here.' She was a thin, dark-eyed girl and deadly serious.

'I want to burn some sage.' The sage didn't want to be sacrificed and wouldn't light. I tried not to giggle. Finally we filled the room with smoke and wafted away all the bad vibes. It was huge fun and didn't involve me being female at all. I rather wished it could go on all day.

The afternoon session began with an exercise that I had not done before. We were dancing in twos as if looking in a mirror. It was an odd sensation. Normally when I look in a mirror I'm thinking, 'Good grief what a sight. Time for a haircut/trip to see the electrolysist/cosmetic dentist/plastic surgeon.' This was different. In this alternative mirror the face looking back at me had total acceptance of herself and was looking at the reflection with pride. It made a very pleasant change. 'Shame these mirrors aren't available at Peter Jones,' I said – at a moment when we weren't supposed to be talking.

Then, just when I was beginning to really enjoy the exercise the chief goddess said, 'What happens if you peel off a layer of clothing?'

No, I was not going down that road. I peeled off a sock. Twirled it round in the air and threw it across the room with gay abandon. I was grinning happily. The voice intoned again. 'And another one.' That was OK – I had two socks. But the women all round me were dancing in twos and taking off their clothes. More worrying still, something weird had happened to my reflection. She didn't appear to be wearing much.

So what would you do in a room full of women who are dancing and removing their underwear? I could have run for the door, I suppose. But then I'd risk looking fearfully inhibited and have to endure a concerned phonecall from the chief goddess later that evening. Then, just when I least expected it, a helpful comment from Mr Masculine, 'It's no more than you do at the sauna. You don't get shy there. These are all girls, you know. What's your problem?'

So, off came the clothes, the underwear, everything. Picture the scene. Seventeen women, colours and sizes various – and me with them, prancing around in my very own birthday suit. The things I do in the name of enlightenment.

Of course, all the bodies were beautiful. This was obviously the 'lesson'. The same old reminder of how crazy it is to think that we need to be thinner, taller, or whatever. We are perfect just as we are. It was all very reassuring – until the next thought occurred. We were naked and this was Saturday. Sunday was still the second day of the weekend and no mention had been made of it having been cancelled.

'Bring your goddess dress tomorrow, and your music,' said our chieftess when we were all fully clothed again and sitting back on the cushions in our fairy circle.

On Sunday morning a circle of chairs stood in their place. Everyone was wearing beautiful dresses and looked radiant. I was in a place that could be described as 'quite scared'. What on earth was she going to ask us to do today? This was the moment of 'initiation'. We were each to do something one at a time. I tried not to let my imagination run away with me. I knew one thing: if this was about being free to 'pleasure yourself' in front of others, call me inhibited if you like but I was leaving.

There was no explanation about the process. The leader was

to go first. She handed her music to one of the women and started to dance. Suddenly I woke up and paid attention. I moved from super-cynical to agog with wonderment in twenty seconds. This was not a dance and, thank God, it wasn't about doing it in public. This was something I'd never seen before and made me question everything I had done in my life until that point. As she moved she peeled off her clothes. But this was not about taking off clothes. Somehow she expressed a part of herself that was so real – the clothes just got in the way.

Scales fell from my eyes as I watched her. 'This is a woman,' I thought. 'Sexuality dancing.' This was the timelessness and receptiveness which yesterday had sounded like theory. I watched her. I wondered where I had been all my life. She stopped dancing. They wrapped her in cloth. They gave her water.

The next woman got up. A black woman who had brought drum music. She started to move. She was inhibited by her clothes so she also took them off. Suddenly I believed in ancestors and power being passed from one generation to another. We were transported to another time, another place, a far-off continent. 'This is a woman.' She became power and strength. Yes, a beautiful strength dancing. Impossible to imagine her going to work on the Victoria Line.

Then a third got up and I saw pain dance. Can you imagine seeing pain? She cried out in a pure grief and with the despair of all women. I'm not sure what century we were in at this stage nor who I was in the room with. And I'd been bothered that this woman had short hair?

Then joy stood up. Dancing to the old pop tune 'My Sweet Lord.' She danced naked before her Lord and I thought of my statue exercise. Here was a woman giving thanks to her God in her dance – thanks for her breasts, for her body, for being alive. We all smiled for her. We beamed at her. She radiated her joy into us, expressing complete freedom and self-love. Thanksgiving. They could learn a lot from this at the Harvest

Festival service in the C of E. Tinned food to give away is one way of giving thanks to God for what we have. This was another.

Then, just when I was convinced I was going to melt into nothingness from the wonder and intensity of it all, lunch was announced. And there I was walking around Highbury with women who I felt more inclined to worship than eat pizza with. They chatted as if this kind of self-expression happened every day for them. Maybe it does. I ate a lettuce leaf or two and wondered how J.S. Bach was going to help me in this situation.

After lunch I saw a warrior woman. Laugh if you like. I know it sounds absurd but when you see an archetype expressed in front of your eyes and hear a woman roar, history lessons about women warriors make sense. She was angry, she was raging. I was glad she didn't have any weapons. I could swear she was wearing a goat-skin. Something out of a prehistoric picture book? But she couldn't have been wearing anything. She had looked like a perfectly normal girl in a rather attractive black dress when she stood up. No clue to what was underneath. Look out, guys!

Finally it was my turn. I felt as if I had not been born. One of the women had offered me a simple white dress and it seemed very appropriate. I was a girl among these women, forgetting that I was older than many of them. Bach sounded and I began to cry. I looked around the circle. Faces of wise women who knew who they were. My job was to let the girl come out and dance. To take a few steps.

No wonder I was always getting told to stop being so strong and clever. No wonder I usually managed to mention to people about the first-class degree. It was suddenly easy to understand that the inner masculine was so strong because this little girl was hardly born. I thought I was someone who loved attention but I was so ridiculously shy. I listened to the Bach. Timidly I took a step forwards, I moved an arm, then lifted the other, slowly to the music. I swayed gently from side to side. I took off my clothes as the others had. I could be naked, emotionally or physically, and not ashamed. That's how Adam and Eve are described in the Garden of Eden, 'naked and not ashamed'. I don't ever remember feeling so vulnerable, so young or so loved.

I had never listened to this girl inside me. I'd had sex with men I didn't really want to be with. A bit like raping myself because I'd never paid attention to my own fragility. I was supposed to have been trained in awareness and yet I had not even learned to listen to myself. My face was red hot. I smiled as they tenderly wrapped me in a sheet and gave me water to drink

I sat back in my chair with another ridiculous born-again look on my face. How could I learn so much in three minutes? I was going to have to start listening to this aspect of myself. Admitting that she was there. And, I know I always say this, but next weekend I wanted to do something really banal. Something truly stultifying. Watch TV, maybe?

The last woman finished her 'initiation'. I looked at them all. To think how convinced I had been that I could learn nothing from these women. I thought that I knew more about being a woman than they did. I tell you another thing I learned that weekend: you can tell nothing by looking at people. Nothing at all. We like to think we know a lot and that we can judge by appearances. Or I do. I pride myself on knowing more about you after I've met you for two minutes than you know about yourself. But it's true that appearances can be deceptive. Very deceptive.

When you go into work on Monday morning take another look at the girl on the reception desk, the bored secretary down the corridor, the smiling nurse or the junior-school teacher that you leave you son with. Women are mysterious and powerful creatures. Any one of those smiling faces may be the wild woman who I met in my goddess workshop. And she roars.

Phase Six: Tantric Sex – Yes! Yes! Yes!

So, now a leaflet in the post inviting me to a tantric sex workshop and I'm not in a relationship. Just my luck. Where were these workshops the last time I had an unimaginative lover? And why would I want to go on a tantric workshop on my own?

'I mean, can you imagine the kind of men I'll meet? They'll all have a well-developed feminine side. They'll all have long, thin bodies.'

'And long, thin willies,' my friend Anna interjected when I complained to her about my predicament.

'They'll wear floaty clothes and have straggly hair and warm, sympathetic smiles.'

'They'll do those double hand-shakes while looking into your eyes,' she grinned.

I started to scream.

It's not that I think I'll be expected to have any sex, tantric or otherwise, with any of these men. It's just that it would be good to want to. To be overcome with a desire to dedicate my body to another participant's learning process.

Perhaps I could take someone else's husband with me. Call up a married girlfriend and say: 'Hi, Julie, I was wondering if I could borrow your husband for the weekend? I'm going on a course to study tantric sex and I need a partner, you see, and . . . Julie? Are you there?'

Or I could put out a general e-mail to all the men in my life on the other side of the Atlantic:

> Unique opportunity offered. Fly to London (at your own expense) and take a workshop (at your own expense) on, er, sex – not that I was suggesting that you need to . . . Oh . dear.

Or what about inviting a complete stranger? There is a rather attractive, good-looking waiter in the new Starbucks on the King's Road. I could try: 'A café mocha, please, and, well, yes, there was something else I wanted, actually . . . I was wondering if you'd like to join me for a weekend workshop to study tantric sex?' He'd probably smile in a long-suffering way and say, 'I'm gay – sorry' and I'd be hugely embarrassed and not be able to drink coffee in there again.

There is one possible sign of hope. The person whom the organisers have arranged to give me a lift to the workshop turns out to be an independent TV and film producer. I did a bit of research and found out which company he owns and what films they've made. Maybe I could sort the next job and the next relationship in one weekend?

The lift was to be shared with another tantric learner. She arrived to meet me looking like one of those Indian pictures of the Divine. Her long legs were clearly visible through floaty black muslin trousers and a small white diamond twinkled enticingly just below her navel. She wore a deep-red top with extravagant jewellery and a beautiful waistcoat that was a sophisticated blend of reds, with golden threads intricately woven through the colour. Her waist-length dark, shiny hair looked like a commercial for some silky conditioner. Her make-up was subtle and perfect and she wore a crimson teardrop in the centre of her forehead. The overall effect was breathtaking.

She spoke with one of those exotic accents that are instantly attractive and mysterious.

I, on the other hand, was wearing a pair of jeans, old trainers and an oversized black fleece. My accent was decidedly Battersea and I hadn't made time to wash my hair which was looking like the 'dull, lifeless hair?' part of a commercial for Head and Shoulders.

A large BMW rolled up and a very thin man with glasses and a large smile got out. 'You must be Stellianna,' he said, turning to shake hands with the vision of mysterious loveliness. 'And your name, was, er?' Why do I do this to myself? 'Er, Isabel,' I mumbled. 'No, I don't mind sitting in the back of the car.'

It was to be one of those dreadful journeys, with traffic jams, a vague feeling of nausea from sitting in the back and snippets of half-overheard conversation from the front. And I was given the map-reading job. 'It's the next turn-off, isn't it? [Thinly disguised impatience] Are you sure?' It was inevitable by this stage that I was going to mess up, make mistakes and humiliate myself. 'Well, I, er, thought the B road would be prettier.' I tried to look blasé as he stared first at the map and then at me with a look of total incomprehension.

And of course his mobile phone kept ringing. He'd say, 'Washington DC? Tuesday? Tell them absolutely not. They'll have to suggest another date.' Or 'The première? Yes, say we'd be delighted.' Or simply 'I can't talk now I'm on the motorway.' My mobile was not ringing, despite the fact that I had briefed my daughter and asked her specifically to 'phone me a lot' on Friday afternoon. She rang once and complained that she'd wiped off the outgoing message on the answerphone. So I was overheard saying, 'Well, just run the tape to the end and then you can re-record it. No, it's the button on the left! Oh [exasperated tone] never mind.' And that was the only time my phone rang. Blasted thing. Who invented mobile phones?

We arrived at a large beautiful centre in Hereford a lifetime later but still in time for supper. Ms Inner Feminine was shouting at me. 'Hello? Attention please?' I washed my hair and put on a dress. Anything to keep her quiet.

After dinner, while we were sitting waiting for the first tantric something to start, an unexpected miracle occurred. I received a note from the TV producer. It said: 'Dearest Isabel, since the moment we met I have felt that special warm vibration. Can you feel it? Your tantric slave, Simon.' Ms Feminine smiled smugly, 'See, I told you it was worth putting on a dress.' Mr Masculine thought, 'This guy's crazy.' I wrote back, 'Warm vibration? Are you sure it's not your mobile phone switched to "vibrate"?' He looked at the note and took up his pen again. Two kids now writing notes to each other in class. This workshop was fun already. 'It's you. You are the perfect woman. A goddess.'

The Goddess workshop had obviously been worth the money. My transformation must have been more complete than I had realised. Not sure about his writing style, though. I scribbled away . . . 'I presume that you work in drama rather than documentary?' I'd already checked him out for hidden cameras. He just went on with his adoration. 'You are beautiful. Your face. Your body. Your eyes. Your eyebrows.'

'My eyebrows?' He wasn't a scriptwriter.

'Will you deny me, oh heartless one?'

'Deny you!? It's Friday evening.'

'Will you let me be your tantric slave and give you total and unconditional love all through the workshop?'

So, would you say no to a tantric sex slave who was offering unconditional love? He was rather thin. I had a quick look round the room. Average age of male participants? Sixty. Average size of beer-guts? Huge. Hair on heads? Very little. Hair on chins? Prolific. Men with an over-developed feminine side always grow beards. It doesn't really fool anyone. One of the very overweight men smiled at me warmly. Anything to avoid the double handshake later. And there was always the excuse that I had to 'use everything for my learning, upliftment and growth'. Best to put these learnings into practice wherever possible.

'OK then, Simon. As you are so impressed by my eyebrows.'

He came to sit next to me, grinning happily. This was a pleasant surprise. Here was I, the woman who goes after men, having a man run after me. I liked this experience. Maybe this was one of the tall, dark, handsome strangers promised by the astrologer.

The first process was to begin blindfolded. It was called 'the awakening'. The leaders had prepared a feast for each of our senses. We were led to another room and sat on cushions while the most sensous sounds filled our ears: gentle drumming, the patter of rain-sticks, bells of all sizes, the deep hum of singing bowls. I slid down into my cushion, healed already by the beauty of sound. Then the sense of smell was to be rediscovered. They had all the wonders of a full aromatherapy shop to pass under our ecstatic noses: citrus, strawberry, myrrh, lavender, sandalwood, peppermint, freshly baked bread, cut grass, vanilla. Then to taste: fresh mango placed sensitively on the lips, dates, pineapple, ice cream, apple crumble (not quite as good as at the convent but a pretty fair second), chocolate, red grapes. Then touch: sea shells, fur, stones, dough, crystal, wax, fluffy leaves, fir cones. Next we were invited to turn and reach out our finger tips to the person next to us. I turned and with a hair's breadth of gentleness touched the very tips of the fingers next to mine. 'Just explore these hands with your sense of touch,' a velvet voice intoned. So we played, these hands and my hands, blindfolds still in place – fingers were intertwined, palms touched palms, thumbs stroked thumbs. A sweet tenderness. An innocence. My white-dressed child was happy to play this game.

Finally we were invited to remove our blindfolds. I opened my eyes. They had been Simon's hands. Somehow he had managed to get himself placed next to me. (I discovered later that he had told one of the helpers we were a couple.) His conquest was going well. I felt OK with him now. He smiled at me. We turned and looked at the room filled with candles and beautiful statues of the god Shiva making love to the goddess Shakti. There were also many-armed symbols of love and the celebration of sexuality. My eye was caught by a large pink crystal ornament in the shape of an erect penis. I imagined putting one on the coffee table in my sitting room for the neighbours to admire. I'd say, 'That, Mrs Jones? Oh it's just a little souvenir of Hereford that I picked up. Do you like it?'

But here, in the candlelight, they looked beautiful. I guess the penis gets a lot of bad press. Women complain about its misuse or how much men are led by it, or deride it when it goes wrinkly or tell jokes about it. Men complain that it isn't big enough or doesn't work well enough, or gets them into trouble or is too active or not active enough. Here the penis was named 'Vajra' (meaning thunderbolt) and was to be celebrated.

So we feasted our eyes on erect crystal peni (plural of penis?) then cuddled like children, went our separate ways and went to sleep. And here ended the first day.

Over breakfast the other participants enquired as to whether we were a couple. 'We're not sure,' he said. 'No, this weekend is an experiment,' I smiled. The deception was complete. They all thought that we were a long-term couple pretending not to be. We touched like a couple, we related like a couple. It was fun. An easy game to play.

Most of the first morning was taken up with the now familiar 'sharing' process. We were twenty-two participants this time, sitting on a circle of cushions. They had been careful to arrange an equal number of men and women. The leaders of the workshops were an odd pair who, of course, weren't a couple. The man would definitely have won the award for the least attractive male in the room. He was about fifty going on sixty, overweight, had longish, straggly hair that needed a wash, comical glasses and a large and unfortunate gap between his two front teeth. I wasn't going to be signing up for any private lessons.

In her introduction the woman told us, 'I've had six children by six different men.' An impressive track-record by any standards. And she went on: 'I've always been interested in sexuality.' I'd guessed that. She was also overweight but she managed to carry her weight like an expression of her sexuality and it made her even more voluptuous somehow. They wouldn't have won any prizes in a fitness competition. But then, I considered, if they'd looked like Barbie and Ken and she'd started by telling us that she'd just had a facelift, they'd hardly have been in a position to teach self-acceptance. They were as honest and open as it was possible to be; they knew their subject and, like all these New Age facilitators, they breathed love.

The sharing was touching, as it always is. Happy couples that had somehow lost their way sexually. Old couples who had lost it completely. Newly weds who wanted to do the sex thing really well. Young couples who were just there to have fun. And then the singles, brave people who wanted to learn this stuff and were not waiting for Mr or Ms Right to come along. Those who admitted, with great courage, that they felt clumsy sexually or just lacked confidence. Simon and I said that we had come to learn as much as we could and to put it into practice. We were so convincing it was silly.

The rest of the morning was mainly loosening up and playing games. Disco dancing – some energetic, some slow, some raunchy – invitations to pull faces at each other, grab bums or argue with each other in non-existent languages. There was even an invitation to say 'fuck off' to everyone. Tantric ice-breakers.

It was easy and fun. Then lunch. Vegetarian, of course. Simon rushed off to make an important phonecall to New York. I sat and ate tofu with a young Chinese professor from Oxford. He had been raised by Jesuit priests and was so cross with what they had denied him in terms of his sexual education he didn't seem to notice that they had given him such a good academic education he was now the leader of his field. I suggested that he wrote his next PhD on the subject of tantric sex. Suddenly his eyes lit up and being an academic didn't seem to promise such a dry future as he'd thought. Simon and I ignored each other. We were a couple after all.

When the first exercise of the afternoon started the instruction was, 'Bonded couples work together – everyone else choose a partner for this exercise'. Simon simply walked straight over to me. Of course, I could have said no. But I was being offered unconditional love and support and, having touched his fingers, I didn't really want to turn him down.

The afternoon lesson was about exploring masculine and feminine energy.

'Walk round the room and celebrate your gender. As you make eye-contact with someone, say the words 'I am a woman' if you are a woman and 'I am a man' if you are a man – to each person you meet. It can be playful, vulnerable, strong, sexy, seductive or however you like. Say this to both the men and the women.'

Most of the time in these workshops I am filled with a feeling of unconditional acceptance of everyone. I make use of the 'the inner beauty I see in you' exercise from Insight. But not always. Sometimes the old bitter, twisted cynic steps in. So when some of these men walked up to me and said 'I am a man' I thought, 'No, I'm afraid I don't agree – I have some clue about what a man is and I can tell you, you ain't it. You have the face of a woman, the energy of a woman, the voice of a woman. Have you ever ridden a motorbike? Initiated anything? Punched someone? Drunk beer? Had sex? It certainly doesn't look like it!' However, I didn't say all this, of course. I simply smiled and gave the required response: 'And I am a woman.'

Then the facilitators said, 'And that is only half the truth, because inside every man is a woman and inside every woman is a man.' So then we were to repeat the exercise. My inner masculine was very happy being allowed to speak. Going round the room saying, 'I am a man' seemed like stating the obvious. The feminine and sensitive men were probably thinking, 'Yes, God help us.' But I knew by now that as I've been a single father as well as a single mother all my daughter's life my inner masculine is not hard for me to access. Even the astrologer told me as much.

And some of these men, none of whom were gay, now seemed to be nearer the truth. 'I am a woman,' they were saying. I was thinking, 'I knew that already.' Other men were afraid to say this so they fooled around, went into 'camp', put on silly voices, acted like little girls. Not so my thin 'bonded partner'. He walked straight up to me, every inch the masculine energy, and said quite clearly, 'I am a woman.' He made it so easy. He was completely comfortable with his masculine energy and com- pletely comfortable with his feminine energy. He didn't need to hide it, disguise it or apologise for it. He simply stated it. And he was happy with me saying 'I am a man' as a simple fact. He didn't seem to be judging me for how comfortable I was with that statement. I suppose he'd already told me I was a goddess. Perhaps he really did accept me as I was.

That was a good thing to know before the next exercise. The instructions began; 'Kneel opposite your partner. The woman likes to give out her energy through her heart. The man needs to receive through his heart. He likes to give out his energy through his sex. She needs to receive him through her sex. When this works, a circle is created.'

Sounds so simple, doesn't it?

This is what we were to experience using our breathing. I breathed out making a movement with my hand from my heart to his. He breathed in to receive me, then he breathed out, making a movement with his hand from his sexual organs to mine, and I breathed in, moving my hand toward my 'sex'.

Now, before your imagination runs away with you, I should add that there was no touching and this was only an exercise about the transfer of energy. But with eye-contact being maintained at all times, you can imagine that this was still fairly intimate. In fact, 'fairly intimate' is a bit of an understatement. It was one of the most intimate exercises I'd ever done in a seminar.

Then we were to reverse it, to experience the energy the other way round. The woman also needs to give out energy through her sexuality and receive from her heart and it is important for both partners to experience both roles. A little empathy leads to a lot of understanding.

Then, just when I was getting totally overwhelmed, they announced dinner. I listened to a woman who was there alone. 'I have been bisexual in the past,' she said, 'but I feel that I now want to have a committed relationship with a man.' Yes, her and a million of my other single female friends. 'I would love to do the one-year training course with a partner. But the one-year singles' course I'm not so sure about.' I choked on my lentil soup.

'The what? The one-year couples' training? You mean they do a one-year course in all this?'

'The couples' course starts in June next year. It's five four-day residentials and lots of homework in the middle.'

'What do they teach that takes a year?'

'Tantra is about learning how to contain the sexual energy that we release at orgasm so that the pleasure becomes implosive instead of explosive or you can rest in the pleasure for as long as you want to. When you can consciously contain this energy it takes you to higher states of consciousness where sexuality and spirituality meet. They can't hope to teach that in two days. This is just a taster weekend.'

'It sounds wonderful.'

'Will you and Simon be doing it? Taking the course, I mean?' I felt I had to come clean with her.

'I'll tell you the truth,' I confessed, 'we only met yesterday.' Her jaw fell.

'But you are both so . . .'

'Yes, I know,' I said hastily, lest she have a chance to finish the sentence. 'It is rather amazing, isn't it? But will we be doing the couples course? I really couldn't say.' She started to laugh. We drank coffee. I liked her a lot. If only I could have that change of sexual preference, life would be so much easier.

'But anyway . . .' she lowered her voice, 'we have to remember that we are here to work on our own sexual growth and understanding. It's really not about who we are with. The real journey is with ourselves.' Suddenly I saw Sister Alison from the convent sitting in front of me. 'The real journey, Isabel, is with yourself.' Good grief, I'm even told this on a tantric sex weekend? Blast the truths of life.

The evening of this course happened to hit Halloween night. They weren't going to let an opportunity like that go by. We were invited to take a different partner. Only of course the 'bonded couples' worked together. Simon, my lifetime lover, appeared at my side. This next exercise wasn't easy. They wanted to use the 'night of dark powers' for all it was worth. The facilitators spoke of darkness, the subconscious, of what was forbidden, of what had been banished. Then the instructions: 'The man should hold the woman in his arms as she goes on an imaginative journey in her mind, down into the deep darkness below death to see what is there.' He held me in his arms. I didn't really want to go anywhere beyond death with him. But he was so loving and supportive it would have been churlish not to play.

I listened to the velvet voice of the fat man with the gap in his teeth and descended into the depths of my mind where I was surprised to meet a wild dancing god. Or maybe he was an Indian sexual demon. I watched in amazement as he leaped and hurled himself around. He was OK safely hidden in my mind's eye. But then the voice said, 'Now bring this energy into you and bring the images to life. Get up, dance.' So I got up and danced. I flung myself around. There was a kind of freedom but as I looked into Simon's eyes, the support of the male Shiva, filled with his promised unconditional love, I knew I was pretending. I felt disconnected with my experience and self-conscious. It reminded me of times as an actress when I'd been on stage and known that I was acting badly. I had not become the Indian sexual demon I saw. I was observing myself being a fraud and still dancing anyway. I did the exercise, but it wasn't real.

Then it was his turn. I got to hold him while he did his inner journey. I don't know where he went but he certainly wasn't pretending. He was crying in my arms. I stroked his hair, being the all-loving mother that I had been instructed to personify. But when he got up to do his dance I left the mother role right behind. Where, I asked myself, had this man learned to move? I thought I was a trained dancer – but ballet class at the Royal Academy of Dancing was never like this.

As he started to dance he played with his sexual energy. I watched him and I could see him wait until he sensed the glimmers of arousal. He moved slowly at first, delighting in his senses. This was too much. I was glad we were in candlelight by this time as my face must have been redder than the satin cushion I was sitting on. He was, quite simply, one of the most erotic dancers I had ever seen. True, he was displeasingly thin, but this expression of sexuality meant I could generously tolerate that. Have you ever seen anyone dance in their sexual energy? It made me shake to watch him. Then the exercise finished. We were invited to stay in the room as long as we liked but to 'please respect the sacred space'. Which I guess meant, in case anyone had done the exercise too well, no bonking.

So the couples lay and cuddled and chatted and laughed. We just lay and held each other. It was so easy to be held. I could have imagined this exercise with some of my former partners. They'd have been saying, 'Well, you didn't get that exercise at all, did you, Isabel? I knew you were pretending. And what really irritated me about what you did was . . .' My ex-husband would have said, 'Nice try'. This man just held me. So you can imagine he was a great trial to be with. Then, one by one and two by two, we all went our separate ways and went to sleep. And here ended the second day.

The Sunday exercises were harder still. We never celebrated All Saints' Day like this in the Church of England. 'And this morning, my brothers and sisters, we are going to celebrate this day of the Lord by our practice of sexual breathing. We will then read the Song of Solomon and sing Hymn number 317, "Glad that I Live am I".'

Here I was praising God in my own sweet way. We were to learn sexual breathing and how to build the energy in the pelvis with pelvic rocking. Also how to hold the sexual energy using the pelvic muscles. This sounds raunchy but after the Goddess workshop it was surprisingly sensitive. After all, there had been no nudity and everyone was free to participate or not as they wished.

Sexual breathing was another exercise to be done while maintaining eye-contact with your partner. I was touched that the woman was to find her rhythm of pelvic rocking and then the man was to take his rhythm from her. This proved to be a bit like dancing. No sooner did I establish a rhythm – squeeze pelvic muscle, breathe, rock forward, release pelvic muscle, exhale – than I'd lose it again. The Shakti incarnation of the female facilitator encouraged me. 'Be patient – this is the first time you've done this exercise together.' Too right it was.

Then suddenly it was Sunday lunchtime and we were in the 'closing sharing'. It was so tender. The couples said that they had rediscovered a connection. One man of about sixty, there with his wife, cried as he looked at her. The newly weds said they had found a way forward. The stuck couples said they were unstuck. The singles said what they'd learned and how touched they were by the support of the group. One woman who had come alone had never done any work of this kind before and had become less and less terrified as the weekend progressed – by the end she was finally able to speak.

And as for me, I felt like a whole person again. I had been taught not to apologise for having a 'well-developed masculine side'. I am a woman, after all, and so to be a beautiful woman with positive masculine qualities of strength and vitality is often a bonus. My ability to see the male point of view is sometimes so accurate I even amaze myself. But I do still want a real Shiva god around to look after me and I know how to be vulnerable too. It's true, I am still learning to listen to my feminine side, but she is alive and well and growing in confidence all the time. So maybe I really am evolving?

But this is not the end of the story. 'What about Simon?' I hear you ask. 'What happened next?' The workshop finished after lunch so that people could enjoy the idyllic countryside. The sun was shining in a blue sky. It was a perfect autumn afternoon. The Indian goddess we had travelled up with was going back with one of the couples. It all seemed too good to be true. It was.

Simon appeared after lunch in a suit instead of his 'walking though the countryside' clothes. 'I'm afraid if you want a lift in my car I have to leave in ten minutes.' I couldn't believe it – his mobile phone was actually ringing. 'I'm sorry, I have a meeting in London at six and I . . .'

'That's OK,' I sighed, looking at the leaves falling over the orchard, 'I'll get my bag.'

I knew he was going to be worried that I may have got a little fond of him. He was male, after all. 'You're afraid I'm going to ring you or something, aren't you?' I asked him. We were half an hour from London. He'd spent the first three hours asking me about my life and telling me how wonderful I'd been.

'It's just that . . . I do have a . . . sort of . . . relationship,' he said.

'Er, "sort of"?' I requested a definition of this interesting adjective.

'Well, OK, a long-term relationship, I guess.'

'How long have you known her?' I asked, having learned over the weekend to be completely honest and open with this man.

'About ten years.' He took a phonecall. 'Seven tonight? No, that's fine. See you then.'

'How long do you expect to know her for?' I asked in a matter-of-fact voice.

He smiled at the thought of her. 'The rest of my life, I expect.'

I was not yet speechless. 'And do you live with this woman?' He wriggled uncomfortably at the inquisition.

'Sometimes.'

'Sometimes? How can you live with a woman "sometimes"? Do you live with her or don't you?'

'Er, yes.'

'Simon, this weekend was divided into those with partners and those without. If you have a sexual partner who wasn't present, why on earth didn't you say so? Why didn't you invite her? Why didn't you tell the group? Why didn't you at least tell me? Why didn't you . . .'

'Oh dear. I hope you didn't think that we could have had some future together. I did offer you my love for the weekend.'

'Yes, but after the kind of intimacy we have just experienced I did at least think that maybe I could ring you sometime. That maybe we could have had dinner, or gone to a film or something.' Another lesson in non-attachment. I crumpled up and started to weep on to the floor of his BMW.

'Listen,' he said, as I lifted my suitcase from his car and walked away. (And every word of this is true). 'I hope I didn't mislead you in any way?'

Phase Seven: But am I Co-Dependent?

The adventure with Simon sent me into the Slough of Despond. Knowing about non-attachment is one thing, but not having anyone to be wrongly attached to is another. Here I am, filled with knowledge on tantric sex and no one to practise with. And we are only talking about looking into someone's eyes. There is no justice in life.

Is it possible that one day I'll have a relationship with a man who I really want to be with? Or maybe when I am totally evolved into a truly actualised person I won't moan any more about not having a man in my life? I mean, Buddha doesn't sit round complaining, 'It's Saturday night again and everyone else has got someone that they adore to spend their time with', does he? People in relationships all seem to give their single friends the same advice. 'When you stop wanting to be with someone they'll just show up.'

This creates an interesting mental game to which, as far as I can see, a frontal lobotomy is the only solution. I have to stop wanting something so that I can have it. But if I stop wanting a 'significant other' in order to get one, then aren't my motives a little suspect? And surely it's all relative? It's not as if I sit in on Saturday evenings pining and reading *The Rules*. Not often, anyway. No, my perfectly balanced inner masculine, inner feminine and I go out with my female friends and my gay friends and my married friends and enquire whether any of them know any interesting single men in Britain and they all shake their heads. Then they add, 'There aren't any in America or Australia either.' One of my friends visited South Africa recently. Her postcard showed a circle of empty chairs with the caption, 'AGM of available men in South Africa'. It seems to be a universal problem.

The only temporary solution becomes to emulate the Buddha anyway and practise this 'not being attached' thing. But I'm not talking about being attached to a person. I'm talking about being attached to the idea of being attached to a person. And the thing I really resent is that I know plenty of people whom I would consider even more dysfunctional than I am and they manage to form nice co-dependent relationships with other dysfunctional people. So why not me? Why can't I just be happily unhappy like everyone else? Why can't I do this evolving process and have a dysfunctional male in my bed? One with a lovely body and an over-developed masculine side? I have to admit I am attached to this idea. As you see.

So, to go back to where I started in this circular meditation on the unfairness of life – this this means I have to un-attach myself. This subject was seized upon recently by a total stranger. I was sitting in a coffee shop, innocently sipping my café latte, which is my habit, when I was complimented by the man on the next table and asked if I would like to chair the following meeting. I said I'd be delighted to, but of what? 'Oh, aren't you an alcoholic?' replied the amazed gentleman.

'No, can't say that I am. Sorry.'

'So what are you addicted to?'

'Er, nothing as far as I'm aware.'

'Mmm', he said in disbelief. 'Tell me about your father.'

I was in good humour, so not about to deny myself a free session of psychoanalysis. 'It would be hard for me to talk about him as he wasn't there. I never met him.'

'I see,' said the bearded character, looking more like Dr Freud every second. 'So how do you model your relationships on this?'

I thought about it. 'That's simple. I have relationships with men who are not there. And my partner, I've definitely never met.'

'There you have it. You are co-dependant. CODA, Co-Dependents Anonymous, for you.'

'Wait a minute, I thought co-dependent meant being dependent on someone else who in turn is dependent on you? Surely if I'm on my own I can't be co-dependent?'

'Are you happy on your own?'

I was beginning to wish the discussion was a little more superficial. Perhaps the current political situation or the world economy? 'Not really.'

'Do you wish you were with someone? Do you feel that your life is not complete without a partner? Do you experience lack in your life as a result of that "other" not being present? Be honest now'.

I ordered a muffin sulkily. 'I suppose so.'

'There you are.' He smiled gleefully. 'I told you so. Everyone needs the Twelve-Step programme.'

I had always considered the Twelve-Step programme as a time-honoured method for curing alcoholics and people with real problems. It had totally transformed the life of an alcoholic friend of mine and I was much in admiration of the system. I had never dreamed that it could have any relevance for someone as evolved as me. After all, wasn't I almost perfect? Wasn't I almost happy on my own and so therefore ready to meet someone? Sigh. Perhaps he was right.

'I didn't know I was an addict till now.' Was this something to thank him for?

'Don't worry. You can go on the programme. Go for six weeks to try it. It's free.'

So they could cure me of my desire to share my life with a man in six weeks? And I didn't have to pay for this?

'Just put your name down here and I'll have them send you the details.'

So the details arrived. A surprisingly large number of people go to meetings all round Britain to admit that they are co-dependent. I had a friend who went. The very same luvvie friend who had persuaded me to take an Insight course all those years ago. Fiona was always working on herself in some way or other. I think she's now one of the most together people I know. She says that she's co-dependent. Of course I still don't think I am. 'But then alcoholics don't think they are alcoholic, do they?' she said chirpily. Fiona found my protestations that I didn't need to do this a matter of great hilarity. 'You are supposed to go to six meetings to see whether you can learn anything.' Oh no, not that 'use everything for your learning, upliftment and growth' thing again.

So I arrived at a meeting. With my friend. Not that I'm co-dependent or anything. I noticed that people tended to arrive in twos, with someone who looked rather like them. Two very thin women. Two punk rockers with studs and pink hair. Two rather overweight gentlemen who looked depressed. I bounced in with Fiona. We are both long-haired and it has been commented upon that we have similar faces. This was not a good start.

The Twelve-Step meeting has a simple format: a few readings, people talk for five minutes each, others listen and then thank them, and then everyone goes home. On the face of it that is all that happens. But the programme is so brilliantly designed that, as people work their way through the Twelve Steps in a serious and committed way, they turn their lives from desperation to hope. Maybe I'd sign up for real at the end; maybe I wouldn't. I was exploring again, I justified to myself. I was allowed to do that. But I felt rather a fraud. I had never been suicidal. I had a job and friends around me. It was remarkably humbling listening to people speak. I said nothing and just sat and listened.

So was I co-dependent? A leaflet had a list of questions to help me identify my shortcomings. Answer 'Always', 'Usually', 'Sometimes' or 'Never'. In the section marked 'Compliance' I did well. Lots of 'Nevers'. I never assume responsibility for others' behaviour. I never have difficulty in expressing my feelings. I am never afraid of anger. I am never afraid of expressing differing opinions. I am not a perfectionist. I do not compromise my own values to avoid rejection. I don't remain in harmful situations too long. So this was OK.

But then came the questions on 'Control Patterns'. Oh. 'Do you offer advice and direction to others without being asked?' Always. 'Are you skilled at guessing how other people are feeling?' Yes. 'Are you calm and efficient in other people's crisis situations?' Yes, always. 'Do you believe most people are incapable of taking care of themselves properly?' Well, yes, but including me. 'Can you tolerate seeing others in pain?' Well, no – and I usually launch right in there with some unsolicited advice.

I suppose I could be just a little bit of a control freak then? I remember an old boyfriend saying: 'You are a very easy person to be with . . . as long as you have your way . . . but your way is usually an excellent one . . . so one may as well let you have it.' But then I left him. I guess because he let me have my way. Mmm. Anyway, that was three years ago and I'm sure I've improved since then. Well, I think I'm sure. Well, perhaps I'm not too sure. Perhaps I'll go to six meetings anyway just to check it out.

By the time of the second meeting, in a different part of town, I was once again firmly convinced that I didn't need to do this. Fiona had complained that she wanted to come with me. You see – she's co-dependent. But I was determined to go without her just to prove how independent I was. Shame really, I enjoy company.

The meeting was difficult for the strangest reason. The structure is such that you can't do anything to help anyone. An amusing challenge for me. For example, a man stands up and says: 'I'm so angry. I just don't know what to do with my anger.' He is shaking. I have a leaflet in my briefcase which reads, 'Anger Release Day – learn how to release your anger and have fun'. So, are you thinking, 'Perfect, give him the leaflet'? If so, I'm afraid you are probably co-dependent too. Sorry. Because, you see, he did not come up to me at the end of the meeting and say, 'Isabel, I wonder whether you know of any way that I can get rid of some of the anger in me?' So if I give him the leaflet – if I leave it 'accidentally' on his chair or drop it 'anonymously' into his bag – then I am giving unsolicited advice, aren't I? Unsolicited advice: lose ten points and return to 'go'.

And a woman did speak with me after the meeting. 'I find all this learning and growing so painful,' she said. Right answer: 'Mmm, I see.' Wrong answer: (as given by me with broad smile) 'It doesn't have to be, you know. It can be fun. Have you heard of Insight Seminars?' I'm obviously a bad case.

Fortunately I have a master teacher at home. My daughter. I can practise not giving her advice on a daily basis. Maybe she'll start asking for it then. 'Mum, do you think I should switch off the TV now and do my homework?' 'I was wondering, do you think it is appropriate for children to smoke? I would value your opinion.' 'Is listening to XFM Radio a better way of spending my time than doing my piano practice?' 'Would it be better to wear a jacket as it's raining?' I can't say that I lack daily opportunities for growth.

And as for Fiona. I've noticed a funny thing about her. She is always giving me unsolicited advice. It's most irritating. We made a deal – she is not to give me advice any more and I'm not to give her any. Our conversation has become very limited. We are forced to become more and more creative in our attempts to influence the behaviour of the other. 'I find it's really good for me to take things easy sometimes,' she'll say, pretending to be expressing a fact about her life if she thinks I've been over-working. But I'm good at catching her out. 'Sounds like advice to me,' I'll say.

Or, if she is depressed, I'll say innocently, 'I was reading when I was at the gym this morning that eighty per cent of depression can be cured by exercise alone.'

'Thanks for the advice.'

At the third meeting the subject under discussion was: 'Take a moral inventory and humbly admit to ourselves and to others when we were in the wrong.' In the wrong? Me? No. I am quite prepared to admit that I may have faults (I'm evolved in that way, you see), but being wrong has never been one of them. If this was an organisation for people who are wrong then it's obviously not the right one for me. I cast my mind back to the last time a friend had accused me of being wrong . . . well, OK, it was the day before. 'You can be so opinionated,' she had said. Did I reply humbly, 'I was wrong – I should have expressed my idea differently'? Nope. I thought, 'Silly opinionated woman.' Good grief. If I am going to have to start thinking about my words and actions and admitting to people I've been in the wrong, there really is some danger that I could become a nicer person. I am beginning to dislike these CODA people.

The fourth meeting I was determined to go to alone again so that I could be sure I was making progress. I sneaked off early on a Sunday morning without telling Fiona, in case she offered to accompany me. I stumbled on a 'Theme Meeting'. They voted on a topic to share about and chose 'Forgiveness'. I sat in my chair and was unusually quiet. I certainly didn't want to consider this topic. Not that I haven't forgiven everyone in my life (including, most magnanimously, myself – for not being perfect), but perhaps there are one or two . . . The only reason that I could come up with for being nice to my ex-husband, for instance, was to take Oscar Wilde's advice: 'Always forgive your enemies – nothing annoys them so much'.

Meanwhile there was a serious meeting going on. The more evolved co-dependent people were being moving and profound again. One at a time they spoke their truth. They spoke of forgiveness in the face of rage. Forgiveness of genuine atrocities that had been committed against them as children. Once again I felt very humbled. I was a pretender among these people. 'Forgiveness.' It was such a beautiful morning and felt so appropriate for a Sunday. This really was an attempt to take the logs from our own eyes instead of taking the splinter from everyone else's. And the questions raised were so profound. 'How do you forgive someone who is not sorry?'

As well as the theme, they were also focusing on one of the famous Twelve Steps. Now, I'm not going to tell you about all the Twelve Steps because I would be unable to resist adding bits of unsolicited advice along the way. Like a truly evolved person I'm just going to stick to my story. At this meeting I had chanced up on a discussion of Step Eleven. For those of you who have never discovered what kind of addict you are, the first part of Step Eleven is: 'Seek through prayer and meditation to improve our conscious contact with God as we understand Him . . .'

I thought that this was very unfair. I mean CODA is not a religious organisation, this was not a weekend with the nuns or a visit to church, and yet even here I was being told that prayer and meditation was a good idea. How could I possibly go on being grumpy and complaining about the lack of a 'significant other' in my life if they were going to encourage me to rediscover prayer? If I were to do this there was a genuine danger that I might achieve the objective for which I came to CODA in the first place.

I stomped home in a temper and blew the dust off a book

called *Teach Yourself to Meditate*. Maybe I could meditate in a very non-spiritual way? After all, I didn't really want to achieve my objective of being happy on my own. I opened my meditation book and attempted a fifteen-minute meditation. I say fifteen minutes but I always fall sound asleep before the time is up. In this effort-free way I can always avoid meditation having any positive effect.

My fifth meeting was on a dark, rainy evening on the other side of London. There were ten of us present – working away on our 'defects of character'. The talk was on 'Just for today I will act in a way that I would admire in someone else'. What a ridiculous teaching. That means live up to my own standards? Ouch. When not working, get up at a reasonable hour, go to the gym, dress well and don't slob around the house, do a full day's work at the computer, don't eat biscuits all day long, send thank you letters for dinner parties, be eternally in a good mood, read proper books, cook real meals. I can't keep up these standards for ten minutes, let alone a day. I don't think I can even approach living in a way that I'd admire. I'm still working towards living in a way that I can tolerate.

I can see that this teaching would be entirely effective if I was in a co-dependent relationship. Trying to live up to my own exactingly high standard would certainly leave me too exhausted to notice any 'defects of character' that my partner might have. And even if I did notice them I would certainly have worked out by now that it is not my job to do anything about them. It's really quite amazing that anyone criticises anyone else about anything. I mean, how many perfect people are there in the world? I've only been to five meetings with this organisation and I honestly can't see myself criticising anyone for anything ever again. And as for giving advice. My friends are going to have to apply in writing.

I'd better go and get dressed now . . . it is nearly lunchtime, after all.

My sixth and last meeting I have to admit I thoroughly enjoyed. It was early on a Saturday morning and I got on my push-bike and merrily cycled off to sit in my circle of chairs. The meeting had a speaker – he was most inspiring. He talked about where his life had been before he had started the programme and how, slowly but surely, he had turned it round, stopped being a control freak, learned to be nice to people, and started his own company in which he had to have very good relations with people at all times. He was funny, too. He ended his 'testimony' by adding 'I could murder a cup of tea and a bacon sandwich'. I laughed. Whatever his 'defects of character' were, he didn't seem too bothered about them.

As we stacked the seats afterwards he invited me to go to lunch. We sat in the café and I told him that this had been the last of the six recommended meetings to decide whether I was going to join the programme or not. 'You don't seem co-dependent to me,' he said. 'You seem far too together.' Appearances can be deceptive, can't they? 'In some ways but not in others,' I said, happily digging into a salmon and cream cheese bagel.

'But you know what your issues are, don't you?' he asked.

'Yes. And I think everyone is co-dependent to some extent.'

'Quite. Are you busy tonight? I was wondering if you'd like to catch a film or something?'

I choked on my salmon. 'Sorry?'

'Can I take you out tonight? Or tomorrow?'

I had come to CODA because I wanted to meet someone – it suddenly all came back to me. No, no! It wasn't true. I didn't want a relationship with this man. Even if he was less co-dependent than I was. I didn't find him attractive. Panic flooded over me. 'How desperate am I to go out on Saturday night?' I thought. I had yet to reach the stage of going out with someone who I was not attracted to just to avoid being alone. Phew, well that's a relief.

'That's very sweet of you,' I smiled. 'But I don't think I'm ready to embark on a relationship with anyone just now.'

'There you are,' he said. 'That proves you are not co-dependent. You know how to say no. You don't make me wrong. You don't accept responsibility for my feelings. You do own responsibility for yourself. Text-book answer.'

'You mean you were just testing?'

'Maybe. But I don't think you need to come back.'

I cycled home. The world is a funny place. I'd given myself six meetings. I'd been given what I'd asked for and found that I didn't want it any more. But I'd learned not to mind other people's business and not to give advice. I'd learned to concentrate on living up to my own standards. I'd learned to think about what I say and do and to consider that I may sometimes be wrong. (Well, let's not go too far.) I had even practised admitting to a work colleague where I had been wrong in a disagreement we'd had. The following day she had been absent, believed to have been suffering from shock. My book on prayer and meditation was no longer covered in dust. And Fiona and I now went to dinner and discussed art and literature.

Maybe there really is hope for me? Maybe there is progress? Maybe I am less co-dependent and dysfunctional than I was six weeks ago? Maybe one day I'll meet a man I'm really attracted to – a man to whom I'll want to say, 'Yes, yes, I'll go anywhere with you and do anything for you'. Maybe one day I'll have a relationship with a man who I really want to be with. Hold on. Didn't I write this already?

Phase Eight: The Bottom Line

Did I tell you I was working again? I like working because I don't have to evolve. And there is another good thing about working in TV. Especially doing research. No one minds how unfit you are as long as you can talk on the telephone all day sounding as if you are full of energy. But as to actually being full of energy – that is a very bad idea.

The answer to the question: 'How are you today?' is either, 'Terrible, I've got a hangover', 'Ghastly, I only had three hours' sleep', or, if you are feeling really good, then a muffled and monosyllabic, 'Fine' is sometimes acceptable in a really successful company. If I ever walked in on a Monday morning and said: 'I feel fantastic, so alive and full of vitality and I'm really looking forward to all the challenges that this series has to offer,' I'd never work again.

The reason I'm telling you this is that here, in the privacy of these pages, I can confess to you the appalling truth. I want to feel in good shape and have a body that I'm in charge of instead of having it boss me around. I had decided, as my energy levels seemed to be sinking from very low to none at all, that the t'ai chi Master had been right – 'ze bodi is veri important'. Perhaps instead of all this thinking about things to evolve I could change tactics all together? I have recently discovered a secret that doesn't involve having to meditate or be nice to anyone. In that

97

famous trilogy mind/body/spirit this is seemingly the easy level. The body. As long as it doesn't involve having to go running or go to the gym. This is good for the body but uses less energy than t'ai chi. I don't have to raise a metatarsal or a gluteus maximus. It doesn't involve exercise at all. So what is it? Have you guessed? (Pause for effect.) Colonic irrigation.

In New York if you haven't been colonically irrigated people look at you in disgust. It would be the same as admitting that you have never washed. So I decided, as I had a birthday coming up, I would treat myself to the ultimate cleansing treatment. A washing out of the entire large intestine using a tube. Seriously. What's more, I'd heard that the person who is colonically irrigating you studies the contents coming out of the tube and lets you know what exactly it is and how long it has been there. Feeling sick yet?

Apparently there are some horrendous stories. Things get wedged inside us and go on silently rotting away like poison. They have found parts of sausages inside people who have been vegetarian for ten years. This is the honest truth. And people who take lots of vitamin tablets in plastic containers – sometimes literally hundreds of bits of plastic can be flushed out of the gut. Am I putting you off your next meal?

So I rang a lady irrigator with ten years' experience behind her. She clearly didn't believe in colonic foreplay. 'How regular are you?' she asked with a directness that I supposed she was used to. 'I mean, how regular are your movements? How often do you go?' I kept silent, amusing myself at her euphemisms. 'When my daughter was younger we called it "doing a poo",' I responded unhelpfully. 'I remember the first one delivered into a potty was a great event.'

'How often do you do a poo then?' She persisted. It wasn't something that I'd ever thought about.

'Er, I'm honestly not sure.'

'Once a day? Once a week?'

'You mean some people only go once a week?'

'Oh yes.'

'Definitely once a day – or more often, especially if I'm running.' Now I was embarrassed. But she continued her line of questioning as if she was discussing the flowers in springtime.

'And when you've been, do you feel complete?' Ah, completeness! Wasn't that what the Road to Enlightenment was all about? I'm not sure she was discussing metaphysics, though.

'Yes, er, most of the time, I think.'

'It never ceases to amaze me just how unaware people are about their own bodies,' she sighed with an air of melancholy despair. Like everything else I obviously have an un-evolved colon.

'You don't know how often you evacuate and you don't know whether you feel complete or not? It amazes me. Oh, I don't mean to be rude.'

'No, of course not,' I reassured her. 'I promise I'll pay more attention between now and my first appointment.'

The next few days were not easy ones. I found I was overcome with a desire to fast, to let not a single solid pass my lips, to starve myself so completely that I would be able to hear her say admiringly, 'Goodness, this is the cleanest colon I've ever irrigated'. But I figured it was pointless. I probably had a burned cocktail sausage stuck somewhere, left over from my twenty-first birthday party. Why not continue with my normal diet of frozen food put straight in the oven?

And, of course, Mr Inner Masculine had views on the subject as always. 'This is all a load of tosh. Normal people have been going to the toilet for years. You really are crazy.' Ms Feminine took a more domestic approach. 'When we clean the house things get wedged in the corners and it takes a little extra effort to wash out the dirt. Why not look after the body with the same care? After all, if it's once every ten years it's hardly excessive. Why not wait and see the results before you decide it's all misguided?'

'Because I'm paying.' Same old story. 'And I'm fed up with her ridiculous egocentric ideas.'

Funny how they both blame me for everything. Must go now, nature calls.

Amazing the effect making that phonecall had on my bowel-awareness. Suddenly my own body, normally totally ignored, felt as if it had some relevance to my well-being. I arrived for my appointment more than a little nervous. I felt less anxious about the actual procedure than the Gestapo interrogation. Do I have the right frequency of bowel movements? Just how unhealthy am I?

I got to the health centre and found, to my huge embarrass-ment, that an old acquaintance was working at the reception desk. He grinned as he saw my appointment for irrigation. 'Blast it,' I thought, now he's going to tell everyone I know that I've got a problem with my bowels.' I wanted to stop and explain, 'Listen, I do not have a problem, OK? It's just that I'm trying to improve on a mind/body/spirit level and I thought it was time I did something for my body. I do not have constipa-tion, irritable bowel syndrome, diverticulitis or anything else wrong. So you can wipe that amused smile off your face right now.' But I knew it was hopeless. If I had said all that I knew he'd just smile even more. So I reconciled myself to the thought of my friends at the pub next week greeting me with the phrase, 'How is your little problem? I was so sorry to hear that you've been having trouble, er . . . down there.' You'd think I could irrigate my colon without someone recognising me.

I thanked God I wasn't Lady Di. When she did this it was splurged on the front pages of all the national newspapers. I saw she even got a mention in the leaflet I picked up in the waiting area: 'Colonic Hydrotherapy was made popular by Diana, Princess of Wales'. Maybe they would add later, 'and fell sharply from fashion when tried by Isabel'.

Her little room was like a doctor's surgery. Normally I like doctors because they make me feel so superior. The wonderful thing about my local NHS lot is that they all look pleasingly unfit. The last time I went there to ask about a muscle I had strained at the gym the doctor appeared to need some explanation as to what a 'gym' might be. He certainly didn't seem too familiar with the concept of exercise and looked as if he was about to suffer a major heart attack.

And then there's the medical. Any 'medical' at the GP's is another opportunity for me to feel self-righteous. 'Any major accidents?' No. 'Any hospitalisation?' No. 'Any prescribed drugs?' No. 'Depression?' No. 'Illnesses apart from colds and flu?' None. 'Last time you went to the doctor?' Can't remember. Yes, I always feel very happy after my dear old GP has wheezed on me.

Today was a different matter. My irrigation doctor looked like an ad for vitamin tablets. Also, her medical examination was far more thorough.

'Do you get wind?'

'Doesn't everyone?'

'Yes, but some more than others.'

My face turned a bright shade of pink. 'My daughter has been known to comment.'

'Do you feel bloated at times?'

'Yes, but they say at the gym that I don't do enough sit-ups.'

She was not distracted by any of my evasive answers.

'If someone massages your stomach do you ever feel any tenderness?'

'For anyone who gives me a massage, yes.'

'In the stomach area?'

'I suppose so.' I wasn't doing too well on her little check-list.

'When you wake up in the mornings, how do you feel?'

'Like death usually.'

'How long do you feel lethargic for?'

'Till I've had coffee.'

'Oh, I see. So you are dependent on coffee to kick start you in the mornings? Do you ever feel naturally energetic when you wake up?'

'No.'

'And do you feel a dip in your energy in the afternoon?'

'Yes.'

'How about the evening? Do you find that you have most energy then?'

'Couldn't say, really.'

'When is your energy level at its highest?'

'Er, couldn't say, really.'

'When was your last period?'

'I'm afraid I always lose track of my cycle.'

'So you couldn't say. You don't know when your last period was. I see. Are your bowel movements healthy?'

'Compared to what?'

'Yes,' she tried to be sympathetic, 'it is sometimes hard for us to know how healthy our colon is. But surely you must have some idea? I mean, are your stools hard? Soft? Average?'

'Doesn't that depend on what I've eaten?' I stared at the floor shamefaced. It really was not a subject I'd ever thought about. 'If I'm not aware of any of this, surely that must mean my digestive system is healthy?'

'Well, let's see,' she said ominously and gave me a cloak. 'Undress to the waist, and lie down here on your side, please.'

This was definitely worse than the astrologer.

She spoke soothing words while she stuck a tube into my bum. 'Now turn slowly on to your back, please.'

'Why do people do this?' I managed to blurt out. 'I mean, it's not natural is it? Surely food passes round the colon quite happily of its own accord?'

'No, it doesn't. That's why colon cancer is the third biggest killer in the country. If we all ate totally natural diets of organic fruit and veg and lived stress-free lives then it would be different.'

She started to flow warm water up the tube.

'You might find this is a strange sensation at first.' I'm glad she said that.

'Say when you've had enough.'

'Enough,' I smiled at her faintly in a I-do-this-every-day-manner. What a curious way to earn a living. What does she say at parties when people ask, 'What do you do?' She stared at the tube with an air of professional detachment. 'We have two pieces of fairly hard stool here. Did you say that you complete fully?' Didn't Freud have lots of interesting things to say about all this? I was glad I couldn't remember what they were.

She flushed in some more water. 'But is this really necessary?' I was convinced at this moment that it was not. 'Surely the colon cleans itself?'

'You see that chart there?' She pointed at a large diagram on the wall. I screwed my neck round to look. 'That is the shape the colon should be. Those are the shapes many colons become – you see, when sacs form, all kinds of things get stuck and constantly release toxins into the body.'

'Enough,' I smiled. My colon felt as if it was about to explode.

'Your system seems fairly blocked.'

'I've been in bed with a cold this week. Maybe that's it.'

'No, I suspect that you've not been completing fully for some time. You've just not been aware of it.' She started to massage my stomach.

'Ow.' I had thought I was fit. Going to the gym. Drinking water. I bet my colon is in a better state than my doctor's.

She stared at the tube. 'Don't be alarmed when I tell you this.'

Suddenly I was alarmed.

'You know that it is very common to get parasites in the colon?'

'It is?'

'I'm afraid that you have threadworms.'

This was too much. 'Worms wriggling around in my gut? Are they alive or dead?'

'These are dead. But there are probably more in some nooks and crannies where they feel cosy. Do you often feel tired?'

'I thought everyone felt tired.' I felt a strange desire to cry. I had failed totally in my colonic health examination.

'It's very common,' she said. 'We'll kill them off with herbs they don't like. Then you'll have lots more energy. More water?'

For a moment I thought she was offering me a drink. 'Oh, OK.' She stared at the tube. I waited for the next revelation. 'Found any old spoons? Pieces of jewellery? It's a bit like emptying the Hoover bag I suppose.'

'There is something else, actually.'

'Really?'

'Candida.'

'What on earth is that?'

'It's a fungus. That's what creates the environment that the threadworms like.' Did she have to mention the threadworms again?

'I have fungus growing in my colon? Lovely'.

'I have some herbs to deal with that as well. You won't know yourself by the time we've finished.'

At least I was getting my money's worth from all this. I suppose the more that's wrong, the more value I get for my money. These Insight courses on focusing on the positive really pay off.

'That's enough for today,' she said cheerfully. 'You'll need to pop to the loo now. Then if you'd like to get dressed. These herbs I'm giving you require that you have no alcohol and no milk.'

'You mean no coffee?'

'I didn't say that.'

'But I drink milk in coffee.'

'Then no.'

'I knew it.' Life is a vale of suffering, deprivation, and tears. Anyone who tells you anything to the contrary has obviously done too many weird seminars.

'How long is the abstinence course?' I implored despairingly.

'Ten days. Starting tomorrow.' That morning a friend with an exceptionally good taste in red wine had phoned up and asked me to dinner the following Monday. That very morning. Why is life so full of sacrifice? Buddha never mentioned that I was going to have to give up red wine and coffee.

'How are you feeling?' the irrigationist smiled radiantly.

'Oh, just fine.' I wanted to kill her.

'It's usual not to have any bowel movements for one or two days after a treatment. Let me know if you have any problems. See you next week.' The treatment was a course of three.

The morning after this first moving experience I woke up an hour before I usually do. This may have been an extraordinary coincidence but the last time I woke up before the alarm clock is not stored in my retrievable memory banks. Even more bizarre was an inexplicable feeling of happiness and well-being. No American men had telephoned. It was most odd. Normally I wake up feeling very grumpy. Where exactly is Robert Redford, for instance, and why isn't he in my bed? I stomp to the shower convinced that I am the most unfortunate human being on the planet and only the first coffee of the day convinces me that God is in heaven and all is right with the world. But I woke up feeling cheerful, lay in bed reading a book for an hour and walked happily to the shower. Maybe the body does have something to do with the mind after all?

That day I didn't want to eat anything. The herbs to kill off the worms had not arrived and I was filled with indignation at the thought of feeding them. No. Ha! I would starve them, get them into a weakened state and then zap them. My weekly shopping bill of organic fruit and veg from Waitrose was ridiculous enough without bearing their comfort and well-being in mind. To think that all these months I had been eating organically. I must have the healthiest threadworms in south London. A fast was called for.

But when the potions did arrive life got worse. My brief moment of inexplicable well-being passed. Not only was I not to have dairy produce but I was also not to eat wheat. Now, as anyone who has ever worked in any kind of office knows, the best bit of the day is the coffee and warm pretzel picked up in the morning. Being reduced to starting my day with black tea did not put me into a state of bliss. All food-breaks became miserable. 'Chocolate anyone?' I couldn't eat chocolate as it counted as dairy. 'Pizza or pasta for lunch?' I couldn't eat either as they both contain wheat. And worst of all the cheerful voice of my work colleague asking, 'I'm just popping down to Starbucks, café latte, Isabel?'

'No thank you. I'll have something herbal.' Roars of raucous laughter at the dedicated coffee-drinker imbibing infusions of camomile flowers. I sat in the corner and worked. Eeyore without his tail.

'So how come you've given up coffee?' asked a concerned colleague in a hushed tone as if offering condolences for a recent bereavement.

'Oh, I just thought I should have a break.' A cowardly lie; there was no way I was going to tell anyone about the threadworms. 'Are you coming down the pub later?' said the cute new director of the next programme. This was hopeless, No alcohol was allowed either. 'No, I think I'll go home and have an early night.'

They stared at me in disbelief. Where was the tireless socialite they had known? What had happened to my ideal of bouncing in, Tigger-like, on a Monday morning, full of life and energy? I

was a mess. If this was becoming more healthy I wanted none of
it.

My second session of being irrigated began rather badly. I had
sat in the waiting room and chanced to pick up an article on
candida in a health magazine. It read,

> As well as cutting out alcohol, tea and coffee it is advisable to
> avoid fruit and sugar when trying to eliminate the disease. Do
> not drink fruit juice because the concentration of sugar is
> attractive to the fungus.

Instead, and here's the bit I really love,

> Drink fresh lemon juice in plenty of water – 2 to 4 litres daily.

When the smiling, healthy irrigator arrived I was not feeling
happy. 'How are you today?' Was there a hint of menace in her
smile as she showed me into her little room with the fresh
flowers? 'In a rage.' I said. 'You tell me I can't drink coffee or
tea, I can't eat bread or pasta or pizza, I can't have alcohol, I
can't have chocolate or cheese or yoghurt or pretzels or buns or
lemon poppyseed muffins at Starbucks. And now this article has
just informed me that I shouldn't eat fruit.'

She nodded appeasingly. I raged on, 'I'd rather have threadworms than die of starvation. What am I allowed to eat?
Potatoes, carrots and mushrooms, I suppose.'

'Actually – would you put this gown on? – those are the only
three vegetables that are not good. Candida thrives on potato;
carrots have a very high concentration of sugar; and mushrooms are a fungus, of course, so they should be avoided.'

I sat on her couch in a state of despair. 'Can I have a list of
things I can eat?' I pleaded as she started my second treatment.
'Yes, of course. Ah, there is a great improvement this week.'

'Really? What sort of improvement?'

'Much more movement. You've been taking the herbs, I can see. There is an old matter here.'

Somehow I don't think she was referring to her outstanding bill. 'Er, how old exactly?' I tried to sound as if I was interested in science. 'Are we talking days? Weeks? Months? Years?'

'It's hard to say but, judging by the texture and colour, I'd say fairly old.'

'I see.' I decided that I didn't like the colour of her lipstick. 'So. What am I allowed to eat then?'

'You can have pasta made of rice or corn, just not pasta made of wheat.'

'I don't suppose they serve that at the Pizza Hut where we go in the lunch-break.'

'No. But if you are going to eat convenience food . . .' Her voice trailed off in disgust.

'What else then? What can I have unlimited amounts of?' I was trying to be enthusiastic about my new diet.

'It's good to drink as much water as possible. But in all other things moderation and balance are the keys.'

She suddenly reminded me of a Shaker-pilgrim-Puritan-type-person. 'Moderation in all things, my brothers.'

'I don't agree with what your article says about fruit, but don't eat too many bananas and oranges.'

She had an uncanny knack of picking my favourites. Then something in the tube caught her attention. 'More candida?' I asked, crestfallen.

'No, some parasites have just passed out.' I couldn't blame them. I was feeling faint myself.

Suddenly she looked quite stern. 'Do you chew your food at all?'

'I suppose I do eat very fast. You can tell that then?'

'Obviously. When food passes out in totally undigested form it tells me that you didn't bother to chew it in the first place. If you're not going to chew your food you could save yourself the bother of eating at all. From the amount of undigested vegetable matter I can see here.'

'I'll put up a notice in my kitchen that says "Eat slowly",' I promised. 'I'll use red felt-tips.'

'You can eat wheat-free Ryvita.' I've always hated Ryvita. I'm sure it's only in the shops so that people can buy it for themselves as a punishment after a dinner they feel they've enjoyed too much.

'And you can have pumpernickel and spelt bread.'

'Spelt?'

'Yes, that's S-P-E-L T. And then of course you can have Barleycup coffee with soya milk and Rooibos tea.'

'Will they have these things in Waitrose?'

'I'm not sure. I always get them at my local health-food shop.'

That was all very well but the health-food shop on Battersea Park Road had closed and been replaced by an ironmongers.

My time was moving to a close. 'You've done very well today.' She said, smiling at the tube. 'A great improvement from last time.'

I attempted a smile.

'Would you like some herbal supplements to help rid your body of the toxins produced by the candida?'

'I suppose so.'

'OK, we'll get you some of those. And do try to be more aware of your body in the next few weeks. Notice what effect it has on you when you eat very late at night – usually you will wake feeling sluggish. Notice how you feel after different types of meals, when you feel energised and satisfied and when you feel bloated and full. Then when I ask you questions next time you'll have grown in awareness of how your body works. This is the first step in learning how to take care of yourself.'

'Er, yes.' I put on my florescent yellow cycling jacket and

pedalled home in joyful anticipation of a piece of black German pumpernickel bread.

It was two weeks until my third and final irrigation session. The herbs had had time to kick in and do their worst. I had gone down with flu and lost half a stone. Obviously the shock of living without threadworms for the first time in years had been too much for my poor colon.

'How are you this week?' I rather wished that she'd had flu as well but irritatingly she looked as healthy as ever. I coughed into my hanky. 'The body has been totally de-toxifying itself,' she said cheerfully.

'No – I've had flu.' I wheezed.

'Yes, it's the same thing. The body has cleared out the colon and now it is clearing out the lungs. How have you been getting on with the diet?'

'Terribly.'

'We need to look more at some of the things you can eat. If you could just undress? So, have you been noticing anything about your body?'

'My breasts haven't grown at all.' Silence. I guess I had to talk about my colon.

'If I go for a couple of days without wheat and then eat bread my stomach bloats and I go around feeling heavily pregnant for a day,' I scowled.

'So your body-awareness is increasing then?' She beamed victoriously.

'And I do tend to notice how regular I am now.'

'Excellent. Have you been taking the herbs?'

'Yes, every day.' I felt as if I should be given a badge – I TOOK MY HERBS.

By this time I was in the indelicate position of lying on the couch with her once again staring at the contents of a tube attached to my rear end.

'I'm seeing much more release this week. This is excellent. There are some old parasites and lots of candida is being flushed out.'

I listened to the running commentary and was just beginning to feel gleeful that the threadworms were finally dead when she said, 'Would you like to see this?'

'Er, yes, I suppose so.' Would I? I wasn't sure.

'Just sit up slowly then.'

I'm glad this book isn't illustrated. 'Now if you look in the tube . . .' she spoke like a biology teacher discussing a science project. 'Initially candida can look white and flaky like mucus but yours is tiny black dots like tea-leaves, which is older. You see, it has sunk to the bottom.'

'Yes, I see.' The water was clear with a coating of gungy specks.

'This in an old candida fungus.' I wondered whether I wanted to know this. 'There is an absolutely huge amount of it. I've rarely seen such a bad case . . .' I winced. 'And it is only starting to release today. That is the herbs, you see. It has created an environment that isn't favourable to candida and so some of it has started to release. You see how much there is?'

'Mmm.'

'Now, I want to teach you how to massage your stomach. Say "when" with the water.' I was still intermittently feeling like a blown-up balloon.

'Yes, "when"'. I tried to smile.

'So, give me your hand . . . You massage your stomach in a clockwise circular motion starting on the inside of the right hip, working up under your navel, and round down to your left hip. Now, you see, if I press here?'

'Ouch.'

'That is trapped wind. You can release it yourself by massaging like this.' She took my hand and pressed in a circular motion on various tender spots. 'The idea is for you to be able to feel it yourself. What can you feel here?'

'Er, feels like something moving along.' Bubbles passed into the tube.

'That's better, you've cleared that now. There is a greater mass today.'

'So, we are celebrating greater mass?'

'Er, yes.' She stared at me blankly. My Roman Catholic humour was lost on her.

'There is old matter here again.'

'Ah, yes, good old matter'. I suppose it did feel good to know that bits of old things that had been stuck in my colon were being flushed away.

'That's all. If you'd like to get dressed. You'll need to take Bifido-acidophilus to continue to put the right kind of bacteria into the colon. Then you need Candtox to remove the toxins produced by the candida and Hebacolenz P to cleanse and de-toxify the small intestine. It's not enough to just do the diet.'

To think I had originally come here because I thought I wanted to be super-healthy. It was going to be a year before I even approached a basic level of colonic fitness.

I cycled away with my three containers of herbs. I knew I wouldn't be troubled by any waste matters for two days. I felt strangely virtuous. OK, I wasn't super-healthy. My stomach, however, was pleasingly flat. My threadworms had gone to join the spiritual kingdom. (Do threadworms go to heaven?) And my colon was at least on its way to health.

Yes, there was a pleasant feeling of smugness. I was 'looking after myself' like it says I'm supposed to in the books. I was practising 'preventative medicine' just as the government wanted. And I was keeping the makers of German pumpernick-el bread in business. Still, I was glad it was over.

I turned my bike in the direction of Starbucks.

Phase Nine: Being Born Again, Again

'You have to give up control to the breath. So re-birthing is the thing to do if you have control issues.' Six weeks of CODA and then being told I didn't 'complete' left me with no doubt in my mind that my control issues were all in charge. 'I thought re-birthing was for people who had awful births?' I asked an alternative midwife who lived worryingly close to Battersea Park Road.

Things were not going well. The last TV contract had ended. After my failure to join them for wheat-eating lunches or alcohol-imbibing social events I wasn't sure I would ever work for that company again. The immediate future was booked in my diary for being-depressed-about-the-job-situation. Perpetual unemployment was looming. Still no relationship. On the horizon were two married men wanting to be unfaithful to their wives and a couple of dinner companions who filled me with an overwhelming desire for sleep. At home I now had a teenager who was unhappy with my radical ideas about getting up before lunchtime. And the cat had died. Being born again, again, was the obvious solution.

'Re-birthing is about releasing memories, feelings or pain that is stored in the body memory on a cellular level.'

'I have traumatised cells now? I see. And what does the treatment for this involve?'

'There are two methods. One takes place in a group and the other is just you and a re-birther.'

I always feel happy in groups. The thought of working one-to-one I find far more scary. I might have to actually let down some of my walls of protection and let her see some chinks in my hard-formed masculine shell. She might ask me a personal question or something. 'I've a feeling one person would be the greater challenge for me, so I'd prefer that.' Blast Insight and their 'comfort zone' concept.

'Really? Most people find groups scary.'

'I'm getting to be something of an expert in a group but I've done very little work with an individual. How many sessions would I need to have?'

'Ten is the usual number. But come to three and see how you get on.'

I thought, 'Ten? At £30 a session?' Surely being newly delivered to the world once would be enough? I had fairly low expectations of what was to happen. The only person I knew who had been re-birthed said, 'Oh, it changed my life.' And then added, 'Just like everything else I've done.' And the thought of going to the home of an unknown New Age-type woman to lie on a bed was scary enough. But I decided that, as an alternative to writing application letters and awaiting polite rejection notes, I could be re-born first thing on Monday morning.

The following week I climbed on to my trusty two-wheeler and cycled over Chelsea Bridge to Pimlico. Ten minutes later I was drinking revitalising tea. My hostess was about fifty. Very warm, motherly and quite sophisticated with an intelligent version of the New Age smile. She had the long flowing hair and long flowing skirts one would expect from a wise Mother Earth-type, but she also had a professionalism that was reassuring. Her taste in art was a little spiritual. The walls looked like *Who's Who in Heaven*.

'Who are all the guru-types?' I asked of the various faces in frames on the wall.

'All the spiritual masters are here,' she smiled. 'Someone for everyone.'

'There's mine,' I said, spotting a picture of Christ. 'Who is the character flying above his head?'

'That is an Indonesian goddess.'

'She's very sexy.' I thought how much Christ would have liked an Indonesian goddess in his life instead of all those fishermen and tax collectors who never understood a thing he said.

'Do you know anything about your birth?' She asked, styling herself on a cushion and picking up pen and paper.

'All I know about my birth records is that I had 'the cutest little feet'. And my mother is dead now – so no.'

'What about the birth of your own daughter? How was that?'

'I was twenty-four and fit so it was pretty good. But it was eighteen hours from first twinge to baby. She was quite happy in the womb. No desire to leave.'

'That's good. Often the first birth experience mirrors our own birth. Is there any particular reason that you've come to re-birthing? How have you arrived here today?'

'I cycled down the Battersea Park Road'.

She smiled politely. There was a long pause. I didn't know where to begin. 'I don't know.'

'It doesn't matter. What is going to happen is that you are going to lie on this bed and breathe in a specific way. It's a breath high in the chest, like the first breath a baby takes after the umbilical chord is cut. You don't push the out breath, you just release it, then you take another breath immediately without out a pause. It's a circular form of breathing. It takes about an hour and a half. You will find that as you do this certain feelings and memories will come up and your body will experience different sensations. This breath will enable your body to release painful events that have been stored on a cellular level.'

I stared at her in horror. I was going to do *what*? Why was the thought of this so scary? Perhaps it was those control issues. Was I ready to turn over control of my breathing and body to this woman? I felt my bike calling me to cycle home again, on a cellular level. If only Robert Redford was here right now . . . I was sure I could lie down and breathe heavily then. I was outside that comfort zone again.

'So, would you like to lie on the bed?' It suddenly looked like a doctor's couch draped in exquisite covers. But I could manage the first requirement. I could lie down.

'Take an intake of breath, like this.' She demonstrated the breathing and I watched her. Then I closed my eyes and copied her rhythm. As I breathed she spoke instructions to me. 'Good. Don't force the exhale. Just let the out-breath release.' I concentrated, breathing into the upper chest and not pausing between the breaths. 'This fills you with oxygen' said a voice, which seemed to be fading into the background.

My body was beginning to feel all manner of strange sensations. My hands, feet and temples were tingling. My calves felt heavy like lead. My speech was becoming slurred and I could feel nothing at all from my neck to the top of my legs. She was massaging my feet and hit a painful spot. 'That's fear,' she said. 'What do you remember?'

Suddenly I was in my bedroom as a very young child. The corners of the room were black and full of eyes looking at me. Ghosts and monsters were hiding behind the curtains. They were waiting to get me if I fell asleep. I knew they were there. I could feel them. Mummy and Grandma were downstairs watching TV. I couldn't shout for help. I couldn't move. I couldn't breathe. Something was moving the curtain.

Then a play-pen. Grandma had gone away and left me here. I couldn't get out. I hated all these toys. I just wanted her to come back. I shouted and cried till I gave up and went to sleep on the cushion.

'My grandmother just left me there every day.' I said. She spoke softly, 'Yes, they thought then it was OK just to let toddlers cry.'

Wow. This was weird. Where did those memories come from? What was this voodoo?

My legs and arms were juddering, it was a curious sensation.

'What do you feel in your body?'

'Tingling and numbness.' I tried to talk to her, but interestingly the power of speech seemed to be leaving me. Friends would be encouraging me to commit to this lady on a regular basis. 'My tung does'n seem to be wor'ing,' I slurred.

'Keep up the breathing. Don't force the out-breath.'

An ache started to develop in my lower back. 'Ow . . . pain,' I moaned.

'Just roll on to your side – keep breathing. Just here?' she said, putting her hands on the exact spot.

'Mmm.'

'That is a lack of support. Hardly surprising for an only child with no father. Have you ever had an anaesthetic?'

'Mmm.'

'Was it by injection into the lower spine?'

'Yeah,' I struggled to get my speech organs to work.

She massaged my lower spine. The pain became intense. 'It really hurts.'

'Don't worry, it's releasing. Just keep going.'

I breathed. She massaged. Slowly it started to dissipate. My calves still felt like lead. My whole lower trunk felt very strange indeed. A dull ache now. My hands, legs, feet and temples were still vibrating. I had lost all sense of time. I don't know how long I lay in the tingling.

'Ease up now.' She spoke softly. 'It would be good to empty your bladder. Don't move too quickly. Sit up very slowly.'

'I'm fine,' I said. A habitual response.

'I know,' She smiled. 'But I'm going to support you anyway.'

She took my arm. I did feel wobbly and I wasn't quite sure where I was. Navigating the stairs was a fun experience, like being drunk. But when I came back into the room a minute later I was shivering.

'Back under the covers,' she said.

'Why am I shivering?' I asked. 'I'm not cold. It's not cold in here.'

'That's your body throwing off fear. What is the ancestral history around fear?'

She was either clever or lucky. 'Funny you should ask that. My mother came from a very old English family. They had their own coat of arms and everything. The motto under the coat of arms is 'Sans Crainte', 'Without Fear'. So I guess it was not encouraged.'

'That has been a good thing and a bad one in your case because whatever fear you did have has been repressed and held by your body. The shivering is releasing it.'

Then slowly the shaking stopped and instead I began to glow. The tingling was replaced by an intense buzzing. A faster vibration of tingle. The place where the pain had been felt very warm and comfortable. She pulled the covers around me. It was blissful. I couldn't quite believe the way my body was feeling.

'Gosh,' I said. 'This feels wonderful. What's happening?'

'The breath just shows what needs to be healed. The heaviness in the calves is unexpressed sadness. The numbness all through the body – well, you need to consider what you have numbed out and why. The blocked speech shows that you are not expressing yourself fully. The pain that released may have been your body releasing the memory of the anaesthetic and may also be related to the lack of support you have. Anyway, it worked its way out of the cellular memory very well. Would you like some tea?'

'Mmm.' I felt very verbose.

'We're not finished. I want to give you some affirmations.'

She produced strawberry tea with chocolate and ginger biscuits and then wrote on a piece of paper.

I am now willing to release my ancestral patterns.
I am now willing to have my needs met.
I am now willing to receive love and support from men.

'This is called overturning core beliefs,' she said. 'You need to work with these every day. Repeat them to yourself as many times as you have habitually repeated the opposite – such as "I never have any men in my life".'

'Mmm, very good. Could we add the word "available" to the last one?' Call me unreasonable.

'Say them in a way that suits you.' She was flexible about redefining my core beliefs. Always a good sign.

'When can I come back?' I had been planning to ignore her suggestion of three sessions and just come once. Now the co-dependent in me wanted to rush back to a meeting and say: 'Go do re-birthing. It's much more fun than focusing on your defects of character.' If we are living in a self-indulgent society we may as well go for it 100 per cent and have fun too. Why choose a therapy that makes you miserable?

'I'm afraid you will have to go now.' She woke me from my bliss-inspired daydream. 'I have another client.'

'Mmm.' It was hard to leave this new mother so soon after birth.

I climbed on to my bicycle. Yes, I had been re-born and I even felt like an evangelical again. I wanted to tell everyone about this. I needed a flag, a drum and a megaphone. I've always wanted to join the Salvation Army. Roll on next week.

But the second session was different. I couldn't remember anything in detail afterwards. I could remember my hands feeling like a pair of rubber washing-up gloves that had been blown up like a balloon. She said hands were to do with asking. I needed to ask for what I wanted. And I hadn't wanted to scream at her, 'I do ask. I did ask. I asked the last man I loved to be with me in every way I knew how.' This wasn't Simon, by the way, this was . . . Well, I'm not explaining *all* my secrets to you. I didn't tell her anything, either. I didn't say anything at all.

I had been given a new affirmation, which made me laugh.

I am now willing to be with a man I want – who wants me.

Did you ever hear of anything so absurd? Mutual attraction? This may happen on planet Zog but everyone knows that this isn't possible in human relationships. Peter likes Jane. Jane likes Tom and Tom is gay. Right?

I admit occasionally Jane thinks she likes Peter and they get married – but then Peter discovers that he really would be happier with Susan, Tom's sister. Peter then leaves Jane and moves in with Susan (but has to pay all the money he earns to Jane) and Jane ends up spending her evenings with Tom and his lovers. Then one of Tom's lovers gets confused and has an affair with Susan, who was bored with Peter and also bewildered by the attention of Liz. And Susan and Jane end up taking the children out and complaining that there are no interesting men in the world. Write your own variations based on any group of friends you have.

The one thing we all know is that never, at any point, are two people mutually and equally attracted to each other. But here was this crazy woman wanting me to repeat this piece of unlikely fiction while doing deep breathing under a silk blanket. She asked me questions but I didn't reply. Any question which might have got anywhere near an emotion was ignored. My hands exploded and made a mess all over her beautiful carpet. And that was all.

Do you hear the stamping foot? I didn't want to be healed of anything by this woman. I didn't want to leave any of my issues behind. My level of resistance was so huge even I noticed it. I've done awareness seminars, you see. I got home from that session and scribbled furiously on a notepad: 'I don't want to cry with a woman in the room. I'd rather stay stuck. I don't want to take this work to a deeper level. I don't care how understanding she is. I will not let down my shields with her. I don't want to. I don't have to.'

This was resistance, all right. Before I had joked about having control issues. Now I was experiencing them in stereo, technicolor and full seat-vibrating 'sensurround'.

Then a voice in my head. 'Isabel, what would you say to someone who shouts, "I don't want to go to the doctor. I don't want to go to the doctor"?' I guess it's obvious. They need to go to the doctor. And not just any doctor. The one they are shouting about. 'I don't want to work with a woman,' I raged on to myself.

'So work with a woman then.'

'I will be in control. I'll show her how tough I am. I don't want to be vulnerable in front of her.'

'Why not?'

'Cos I don't want her to see the pain underneath.'

I didn't stop to ask where this voice of wisdom came from. I just listened sulkily.

It wasn't that this woman was bad at her job or that I didn't like her. I did like her and the way she worked was superb. That was just the problem. She worked with such sensitivity it was hard to hide from her.

I could cry with a man but not with a woman. It was obviously an unresolved issue with my mother who had given me the 'strong single parent' modelling. But knowing why my fear was there didn't make it any easier. There was only one thing for it. Damn and blast the Road to Enlightenment. I was going to have to go back.

There is something I need to explain to you. This 'core belief' thing. The idea is that I may say 'I am willing to be with a man I want who wants me'. But, based on current reality (and in spite of CODA), I am not with one. With me so far?

You can apply the following irritating little theory to anything in your own life that you want but don't have. The idea is that you have a subconscious resistance towards it and somehow the world knows that. So if I enter into a relationship with a man I would like to spend my life with and I think, even on an unconscious level, 'Of course you won't want me', then he'll pick that up and back off.

Or if you have a belief that you will never be rich? Guess what? You won't be. Many of these ideas are so clever it drives you crazy. Insight have them all in shorthand:

> There are those who say they can and there are those who say they can't, and they're right.

So you need to change the belief. Easier said than done.

My re-birther suggested the following method. Write down the new belief and then write next to it the objection that comes into your mind. Then you write the new belief again. It's like doing lines, only much more interesting, because you can watch the shifts in your thinking happening before your very eyes.

So, to continue 'sharing' with you about my 'process'! It looks like this:

1.) I am now willing to be with a man I want who wants me.	This is a silly piece of homework and this woman is mad.
2.) I am now willing to be with a man I want who wants me.	Flying pigs are often seen on Battersea Park Road.
3.) I am now willing to be with a man I want who wants me.	The clouds are made of candyfloss; the moon is made of cheese.

Fifty-four lines later, I had stopped stop playing around and was beginning to look for the deeper level. I wrote:

57.) I am now willing to be with a man I want who wants me.	Being with one? I can't even imagine meeting one.
58.) I am now willing to be with a man I want who wants me.	But all the ones who like me are boring and the only one I think I want doesn't want me.

By the 198th try I had discovered the wiring . . .

But my father never wanted my mother. If my mother never had this, why should I?

And;

My grandmother lost her husband and my mother brought me up alone. Why should I have a man in my life I love?

So this is what she meant by an ancestral pattern. Could this, I wondered, be the basis of the warning that the sins of the fathers are passed on to the sons. It's not that God smites us with these things, but we pick them up – in the same way we inherit an ability to run fast or sing flat.

I don't want my daughter to inherit this belief so I have to change myself. I write the 'new belief' another hundred times . . . with all my objections. Finally I reach: 'Yes, it's true.' For today, anyway . . . It's exhausting work, reprogramming your brain.

I amused myself by thinking about the kind of man I'd like. A man with the mind of Louis de Bernières who wrote *Captain Corelli's Mandolin* and the looks of Robert Redford. Then again if he had the wit and compassion of Bernières I'm not sure I'd mind if he looked like Quasimodo.

I felt a moment of courage and made my next appointment.

The following week I climbed on my bike feeling extremely vulnerable. It's all very well saying that if you wear a helmet when you cycle you will be safer, but there is no protection from a re-birther. I toyed briefly with the idea of cycling under a large truck and taking a short cut down the Road to Enlightenment. The headlines would be good: 'ISABEL REACHES ENLIGHTEN-MENT ON BATTERSEA PARK ROAD' But then I remembered the chocolate ginger biscuits she served at the end of the session. Are there chocolate ginger biscuits in nirvana? I couldn't be sure. It wasn't worth the risk of missing them. Better stay on the earthly plane a bit longer then.

A friend had asked that morning, 'So if you hate it, why do you go back?' I had to stop and explain all about the comfort zone and the benefit of doing things to which you have resistance. In trying to convince her I had almost convinced myself. But not quite.

I cycled along feeling determined to do the work at the

deepest level necessary – despite the fear. But Mr Inner Masculine was very unhappy, 'I hate all this support and understanding . . . all this feely stuff,' he said. 'Can't we just go to the gym?' Suddenly I understood why so many men are frightened of women. We want to talk about 'feelings' we 'understand' . . . it's very intimidating.

I've only got to hear a female friend say to me, 'How are you feeling?' and my inner masculine side is ready to go out and learn cricket. It can feel so invasive and can produce a shutdown reaction in me rather than a willingness to open up. Women have been moaning for years (not me, of course) that men don't talk to them. So just don't ask the question, girls! Anyway, most guys relate better to a good blow job, I've found. When he wants to talk, he will.

My inner masculine and I chained up my trusty steed (well, bike), I strapped on my armour and walked into her house. A plant screamed at me, 'Water!' and I stopped and insisted on watering it for her. She smiled benignly, recognising my feeble attempts to put the work off for another thirty seconds. I sat down and said, 'I don't like you cos you're understanding and supportive. I don't like your silly homework, either.'

'How do you feel about the statement: "Men I want stay with me"?' she asked. I tried to repeat it but I still couldn't help grinning cynically. 'A bit more work to do there,' she said. Highly trained you see.

'Would you like to lie on the couch and start the breathing?'.

'No, no, no. I wouldn't.'

I hoped to divert the session with a display of resistance. It was hopeless.

'Lie down and breathe and shout about how much you don't want to shout,' she ordered gently.

I started to tingle all over. It felt very nice and it made it hard for me to be quite so cross with her. 'What are you feeling in your body?' I didn't answer her. 'What is happening in your face?' She asked. Once again I didn't answer her. It wasn't that I didn't want to answer; I just didn't feel safe. But here I was, lying on the couch of an experienced and empathetic woman who only wanted to support me. Unfortunately she was a step ahead.

'You don't feel safe?'

'No.' I could say that much.

'Did you feel safe with your mother?'

'No.'

'So as a fatherless baby you took on the role of courageous child and became your mother's protector?'

I went on breathing and tried to ignore her. I thought about the price of Ryvita in Waitrose.

'Did you ever feel safe with anyone?' That was it. Blast her. She'd hit a nerve. I remembered the one man I'd felt safe with. He had left me too. Like my father. Before he even knew me.

She had somehow reached all the pain I knew was buried in me somewhere for the man I had wanted and lost – by turning me into the child who had lost her father. Tears started to stream down my face. I wanted to shout out, 'No. Please don't leave, please, give me a chance.' I had wanted to feel safe and protected for so long. As far back as I could remember I'd forced myself to be strong. I had finally, a lifetime later, met a man who had learned to be stronger than I was and he had 'abandoned' me too.

'What are you thinking about?' said Ms Sympathy-and-Understanding.

I certainly wasn't going to tell her. Then suddenly a picture came to my rescue.

I saw myself as a child as running barefoot over the shingle on Brighton beach. The stones hurt but I wanted to be strong. I didn't want to feel pain. I walked over the beach every day refusing to wear shoes to protect my tender feet. It was ex-cruciating. I guess I wasn't very sophisticated in my choices of ways to numb out feelings. But it had worked.

'What are the sensations in your body?'

My hands were still tingling. And my calves. But aside from this hardly any sensation. I felt numb. 'Nothing much,' I whined.

'That's OK. Just relax now,' she whispered. I started to cry again.

'Why, when I met someone I could really have loved, didn't he want me?' I wailed like the abandoned two-year-old she had turned me into. Bloody voodoo breathing.

'Maybe you told him to go. You said men you want leave, didn't you? Or maybe it was his issues. Who knows? But you aren't going to do that any more, are you? Because men you want stay with you, don't they?'

Despite everything, this woman really did humour well. 'Men I want stay with me.' I saw myself saying the line in a Woody Allen movie.

The session finished. 'Well done.' She was looking supportive again.

'Why are you being nice to me? I haven't done anything to you,' I winged.

'Tremendous work today. You allowed yourself to be vulnerable despite your resistance to working with a "mother" figure. And we found out that you have never felt safe or protected and that you have a tendency to numb out feeling. It's just a question of bringing these things to awareness so then you can move through them, as you are doing. Fabulous work.' I was feeling utterly pathetic.

But then she brought the strawberry tea and chocolate ginger biscuits and I thought that the world was a wonderful place full of joys and delights. Raindrops on roses and whiskers on kittens. I even felt a passing affection for Julie Andrews.

Then she said, 'I'm giving you the phone number of Roger Woolger, a friend of mine who deals with past lives. I think it would be valuable for you to go and see him.' She pushed a piece of paper into my hand.

'I don't believe we have past lives.'

'No, I didn't think you would. Nevertheless, give him a call. You might be surprised.'

I cycled home feeling as if I'd been emotionally irrigated. Maybe it was relief that the three sessions I had committed to were over, but I had a smile on my face for all the world. I even stopped my bike in the park to pat a friendly dog. I'd been taking the affirmations daily and, although swallowing herbs is easier, I was becoming convinced the re-wiring job was done. Men I want stay with me? They'd be crazy not to.

But past lives? You've got to be kidding . . .

Phase Ten: Past Lives with Wooden Doors

I was being haunted by a piece of paper. I knew that somewhere, lost in the bottom of a huge untidy shoulder bag, something was whispering 'Past Lives' and a phone number. I held out for two weeks and then my curiosity once again got the better of me. I rang the number. An efficient secretarial voice informed me that it would not be possible to attend a private session as, 'Dr Woolger lives in America and is rarely in this county. I can send you details of his workshops but you need to read his book before you attend.' Homework before a workshop? This was new. They were obviously determined to prevent me from raising uneducated or naïve doubts about my previous incarnations. These Americans are too much.

Other Lives, Other Selves dropped through my letterbox with an ominous thud. It was so heavy it woke me from my blissfully unaware sleep. I grumbled up the stairs to fight with Sellotape before the first coffee. The cover showed the silhouette of a faceless man emerging through fluffy white clouds. At least these American New Age books are always an easy read.

In order not to make a complete fool of myself I would have to wade through it. In two days. Still, it was a good excuse to lie in the sunshine wearing the now compulsory factor 50 no-chance-of-a-tan-with-this-on cream. I suppose someone has to live like this to keep the economy balanced, right? Someone has to just spend money instead of actually earning any, don't they? I must study economics. Some day.

I filled my large portable coffee mug, picked up a rug and collapsed into the garden. I was careful to bring my mobile phone in order not to miss all those important calls from TV companies, eligible men who want me, etc.

Before I opened the book I noticed the subtitle: *A Jungian Psychotherapist Discovers Past Lives*. Already I felt a weight of ignorance upon me. Why have I never studied Jung? This was obviously going to be as bad as my time with the infernally well-educated Christians. If I raised any doubts about the basic premise of whether I have been here before I would be laughed at. Or, worse still, patronised in a loving way and spoken to like a curiously eccentric being who still believes the earth is flat.

Then I read the first line:

> When I graduated from Oxford University in the mid-sixties with a joint degree in behavioural psychology and analytic philosophy, my mind had been put into a carefully tailored straight-jacket, though I hardly knew it at the time.

The idea of studying my past lives with an Englishman was difficult to grasp. To even imagine an old Oxonian 'sharing' was beyond my imaginative faculties. And I was soon wishing that I had been to Oxford myself instead of spending my childhood singing. Notes began to appear on the side of my page – 'Read up on theosophy'. 'Which bit of psychology is parapsychology?'; 'what the . . . is cryptamnesia?' Literary references were profuse, Dr Woolger naturally assumed that I had read *Oedipus Rex*, *The Brothers Karamazov* and *King Lear*. I have always intended to read Jung's *Memories, Dreams and Reflections* but I've never actually done so. Not that I'd admit that at a dinner party. And one is, of course, also familiar with the yogic texts, Chinese alchemy, *I Ching* and *The Kab-*

balah and one has practised diverse forms of meditation and made a detailed study of *The Tibetan Book of the Dead*. Well, *obviously*.

Dr Woolger was certainly keen to avoid unnecessary questions in his workshop so he proceeded to work through all the major areas of thought on the subject of life before conception. I'll do you a super-condensed version.

The first group of people who claim to know anything about what my ex would call 'all this nonsense' are the psychics. As far as I can see these are the interesting characters who like to commune with the spirit of your dead grandmother or to have books 'channelled' to them from 'the other side' so that they don't have to concern themselves with punctuation. Psychics are frightfully useful for convincing the sceptics that there is another side because they usually get Grandma to tell them lots of things that they couldn't possible know from any other source. This leaves the bewildered non-believers uttering phrases like, 'That was amazing' and then not thinking about the matter any further.

The second group of people wear white coats and live in universities. They have tape recorders and interesting looking machines and spend many long years trying to either prove or disprove the truth of past life experiences using statistics. This sad group are usually shunned by the rest of the academic world, eat convenience food and have pale skin because they rarely get out into the sun. Eventually, exhausted by too much data, they die an early death and are often said to haunt universities with a gleeful 'I told you so' enthusiasm.

The third group is highly revered. They have actually read the *Bhagavad Gita*, are usually Buddhists, Hindus or Taoists and laugh at anyone who dares to think that reincarnation is not a fundamental truth of existence. Apparently they are joined by almost everyone who lived between the sixth century BC until AD 529 when the Emperor Justinian woke up with a headache one morning and, unable to find a coffee, closed the University of Athens. More recently added to the names of this list are a few people whom it would be hard to dismiss as gullible: Goethe, Benjamin Franklin, David Hume, Schopenhauer, T.H. Huxley and Tolstoy. But not, apparently, Roger Woolger.

Just when I was beginning to think I could work out the old Oxonian I found that he was in a fourth group. Past-life psychotherapists use past-life regression in the same ways that more conventional therapists use childhood memories. He declares:

It doesn't matter whether you believe in reincarnation or not.

He is concerned with helping people (especially those who go to too many seminars) and not with promoting a doctrine or proving a theory. He just asks us to believe in the 'healing power of the unconscious mind'. Oh, that old thing? The unconscious. Do you know that despite all the workshops I've done I'm still not conscious of it. But can I believe it can heal me? I suppose so.

Can't say that I'm that fond of my unconscious. That's the bit that makes my dreams up – I know that much. Rarely do I wake from a night of virtual sexual passion with Robert Redford or a glorious surreal fantasy of flight and chocolate. I wake up most mornings in the middle of an argument with my daughter that is an exact replica of the previous day:

'So, a letter from the headmistress again, complaining about you wearing "unsuitable shoes"?'

'So, what do you want me to do?'

'Stop wearing the shoes.'

'But I like them.'

'Yes, but they are unsuitable.'

'No they're not.'

My unconscious has to work overtime and still can't unravel the logic of a teenager.

Still, it was a relief that I wasn't going to have to alter my entire belief system. He went on,

> It should be clear by now that the therapeutic approach to past lives places primary value on the subjective experience of the client and leaves the question of historical truth or doctrinal orthodoxy entirely to one side.

'Yes, Dr Woolger. Absolutely clear, Dr Woolger.' Then a fat cloud came and sat on the sun. It was lunchtime and still my mobile phone hadn't rung. Lunch has always been a problem since I met the colonic irrigationist. My fridge always presents me with a collection of foods that I'm not supposed to eat. Or a lettuce. I pulled a terrified lettuce from the fridge and consumed it, also sacrificing a couple of slices of forbidden bread and an absolutely vetoed lump of cheese. I then forced myself to write a letter to a TV company for a job I didn't want and decided to spend the afternoon in the garden with Dr Woolger. I couldn't accuse him of being dull. Mad, possibly, but not dull.

He went on trying to educate me. Apparently many people have 'past-life memories' that come to them in dreams, visions or while they are meditating. Many children simply remember who they were in a previous incarnation. Some professor called Ian Stevenson has 'rigorously researched' cases of children who remember detailed facts from the lives of deceased individuals they claim to have been. What is the intelligent reader such as me (and you, of course) to make of all this?

There are three schools of thought open to us. We can fall into the 'load of tosh' school, more academically known as the *tabula rasa* position which claims that at birth the mind is a 'blank slate' (one knows that because one speaks Latin, doesn't one?). This basically means that, as we have only one life, 'past-life memories' come from TV or from stories we've read or overheard and that all our psychological disturbances can be blamed on our parents. This is Siggy Freud's position. Makes you want to rush home and make babies, doesn't it? Just so they can shout, 'It's all your fault' at you when they are thirty.

The second position is a great one for waffley New Agers or those who want to appear mystical and broadminded but not to have to think too much. This is the Great Memory position. Or what you may have heard referred to at fashionable cocktail parties as 'the collective unconscious' or even the 'Akashic record'. If you want to sound really knowledgeable and bluff your way in New Age circles you say, 'I feel that we all have the capacity to dip into this vast universal stratum of the unconscious which is a collective memory bank for all mankind.' Watch the use of the word 'mankind', though – not very PC. It's OK to be open to the concept of the collective unconscious as long as you are closed to the use of certain nouns.

Now – and this is where it gets exciting – if you want to move even further out than that, then you simply ask, 'How it is that specific memories seem to come repeatedly to some individuals and not to others?' And see if anyone has a reply. Why do certain remembered images or events have an eerily uncanny familiarity about them for some people? The trouble with the reassuring 'collective unconscious' solution is that particular memories really do seem to belong to us individually.

So this leads us to the third option, which is the reincarnationist position. But this is not straightforward. Even if you enter into this position you still have to work out which bit of it you stand in. Woolger warns against a 'sentimental picture of the evolving soul as it progresses through karmic high school'. Climbing on to his soap box he declares,

For lack of serious grounding in traditional spiritual psychology, writers of popular metaphysics fail to make the proper distinction between the ego personality and the greater soul.

The ego self does not reincarnate at all, only the soul and even then it is far from clear to what extent progress is linear and historical.

So is everything clear to you now? No? I thought not. Never mind. That's enough theory anyway. I was impatient to know what exactly was going to happen on this workshop. Who was I in a previous life? Was this new self-knowledge going to give me a new aura of glamour? An opportunity to feed the ego so derided by Dr Woolger? Perhaps I was married to Henry VIII? Perhaps I was a mystic Sufi and, to become more enlightened, all I have to do is tap into the knowledge that it once took me a lifetime to acquire? As I flicked forward a chapter or two I realised that no such joys awaited me.

It would be as valuable to focus on happy past lives as it would be for a physician to treat a mangled leg by examining the healthy one.

Apparently the focus was to be the miserable and the traumatic. The book contained countless case histories of clients who had remembered being hacked to death, gassed, hung, drowned and numerous other delights for a sunny Saturday afternoon. Oh, yippee. This sounds fun. Ten cases and a bit more theory later, I closed the book and decided that maybe sunbathing was a matter of great importance. But as I lay frying I remembered an unsolved mystery of my own.

Once upon a time on a bed, one of the gorgeous Americans in my life took me on an imaginative journey. As I lay there with my eyes closed he intoned, 'Now, go back to the age of six and tell me what you see.' I described my grandmother making cakes and the doughy smell coming fresh from the oven. 'Then go back to the age of two, what do you see?' I described leaves in the garden, a blue sky, warmth. 'Now I want you to go back further, before birth into a previous life – don't worry if you don't believe in all this, just tell me what you see.'

I saw a wooden barn door, with a cross-piece diagonally down the door from left to right. The image was quite clear. The door was locked from the outside and I was banging on the door. I was locked in the barn with three young children from whom I felt quite detached. The men had locked the door and gone away. I didn't know if something had happened to them or whether they intended to return, but I couldn't make anyone hear me. That was the image. Along with it went a nasty feeling that I died a horrible death in the barn along with the three children – a death of dehydration and starvation. I never got out. I thought if that had been my fate it was no wonder that the image of the door had been so clear. I must have spent several days looking at it, refusing to give up hope. Even now I could see the door clearly in my mind's eye. Until now I had ignored this image. Not knowing what to make of it, I had put in on hold till 'later'. This weekend it seemed, was 'later'.

Or maybe I had been lying in my garden under the sun too long. I swayed towards the house and into a cold shower.

I am rarely scared before workshops any more. I've learned that going beyond my comfort zone is exhilarating. But this was something else. This was venturing into a whole different dimension in which I knew lay desolation and dehydration. Suddenly even Waitrose seemed like an agreeable prospect. I suppose I'd been scared by the re-birthing but this time the quality of my fear was more vivid. I confess I even resorted to phoning a couple of my ever patient and loving friends, who, sighing with despair when I told them what I was up to now, offered to pray for me over the weekend. An offer which, shamefaced, I gladly accepted. When leaving this life it is mightily reassuring to know that someone is asking The Holy Spirit to go along with you.

I arrived in a room in Holloway Road to find a horseshoe of thirty chairs. At least it wasn't a circle and at least it wouldn't be all women. Then some women arrived. Then more women arrived. Then even more women arrived. I began to get irritated. I know this sort of work is pretty weird but you would think that some men would have the courage to explore these possibilities. I sighed deeply. At 10 a.m. the appointed starting time, we were twenty-three women and one man. Then a second man arrived, aged about seventy, dragged in by his wife, and finally a third, aged about twenty, dragged in by his sister. I could have jumped up and down with rage. What's wrong with 50/50 as a ratio?

Roger Woolger tumbled in. Instead of the heavyweight intellectual I had anticipated from the book he was a rather amiable fatherly type with long Denis Healey-style eyebrows, a body that was obviously a stranger to exercise and a rather buffoon-like smile. Very reassuring.

You know what happens next, don't you? Yup. We go round the circle and explain why we are there. Most of the women were therapists, homeopaths, psychotherapists, or 'body workers' of some kind. We also had a biochemical scientist, an architect and a singer. I'm sure someone said 'I'm an acromatherapist' but I didn't put my hand up and say, 'a what?'

When it got to me I amused myself by claiming to be a 'writer'. I added, 'I have two fears about this workshop. The first is doing the work at the deepest level. The second is not doing the work at the deepest level.' I was scared but I didn't want to cop out.

Then the woman on my left spoke: 'I'm a sensitive and I've been picking up on your nerves, but now you've spoken I feel better.' I was flabbergasted. She proclaimed 'I'm *a* sensitive' the way you would say 'I'm *a* mother'. Only she said it in a very loud voice suggesting a complete lack of the quality with which she identified herself and then accused me of upsetting her by being nervous.

A softly spoken Asian girl was next. 'I come from the Jain faith and we are brought up with reincarnation but no one ever seems to want to explore the doctrine experientially. I've had several images in dreams that I think may be from past lives and I want to try and find out about them, but I won't tell my family I've come here or they'll think I'm crazy.'

One woman told her story and added 'I should hate to have another life like this time round so I'm doing all I can to learn how to prevent it.' A charming looking elderly woman had a recurring nightmare she didn't understand. 'I can't shake it off, even though I work with dreams. Then I saw you in a dream, Roger, so I thought I'd come here.' She had an MA in transpersonal psychology, whatever that is, so I guess she knew what she was talking about.

Views on reincarnation differed: 'I don't know if I believe in past lives but it interests me'; 'I came to the conclusion when I was small that there was more than one life'. The young man who had been dragged in by his sister said, 'I'm a research scientist and I don't believe in any of this. I don't want to be here and I've done just about everything I can this week to avoid it. The scientist in me says this is all nonsense.'

I liked him enormously.

When the intros were over Dr Woolger started on his chat. He checked how many people had read the book, saying, 'There's a test tomorrow morning'. I'd have been happy if there had been. I'd read all the arguments, counter-arguments and case histories with fascination. Instead of joking he could have done the test and thrown out anyone who hadn't read the book to make more time for the rest of us. Good thing I wasn't in charge.

Then suddenly he looked serious and said: 'This is an introduction to past-life regression as therapy. It is not a training for you to go away and practise. Please do not try this at home. It's a bit like opening Pandora's Box, quite easy to get someone into a past life but what you do when you've got them there is another question. Don't go there alone. However, this is a very fast and very powerful kind of therapy. I do this because it works and I'm a pragmatist.'

He'd stumbled on past lives from his own more conventional work as a therapist.

'We are carrying all sorts of fragments of other human beings in us. This is the mess we call 'karma'. This work is specifically to do with the fragments that are blocking us. Old stories that have fear in them can leave an imprint. I was born with an irrational fear of fire despite the fact that I'd never seen a fire. It turned out that in one lifetime I had been burned at the stake.'

He continued our education. 'Freud couldn't find the origins of phobias in early childhood. That's because they weren't there.'

He smiled smugly and then told us the story of Edgar Cayce, an American Christian fundamentalist who became a recognised expert on past lives, which was damned inconvenient for him as he wasn't supposed to believe in them.

I was bursting to find out how he was going to reveal our previous incarnations to us. 'We are not going to use hypnosis because it's long and complicated. We use the imagination and free-association with images and feelings. People like to play down the importance of the imagination when used with the unconscious.'

The first 'process' was a game called 'The 10p Psychic'. We sat opposite a partner and gave them 10p. They had to play the psychic, look into your eyes and say the line 'In past lives I see you as . . .' and then tell you.

Dr Woolger gave instructions to the 'psychics'.

'A number of things might happen. You may look into the person's eyes and see many things in quite quick succession. If so, just go on telling them about all the different people. Or you may just see one or two and want to go into more detail. That's fine, then just tell them the story. Or you may see nothing at all, in which case, well, for 10p, make something up.'

I sat opposite a black singer and looked into her eyes. I gave her my 10p and, like a racehorse, she was off.

'I see you as an African woman in a beautiful tribal dress with ornate jewellery of bone around your neck. You are tall and very elegant. Now I see you as a young Arab boy on a horse, riding out into the desert. You love riding and there is a great sense of freedom. You must be about eighteen or nineteen. There is a huge energy, a *joie de vivre*, but something happens to you. You die in the desert and your horse is left wandering. You died with a feeling of how unfair it was because you loved life so much and you didn't have enough time. Now I see you as a master of a ship, a galleon ship. You are the leader, a strong leader, but there is a storm, I see lightning and something is wrong, maybe your crew mutinied against you, I'm not sure.'

Where was she getting all this from? She galloped on.

'Now I see you as a whale! You are injured, there is a boat. But I see the sea and the sun and the sky. You love the sea. Now I see you as a racing-driver. There is a black and white car, an old fashioned racing-car. You love racing. Now I see you as a tribal woman again, you are carrying something on your head and your child is with you. You are going to hand over your child and all her possessions are in the basket. But you are not sad. It's a joyful giving. Maybe to a marriage. Anyway, the time has come and you are both joyful. Now I see fire. You are a firefighter. Now I see you in a wagon like those of the Wild West. You are a woman but you are holding the reins, it's a race for land and you are racing the cart. You have a lot of spirit.'

Finally Roger asked, 'Is there a theme?' and she said, 'Yes, you have a wonderful sense of fun and joy and you love life wholeheartedly.'

I sat amazed. It was worth 10p, even if it was all made up.

Then I smiled as she handed me 10p. I looked into her eyes very carefully. I was slower than her. I looked and looked. There was something in her eyes that looked very young, a little boy of about eight, white, who was unhappy working for a man who didn't care about him. Perhaps a chimney sweep who died suffocated by smoke. I told her about the chimney sweep, but not about the suffocation. I couldn't bring myself to tell her that. Then I saw something I thought I saw that was cruel in her, a tyrant. Ancient Egypt came to me somehow. Yes, I told her that I saw her as a Roman in charge of driving the Israelite slaves. She had a whip. Then I added, as if for justification, 'I don't know what happened to you in that childhood to make you that callous, but it must have been totally loveless.'

Then I looked again and saw someone very old. A wise shaman or witch doctor of some kind. I saw him feared by his community and yet also revered by them. He was a healer, working with all kinds of magic using herbs and plants and also calling on spirits to help him. He was lonely in this work but also genuinely able to heal others.

Then I saw a white woman in a crinoline with a parasol. She was very pretty and knew how to use her feminine wiles to get exactly what she wanted. She had wealth and power.

Then I saw great humour. A jester who was loved by all the court. Again, a man of great wisdom who hid behind his wit and buffoonery but who actually looked after everyone, guiding them with tact and jokes.

'And is there a theme?' Dr Woolger finally asked.

'I see you as a soul of enormous experience, a wise soul who has been through many lifetimes and has learned much. A wisdom and a kindness.'

The young black singer smiled at me. At least, I think it was her.

Conversations broke out after this exercise and many people wondered how much was projection by the 'psychic' and what was the point of the exercise. We in the West, it seems, all need to put a process like that into a box in order to understand it. One woman asked 'But is it true?' and everyone laughed. I was sufficiently out of my intellectual perspective by this point to not mind. Maybe that was the point of the heavyweight 350-page tome. To exhaust our brains so that we would be ready to enjoy ourselves when we arrived. It didn't seem to matter to me whether these lives were true, made up or projection – I loved the images, especially the young Arab boy riding out into the desert with his love of life and freedom. It made me want to go and buy a motorbike to 'honour my inner Arab'.

Lunch came and we all went to the pub. Fish and chips never tasted so good. Conversation suddenly took on a whole extra dimension. The body-worker spoke to the young Asian girl. 'I love India. I've lived there a lot.' Pause. 'In this life, I mean.'

Our afternoon was to start with travel. We lay on the floor for a bit of guided imagery.

'I'd like you to look around the world and call in on some of the places that you feel attracted to. Notice which countries have a particular appeal to you and when you've paid them a quick call you can visit somewhere else.'

I liked this game. I zapped down into St Mark's Square in Venice and fed pigeons and then beamed over to an Amazonian jungle to see the monkeys.

'Now notice any countries that you feel repelled by in any way and see if there are any places that you don't want to visit.'

I scanned the world and, much to my surprise, found that there was an area of central North America that made me feel uneasy. Maybe that was the location of my wooden door. The instructions in the background went on.

'When you notice anything that has a charge for you, go there. It doesn't matter what period of time you are in when you arrive. You can visit at any period of history that seems to draw you. Just go down and see what picture you see.'

I saw a large, medieval-looking cooking pot in a room with no floor. A crude hole had been dug in the ground for cooking over. I seemed to be bent over the pot in which was a rather disgusting slimy substance. Something that was supposed to be stew, only there was so little grain it was more like water.

Then he brought us back to Holloway Road and gave us all paper and pastels to draw the last image we had seen. I took black and drew a rounded cooking pot hanging from a tripod. Then I drew the figure of a woman in a crude sackcloth dress with a cape pulled around her. I coloured her in red to indicate all the pain that her body was in. She was stiff, malnourished and ill. Her shoulders were stooped. 'Give your image a caption, like a newspaper headline,' he said. I called mine 'Desperation at Home'.

Then he asked who would like to work with the image. I volunteered, of course, along with six others. He asked us to hold up our pictures for a group consensus. I came in second, behind a woman who had drawn a Russian-looking soldier. One of the helpers smiled at me, 'We'll use you too if we have time.'

As the woman lay on a blanket in the middle of the room I was glad it wasn't me.

He asked her to describe the clothes she was wearing in the picture and spoke to her as if speaking to the Russian. The soldier was standing in a village, there was no one there. She said: 'I don't know what I'm waiting for. Everyone's gone.'

Roger spoke softly. 'We are going to go back in time to the last major event to see what happened. I'm going to count three. One, two, three – and what do you see?'

'It's a charge. Lots of people, all fighting. It's chaos. I've lost the plot. I'm supposed to be in charge but I don't know what to do. I've lost control over them. They are running riot. It's like I'm paralysed.'

'So what do you do?'

'I walk away in the opposite direction.'

'Are you deserting?'

'Not really, because I feel as if I have no role. If someone told me what to do I'd do it. But I don't know what to do. I get to this town but there is no one there.'

'How long do you wander for?'

'A couple of days. I'm hoping I'll find someone who'll tell me what to do. My neck hurts. Something has happened to it.'

'Let's move forward in time to the next thing that happens. One, two, three . . .'

'There are people but they are talking about things I don't understand. I don't know if I can connect with them. They are not like me; I don't understand them.'

'Are you in a state of shock?'

'Maybe. There is a distance. I'm there yet I'm not there. I go with them.'

'OK, let's see where you end up. One, two, three . . .'

'I'm in a building, wandering around. I'm disconnected. Nobody bothers me. I find a corner to sleep in. Everyone is busy. Nobody speaks to me.'

'We'll move forward a couple of days.'

'I'm still in the corner, curled up. I don't need to eat or drink. I've opted out of life. It gets harder to move because I've been here so long. It feels like I'm not here because everyone walks past.'

'So no one came?'

'No one. I'm not surprised no one came because no one could see me.'

She started to weep.

Roger said, 'That's all right, soldier. You can cry now.'

She cried and coughed. 'No one could see me. No one cared.' She wept uncontrollably. 'Nobody cared.'

Then Roger asked, 'If there was something you could say to those people, what would you say to them?'

'I'm here; I want to join you.'

'Is your body dead now?'

'Yes.'

'Are you ready to leave it?'

'Yes. I've left it. It feels like flying in the dark. I'm looking for my men. Yes, I've found them. We are together again.'

'Now say to yourself "The battle's over".' Imagine all the soldiers around you and I want them to *see* you.'

'Yes, they can see me.' She laughed.

'Now, in this life have you ever experienced a feeling of not being seen?'

'All through my childhood.'

'Is there anyone you want to be seen by now?'

'My son.'

'What do you want to say to him?'

She cries again and says, 'I'm not going to hide from you any more. I want you to see me.'

'So you have a tendency to go away when things get stressful. You are not on the battlefield any more, so you need to be fully present. People care about you today. And people see you. Look. Open your eyes.'

She opened her eyes. A room of faces looked at her, smiling. I felt like a Russian soldier in a barracks of men. Real camaraderie. She laughed. 'Gosh, I forgot you were all here.'

It had been an exhausting session even though it lacked the real trauma of some of the case histories in the book. Roger told us that once a room of people had seen red lines appear across a woman's neck as she had recalled a hanging.

He entertained us with some tales to take us till 6 p.m. I was mightily glad that there was not time for my story. And I suppose the better part of me was mightily irritated that we sat for the remaining hour and just chatted. Roger said, 'Maybe somewhere in Russia is a house that will be a little more peaceful now.'

People asked whether, in 'the spirit world', people always forgave. Apparently they almost always do. One client who had been burned at the stake went to find Calvin. Calvin said, 'I suppose I was a little strict.' Another client had gone to shout at St Paul about his treatment of women. St Paul had replied, 'It's true that I didn't understand women very well.'

One of the women told us a story about a job she'd had in an ashram (in this life). She was a devout Jew and not a believer in reincarnation. An Indian man came to work at the ashram and she felt very fearful of him. So much so that she was amazed to find herself hiding the knives in case he attacked her. She was much shamed when she spoke to him after a prayer meeting and found him to be a softly spoken and gentle man who was a pacifist and lover of silence. But then he said to her, 'I know you. I murdered you in a previous life. I stabbed you in the back.' She had said nothing to him about her fear or that she had hidden the knives when he arrived. This incident had convinced her of the truth of past lives.

When 6 p.m. came I headed for Starbucks feeling a great need for all that was familiar, banal and bad for me.

The Sunday-morning exercise was to learn how to be guides for each other's 'regressions'. We were handed sheets of paper with instructions on how to guide someone through their story. There were four qualified assistants on hand as well as Roger in case anyone needed help. The key principle was to ask what was happening and not to ask 'Why are you there?' 'Why?' questions tend to move people out of feelings and into their heads. The guide does not want the regressee saying, 'I think it's something to do with the fear of witches that was prevalent in this century.' Instead we were to ask 'What happens next?' to elicit a re-experiencing of events that would sound more like, 'They are tying me to the chair, they are drowning me.' We were told to give commands. To ask questions such as: 'Would you like to go forward in time to the torture chamber now?' would be unlikely to receive an enthusiastic 'Oh, yes please.'

My partner had drawn a picture that looked like an advertisement for a holiday in a pacific island. Her caption was 'Life in Paradise'. I felt very envious and wondered whether she had missed the point. I started to question her and was told of warm sand, a beach, collecting food from nature to feed her husband and child. It sounded dreamy. 'How old do you think you are?' I asked.

'Oh, about eighteen, and I'm very happy. I have a daughter. My husband is a fisherman.'

I wondered where all this was leading. 'So let's move forward to a significant event,' I said, 'One, two, three . . .'

Before I had time to question her any further she was running to the beach, her child was in the water and she was trying to rescue her – drowning herself in the attempt. 'I can just see blue, translucent blue. I know I can't reach her in time. I've failed her.' She lay on the blanket with tears streaming down her face.

'So you both died?' I asked. 'What about your husband? What happened to him?'

'I don't seem to care about him. I'm a spirit now and I'm looking for the spirit of my daughter. There she is. She is running to me. Holding me. It's strange because we don't have bodies but it still seems that I can hold her. She says it wasn't my fault.'

She goes on weeping softly. I had put my guideline notes down by now and I just trusted that I'd know what to say. 'Is there anything else you need to say to her now?'

'Yes, that I'm sorry.'

She went on talking to her daughter in a spirit realm, while on the Holloway Road I just watched and waited. Finally she finished and opened her eyes. 'Does any of that tie into your life today?' I asked innocently.

'The water. Drowning. I never realised. I've always had an

irrational fear of putting my head under the water. It's so bad that I won't even stand under a shower. And, good God! I've always known that I've been over-protective as a mother. Isn't this stuff weird?'

At lunchtime I found Roger Woolger sitting in reception alone. He was waiting for a 'woman from the BBC' who had come too early and, having been asked to return at the appointed hour, had now disappeared completely. Seizing the opportunity to ask questions of my own, I sat down and he shared his strawberries with me.

I told him that meeting him was a pleasant surprise after the rigour of his book and, like a star-struck adolescent, asked him to sign my copy. 'Where does God come into all this?' I asked, keen to discover whether he thought there was a guiding love beyond all this karmic confusion.

'Love is what's it's all about,' he smiled. 'But I don't think there is an interventionist God. God is beyond the personal.'

'What about the nuns who dedicate their lives to prayer?' I asked. 'Is that just sending the world good vibes?'

'I was going to become a priest once . . .' he said. 'Have you read Simone Weil?' I had not.

The woman from the BBC walked towards us. 'One last question,' I said.

'Mmm?'

'In your opinion, is it true that we meet people in this life we have known in former ones?'

'The law in the spiritual universe is one of attraction. That's what we mean by kindred spirits.'

Then he was whisked away, giving me time to eat three biscuits with jam in the middle as a preparation for the afternoon session.

I found myself lying on a blanket and my partner was saying to me, 'Look down at your feet. What are you wearing?'

'Nothing. They are black with dirt, and bleeding. I seem to

have some skin disease. My feet and legs are raw and dry and my skin hurts. I am ill. My whole body is stiff and in pain.'

'What are you doing?'

'I'm supposed to be making food, but there is nothing to cook. I'm angry, resentful that the men have all gone and left me with these children. I am starving, desperate. I can't cope on my own. Everything is getting worse and worse. There is nothing to eat. I can't go on.'

'What happens next?'

I saw a picture of 'myself' going out to look for the men. One or maybe two of them are fathers of the children. There seems to be a group of them I'm looking for. One of them I love but he has never treated me well.

'I'm looking for them.'

'Do you find them?'

'Yes. I'm pleading with them for help, but they seem to despise me. Perhaps it's because I disgust them with my skin infection. They tell me I'm mad. Then the one I love drags me back, holding on to my clothes. He's violent. He doesn't hit me but he pushes and shoves me. He is the father of one of my children but the child was not conceived in love. I don't understand. I just want to love him. I'm not an old woman. I'm about thirty-five but I'm stooped, and sick.'

'What happens next?'

He throws me into this barn where the children are and locks the door. Then he rides off on a horse with the other men. I bang on the door. I try to get him to hear me. Or anyone to hear me. I can't get out. The children are crying.'

'Let's move forward in time and see what happens. One, two, three . . .'

'I'm lying on the ground. I'm very weak. I haven't drunk anything for days. Two of the children have died. The third is making a moaning noise but I can't do anything. I'm still looking at the door. I don't think they intended to kill us. I think they thought someone would come and let us out. Or maybe they knew we'd die. But I still wait. I can't give up hope.'

'So, let's see if anyone comes. Let's move forward in time.'

'No, no one comes. I have died now. For a while my spirit waits in my body, to see if anyone will come, even after death. But no one does. I think that maybe they were all killed, so I look for them. From the spirit world I see them drinking in a kind of tavern. They are not thinking about us at all. He didn't think, the one I loved. He didn't understand.'

'Let's move forward in time until after his death. See him standing in front of you now.'

'He is smiling. He says, "Can you forgive me?" and I'm confused. I want to forgive him but even as a spirit I don't know how.'

Then suddenly as I look at this face in my mind's eye he looks familiar to me. The smile, the eyes, and suddenly I thought I recognised one of the Americans in my life. The one who had gone away, who had left me. And I got very confused not knowing what time zone I was in or who I was speaking to. I tried to get my mind back into the scene and answer the question. 'Can you forgive me?' I stood before him, helpless. It would have been easy to say the words but I knew that wasn't enough. He had taken me sexually and not in love, I had borne his children, and then he'd killed me by his neglect. And the children too. How could I forgive all this?

I decided I would leave the question. I would ask for the help I needed. I finished the exercise and walked over to Roger. I suppose he got questions like this every day of the week.

'Er, I'm standing in a spirit realm before a man who has as good as raped me and then been responsible for me dying of dehydration and starvation. He now wants my forgiveness and I want to forgive him but I'm not sure how. Any tips?'

'It's no good forgiving someone if you are still angry. Let the anger out, then you can forgive them. The clue to compassion is

empathy. You have to understand what it was like to be him.
You have to really think about that. Then you can forgive him.'

'Yes, Dr Woolger. Thank you, Dr Woolger.'

Other people were still living their scenes. The sceptical
scientist who had been dragged in by his sister appeared to
be murdering someone. He had a cushion by the neck and while
strangling it was screaming: 'You will never, never, do that to
me again.' I thought cheerily to myself that whatever his
scientific objections to this sort of process the stuff seemed to
be working for him. One of the experienced helpers was watching carefully, presumably concerned for the safety of the cushion.

I decided not to go back but just sat with my 'guide', who
casually asked me, 'Is there anything in that scene that seems
familiar in this life?'

My life flashed before me. Men who went away. My father
who had left my mother before I was born. The men who were
not around to help my mother bring me up. My ex who had
gone off and left me with a small child. And the last one who
went away, who I had just wanted to love. And who hadn't
understood. Men who weren't there! Even yesterday morning I
was more bothered than anyone else about there only being
three men in the room. Hopeless species.

'Er, yes,' I said.

Finally we were back in our horseshoe of chairs. Roger
played us some Bach. Then he spoke to us.

'The past is over. The only reason to remember past lives is to
put them in the past. These inner characters are like complexes.
Everyone knows that we have complexes but if we are not
aware of them then they run us. If we are aware of them then we
run them. People are afraid of the idea of multiple personalities
but we all have many personalities within us. I have an inner
monk who always expects the Lord to provide. I have to tell him
that we are in the twentieth century now and I have to have a

bank account, but I like his optimism. If I find myself having thoughts that I know are not really mine then I recognise them. It is important for someone who has a loving family in this life to stop feeling unloved just because, once, they may have died alone.'

There was a calm in the room. He spoke gently.

'I found when I started doing this that my sceptical mind kept asking, "Is it this life or is it a previous life?" Then it stopped being relevant and I just had a clarity about the whole issue. Once you accept that we are carrying residues from previous incarnations it explains a lot of things. These are like parts of yourself that need to be welcomed back in.'

My own sceptical mind was still wondering. Was my starving and deserted woman a reality from a previous lifetime whose imprint was somehow influencing my behaviour and my expectations, or was she just a shadowy figure from a dark corner of my mind, an imaginative creation of my subconscious? There was no possibility of knowing the answer but either way the challenge was the same. That guideline from Insight again, 'Use everything for your learning, upliftment and growth'.

I needed to find a way to reassure this character, to feed her, look after the old body and let her know that lost love didn't have to be for ever this time. Ho hum. All in a day's work.

The workshop ended with some readings and one fitted my story rather well so I gambolled up to him afterwards and copied it down. It's from *The Conference of Birds* by Farid Attar.

All those who are wounded by love must have the imprint on their face, and the scar must be seen. Let the scar of the heart be seen, for by their scars are known those who are in the way of love.

Phase Eleven: Being Rolfed, Initiated, Stoned and Kneaded

A week after the past-life workshop I felt exhausted, traumatised, and tense. My shoulders seemed to be so stiff that they were up round my ears. I mooched around wondering whether my tension was mine or hers and shouted at everyone. For once there was an easy solution. I needed a massage. I wanted a little pleasure and if I also happened to be looking after an imprint of a previous incarnation, so much the better. I would pay for a massage and make that overdue contribution to the economy that I'd been meditating on while sunbathing. That decision taken, there was the problem of finding someone who would do a good job.

I don't know about you, but I hate a massage that seems to just move the skin and leave the tension in the muscles totally untouched. 'A little harder, please,' I've been known to request. For a total of thirty seconds the masseuse presses harder before returning immediately to a gentle tickle. I hate this. I'll sometimes implore, 'Could you work a little more deeply, please?' for a second time and, again not achieving the desired response, will have to lie listening to Mr Inner Masculine raving at me: 'You see? This is a total waste of time.'

So I asked my personally developed circle of friends for recommendations. Vicky, a masseuse herself, didn't mind at all that I was looking everywhere. 'If you want a deep massage you need to be rolfed.'

'Rolfed?' It sounded rather radical.

'It's to do with realigning the body and it's supposed to be very painful.'

Yes. Pain. That was what I wanted. Those wonderful moments when someone has their fingers right on a knot that has been keeping my shoulders around my ears for months, and they are pressing. Hard. I wanted pain. I'd do it.

Three phonecalls later I had found a rolfer. An American who already had me dreaming up unlikely fantasies about him based on one phonecall. His voice was all silky. I could hardly wait to lay my semi-naked body on his table. Once I'd established with a few cunningly placed questions that he wasn't gay, I'd started to flirt incorrigibly over the phone.

'I'm not ticklish any more.' It was the female-needs-looking-after approach. 'Do you think there is anything in rolfing that could help me recover my ticklishness?'

'That's a very interesting subject.'

'Perhaps you could use me as a research project?' Really. Sometimes I even shock myself.

I was excited when the day came. Fiona, my co-dependent friend, wanted to accompany me. I'd talked so much about how sensuous this guy sounded she was curious to have a look at him. When she arrived and caught sight of him her eyebrows moved into an interesting zigzag shape.

Don't you hate that? Voices can be so misleading. He had lived in Japan for ten years and appeared to have become one of those nervous, highly stressed, overworked and undernourished types seen wedging themselves into the Tokyo Underground every working day. Even his face looked Japanese. It was most odd. 'Hi, I'm Peter,' he said in a broad Californian accent. I smiled, feeling rather faint with disappointment.

'May I have a glass of water?' I asked.

'Sure.' And he disappeared.

The rolfing room in Camden Town was small and not well heated. I took off some of my clothes rather resentfully and sat on his table feeling cold. A month later he returned with water.

'Could you stand up, please? I need to look at your alignment.' I've always prided myself that, as a result of my dance training, my posture is very good. He walked around me as though examining faulty goods. I waited for him to say, 'Well, OK, but can I have a discount?' Instead he scowled. 'Could you sit on that chair, please?'

'Certainly.'

'Now stand up again, please?'

'Now sit down again.'

'Now stand up again.'

'Now sit down again.'

'Now stand up again.'

I was paying for this. 'Now, could you walk?'

'Well, no.' There was no space to walk without climbing on to the table or knocking him over. I took one step forward, turned and took one step back.

'And again, please. And again, please.'

Eventually, when he had thoroughly studied which bits of me needed realigning and which didn't, I was invited to lie on the massage table. Now you wouldn't think it would be difficult to design a massage table, would you? Wide enough so that you can lie on it? This one didn't do the job and I observed with mounting irritation that I was forced to wedge my hands under my legs to prevent my arms falling off the sides.

Then the rolfing started. He laid his hands on my back, pressed quite hard and then drew them downwards. And it was painful. Not, however, the delightful pain of muscle tension being released, rather the curious sensation of skin being stretched. He used no oil or talc or anything to make the drawing-down process pleasant. He just pulled on the skin. I was sure of one thing: I didn't like it.

He worked in silence. There was no friendly voice saying, 'That OK?' I didn't feel I could really say, 'Listen, this hurts.' I had been warned, after all. It was intended to. And he didn't do much. 'We'll just work on the upper body in the first session,' he had said on the telephone and I had said, 'That's fine,' imagining my back and neck in a state of total joy.

He went on prodding and stretching. I could see this would be an effective treatment for someone whose skin was, for some reason, too small for their body. I wonder, has there ever been such a problem? I seemed to be suffering from it. 'I'm sorry, Isabel, but we just need to extend this skin for another inch.' No, he didn't really say that.

He slid his knuckles down my back. The pulling-pushing sensation could hardly be described as massage. Did people really come and have this done on a regular basis? Then my neck was stretched. I wondered why he didn't just use an old-fashioned rack from the Tower of London and save himself the trouble. Then there were some brief moments of pleasure as he massaged my head and he was finished.

'That's enough for today,' he said with the deadly serious Japanese tone. 'The body needs to adjust slowly to the rolfing process.' I wondered why it would want to do that but I wasn't about to discuss it with him.

'Would you like to book your next session now?' he asked, metamorphosing chameleon-like back into an American.

'Er, no. I don't have my diary with me.' I lied, hoping it wasn't about to fall out of my bag. 'I'll give you a call, OK?'

I staggered out to meet Fiona, who sat with her book, smirking, in a coffee bar. 'So how was it?' She asked cheerily. I relayed my tale of woe and stretchmarks. 'I'll tell you a secret then. I was hoping that you'd hate it because I want to send you to my masseuse. I'm going to give you the first session as a present.'

Wow, maybe this was heaven rewarding me for the experience I had just been through.

'Ring this number. He's a very good friend of mine. He's called Jeremy.'

The second possibility of bodily contentment sounded interesting. It was called 'kahuna' and was originally practised in Hawaii. It should be worth a trip.

As it turned out, a trip was what was needed. Fiona's friend Jeremy had inconsiderately moved to the countryside outside Bath. I wondered whether I wanted to spend a day travelling for a massage, no matter how good. This time Mr Inner Masculine had changed his tune. 'These kahuna sessions are normally £80. I think we can afford the fare to Bath if we are not paying for the session.'

'Anyway, I love Bath,' chirped Ms Feminine. So a day came when I arrived at Bath station to be met by a smiling kahuna specialist. Jeremy was attractive, dark-eyed and mystical-looking, as if he knew my every thought; and, for once, I'd found a man who wasn't thin. I looked at his muscles and hoped he was going to be using their full strength on my knotted body. While we drove to his home I enquired about the discipline.

'It was practised in the Hawaiian temples as an initiation.' He had suddenly become as serious as the rolfer. Obviously massage is a serious business.

'An initiation to what?' I tried to lighten the atmosphere as glorious Georgian crescents sped past the window.

'A right of passage, really. For example, into womanhood.'

'Really?' I wasn't sure I wanted to ask any more questions. What exactly was Fiona up to?

We arrived. 'If you'd like to enter?'

The 'temple' looked very like a temple. Drums, swords and masks adorned the room. Where the altar would have been was a massage table. I was to be laid out like a ritual sacrifice –

which made me somewhat uneasy. But it was also very well heated, I noticed with pleasure.

'We will not be speaking during the initiation,' he said. 'But if you want to make sounds or noises of any kind feel free to do so. Also, keep your breathing free as this opens you to the work. Do you have any final requests?' I think he actually said, 'Do you have any questions?' – It just felt like 'final requests'. Anyway, the answer was the same. 'No.'

'If you could take off all your clothes, lie face-down on the table with your head over the hole, and cover yourself with the cloth.' And he left the room.

All my clothes? All my underwear? Well, as they say, in for a penny in for a two-pound coin. I removed all my clothes and prepared myself for the arrival of this complete stranger. I reasoned with myself, 'This is a massage.'

I lay on the altar and covered my nudity with a fine cotton sheet. A few seconds later I heard him tip-toe silently into the room. I couldn't see anything except the floor. He hovered, and walked around arranging me. My hands, despite the fact that the table was wide enough for my arms to relax, were placed under my hips. My legs, which I had together, were separated so they fell apart. Was there something about this massage that Fiona hadn't told me?

Slowly, he removed the sheet and then started to spread oil liberally all over my back. At least I wasn't going to get stretched skin. Then he started to 'work on me'. He didn't just use his hands, he used the whole top half of his arms. He slid around in a continuous circular motion while breathing long, slow, deep breaths and grunting on the exhale. It was surreal but very pleasant.

I'd been warned that it may produce visionary experiences, or that I may be overcome with feelings. Maybe, in spite of my numerous re-births, my feelings were still blocked, because the only thing I was experiencing was a desire to stay right where I was. He moved to grunt about the other side of my back. He arms slid around in circles. It felt pleasant but I did have a voice inside me telling me that he was sliding right over the problem. I was not at liberty to say, 'A little harder, please.' He was obviously exhausting himself.

It was very relaxing and I kept having to remind myself not to fall asleep. I didn't want to miss anything. Then as he moved close in to me I caught sight of a leg. All the way to the top. He was naked. I was lying naked, spread out like a pair of shears, with a naked grunting man. My body was torn between extreme relaxation and extreme panic.

Maybe at this point I should have got up and said, 'Look, I don't know where all this is leading but I'd be deeply reassured if you'd put some clothes on.' Except by this point he was massaging my feet and lower legs and it felt so good that any desire to leap to my feet and start questioning him was overpowered by pure pleasure. I decided I might as well enjoy the good bits and if there was more to this experience than I'd bargained for I'd move and start the 'anger release' then.

He slid his hand under my stomach and, with a movement of impressive style, flipped me over. I kept my eyes closed as he started on my feet once again, presumably to work his way up. The grunting continued. I was very tempted to peek. Was he naked and, if so, was he aroused? If he was did I want to know? What if he was? Would I bolt for the door, quick? As he started on my stomach my inner feminine suddenly spoke, 'Excuse me, but this is so nice I'd rather not know.' 'Are you crazy?' Mr Masculine shouted back and before I knew it, I'd snatched a peek.

Thank God he was not naked. He was wearing a G-string. The manufacturers had possibly been having a hard year and wanted to economise on material. No wonder I hadn't been able to see it. I looked at him to see if he was looking at me looking at him. His eyes were closed. That was a relief, too. The idea of meeting the eyes of a complete stranger who was grunting while massaging my naked stomach could have complicated the situation still more. I closed my eyes, offering a silent prayer of thanksgiving to the Lord and Buddha and any old Hawaiian deities who happened to be about.

He was now sliding his arms over my chest. Now, I know what you are wondering. You're thinking, 'But was it erotic? Were you aroused by all this?' And the answer, I'm afraid to say, is 'No'. I was lying there thinking, 'What's wrong with me? Shouldn't this experience be erotic in some way?' But it was just very relaxing and very pleasurable. He moved to the back of my neck but didn't stay there for nearly long enough. Then my arms and hands. My arms felt like dough and the hands felt very intimate.

He had skipped over all the rude bits and, despite the nudity, it was all in the best possible taste. Finally the grunting sounds came to an end. He lifted the sides of the sheet I was lying on and wrapped me up like a cocoon.

I lay still and opened my eyes to look. His eyes were still closed while he stood with his legs apart and his arms folded, breathing heavily. After about five minutes he finally opened his eyes and looked at me. The tension in the atmosphere was palpable.

'Could you do that again, please?' I was attempting to be humorous and smiled broadly to make sure he understood that. The sides of his mouth flicked upwards briefly. His voice remained intense.

'You can use the sheet to wipe off the excess oil. Then, if you'd like to dress, we have some time before you need to leave.' He left the room and five minutes later we were both standing in his kitchen wearing curiously twentieth-century clothing. I didn't know what to say to him.

'Fennel tea all right for you?' I had never drunk fennel tea. 'Oh, absolutely. What a lovely home you have. Have you been here long?' I uttered the kind of inane chatter that I most loathe.

'For a while.' He was obviously longing to say, 'So, how was it for you?'

We finished the tea and drove back to Bath station. After a silence I said, 'Strange, without love or affection, physical intimacy like that.'

'And spiritual intimacy.'

As I climbed on the train and waved warmly I pondered this last comment. I was glad it had been a spiritual experience for him. I hadn't wanted to spoil it by telling him it had been a purely physical one for me. I felt good, that was for sure. I felt very calm and relaxed. There was just some tension in my shoulders and in my neck. I needed a good massage.

There is a way to be stoned that does not involve either the ancient punishment for adultery or the excess use of drugs or alcohol.

Have you inadvertently flipped to the wrong chapter? Weren't we discussing massage? Yes, there is now a form of massage known as 'stoning'.

I happened to see an article about this in the middle of my search for the ultimate massage and, although strictly speaking it wasn't part of the plan, I couldn't resist it. I've always been very partial to stones. My home is full of them. You know, those eccentric characters who are incapable of spending the day on the beach without robbing the natural environment of its riches and hobbling up the beach at the end of the day, pockets laden with rocks? Your narrator is one of them. It takes all sorts.

Now, you may wonder why anyone would want to be massaged with a rock when the human hand is surely softer? To discover the answer to this question I had to go to Harley Street, of all places. You wouldn't have thought that a street so prestigious for expertise in the medical field would have people getting silently stoned behind closed doors would you? But sure enough, there is a woman hiding there who does weird oily things with hot rocks.

I cycled from Battersea to Harley Street (I wanted to put that in so that everyone who knows London can be impressed with how fit I am) and arrived just in time for her to be ready with a glass of mineral water. 'This works best if you remove all your clothes.'

She looked rather medical, like a young nurse. I was getting used to taking my clothes off and with no kahuna swords on the walls I just lay on her pleasantly wide massage table feeling happy. She had filled the room with a wonderful aromatherapy-oil scent called 'energy'. It made breathing a sensuous experience. And somewhere there was a tape playing plinky-plinky New Age music.

The first part of this new experience involved sitting up and then lying down again on to a row of hot stones that had been laid out to heat up the muscles on either side of the spine. Damned clever. Don't you find that when you lie down on a stone beach, no matter how much you wriggle there is always one stone that insists on digging itself into your back? This was a blissful re-enactment of that experience. As I lay down on the stones each one was perfectly placed to match all the major muscle groups. I sighed, 'Oh yes, heat just there, and there and there.' Then she put a round, flat, hot stone wrapped in a sheet on to my stomach, and one on my breast bone, and one anywhere else where it wouldn't fall off. It was a great way to warm up.

One stone was put in the middle of my forehead and eight little stones were put between my toes. Then she took two large hot stones and gave them to me to hold. You may be thinking, 'This is all very well for people with nothing better to do with their time.' But how do you know that there could be anything better?

You see, these crazy Americans have come up with a thousand and one ways to produce a feeling of bliss. Maybe it's something primal about stones but they do have something very reassuring about them. Holding a beautiful round stone in your hand does produce a feeling of being 'in touch' with reality somehow, doesn't it?

So if you take that feeling and magnify it by the number of stones that I was currently 'in touch' with, you can begin to imagine the effect of all this. Granted, I did feel slightly daft. The days when I was dubious of the latest American fad to hit London were long gone. Now I just wanted to try them even if they did make me look as if someone was trying to bury me.

Then an oily stone started to massage my arm. I suppose her hand must have been connected to it at some point but I couldn't be sure. She was so skilful that it was hard to tell what was her hand and what was the stone, except that the stone was hotter. I began to feel a rush of affection for the stone. It was so good at massage. I'd had grown men in my life who claimed to be experienced lovers who couldn't make my arm feel as good as this stone could. Yes, I was fond of this small rock.

She moved to work on the other arm. A new stone appeared in my life. As warm and tender as the last. It understood my arm. It knew how to hollow itself round every tightened sinew. It knew how to slide itself along any aching tendon. My affection was growing deeper. I was interested in dating the stone.

There seemed to be battalions of them lined up to please me. No sooner had one cooled down than it was replaced by another. 'You are allowing them to give you their heat,' she said.

'Doesn't everyone?' Surely I wasn't doing anything special?

'Some people do not receive the heat. They are resistant to it. With some clients I don't need to change the stones at all. Everyone is different.'

Finally I have found something in life for which I have a talent. Receiving heat from stones. Then some little pebbles started to make love to my face. They slid around happily. So intimate, so gentle. I wanted to proclaim my tenderness to them, 'Oh stones – how I do love thee.'

Then I had to turn over. As I lay down there was a round, flat stone that fitted perfectly into the pelvic girdle. It was like lying on a hot water bottle only twice as good and even quite sexy. Heat up against the pubic bone. My potential new relationship was feeling very promising. And the uncanny feeling of being understood was becoming increasingly worrying. Maybe this is what I'd been doing wrong all these years? Trying to have relationships with people.

A stone started to express its devotion to my neck. I had a knotted muscle on the right-hand side that had been there for years. Many the masseur that had skimmed straight over it. But not this stone. The heat was wonderful and the scented oil meant the stone could slide into the problem without being at all painful. I was lost. 'Oh yes, stone, yes. Where have you been all my life?'

Then my shoulders, and down my back. The stones pushed their way down on my shoulder muscles as if trying to bury themselves. I said 'Ow' but I wasn't complaining. For my back, two twin stones slid up and down either side of my spine. They moved down my legs and started on my feet. So few men understand what an utter source of bliss the feet can be. Did you know that the tips of the toes, like the tips of the fingers, are among the most sensitive places in the body? The huge number of nerve-endings in the fingertips are what makes it possible for the blind to learn Braille. We have hugely sensitive fingers. And toes. You may not know this, but the rocks did.

A pebble was stroking my foot. There may once have been a man who had felt so passionate about the outside edge of my foot . . . but I couldn't remember him. I was in love with this rock. So warm, so undemanding, so giving, so well rounded.

Then the stones started to speak to me. 'Why are you always fighting your life and treating it as a struggle? Why are you always resistant? Why do you try so hard? Let things happen. Relax. Be gentle.' I was now being counselled by stones. I was ready to make a commitment. It was going to have to be marriage. 'I take thee, stone, to have and to hold from this day forth . . .'

Then a terrible thing happened. A human voice spoke. 'Your session is over now.'

Who was this silly woman? 'Lie still for a while and then sit up slowly.' She left the room. I lay feeling the flat, round stone warm against my tummy. I sat up and unwrapped it from its sheet. It was just a normal beach stone made of basalt but I loved it.

I wanted to take it home. But they are very spiritual things, rocks. Like the nuns, they don't save their love for one person but have a similar level of devotion to everyone they meet. Alas, they would be just as attentive to the needs of the next customer. Blast non-attachment. I sighed and placed the rock lovingly on the massage bed.

As I put my clothes back I felt like Celia Johnson in *Brief Encounter*. I had to leave, to return to my washing-up. I walked courageously from the room. A new heroine for the new millennium. 'Isabel leaves rocks.' Never let it be said that my life is not full of brave and heroic actions.

As I cycled home I remembered other meetings with rocks. The memory at my re-birthing of running over them to hurt my feet. Now I had made peace with them and they were yet one more lump in the universe which I held in deep affection. Gosh, accidental progress along the Road to Enlightenment while in selfish pursuit of the ultimate massage. Sometimes, life is good.

'Would you like to try chavutti thirumal?' It's not often you hear someone say that. Sounds like the answer should be 'No, but I'd like tikka masala.'

Someone rang me and asked this question on a day when I was playing a game with Insight. They have an exercise, (no, this is true) when anything anyone asks you all day long, you answer 'Yes'. The idea is to be open to new things and new possibilities. If someone asks you to do something you really don't want to do, then get clever at saying 'no' while sounding nice.

'Would you like to have lunch with me today?'

'Yes, do you know anywhere that is smoke-free, non-alcoholic and vegan?'

'Would you like to go out with me?'

'Yes, I would. I'm co-dependent, you know.'

'Would you like to have sex with me tonight?'

'Yes. Did I tell you about my threadworms?'

But that's only necessary if you really want to cop out. Most of the time the exercise is just to say 'Yes' to everything that comes your way, for a day. Try it some time.

Anyway, back to the story. So I said 'Yes' to chavutti thirumal and then enquired what interesting new experience I had let myself in for. 'A massage.' Well, here goes, let's hope this Chavutti chap is as tasty as he sounds. I got on my bike and cycled from Battersea to Oxford Street. I was ready to say 'Yes' to all the questions he asked me.

I arrived at the centre to find a mother screaming at her three-year-old: 'You *do* want to do your ballet class!'

'No, no, I want to go home!'

'No, you can't go home!'

Life is full of harmony, isn't it? I toyed with the idea of introducing them both to the 'Yes' exercise but as the young prima-ballerina began to hurl blows at her mother I thought maybe this wasn't the moment for some unsolicited advice.

'Are you the 3:00 p.m. appointment?'

'Yes.'

'Would you like a full session?'

'Yes. Are you Chavutti?' I enquired of the good-looking Indian sitting behind the desk. He smiled graciously.

'Chavutti means foot,' he explained.

'You are named foot? Great sense of humour, these Indian mothers. There must be a good story there.'

'There is. Would you like to hear it?'

'Yes.'

' "Chavutti" means foot and "thirumal" means massage. This is the name of the massage you have come for. It's a foot massage. My name is Ken.'

A massage for feet? From Ken? Another beautiful moment bites the dust. 'You do the massage, do you, Ken?'

'No.' Why wasn't he playing? 'The woman giving the foot massage is called Tracy. It's not for feet. The massage is given with feet.' Stupid Insight games. I was going to be massaged by Tracy's feet? I contemplated making a bolt for the door. But then she appeared. A stocky girl. I glanced at her feet. I wasn't overwhelmed with a desire to become intimate with them.

'Are you Isabel? Nice to meet you.' She shook my hand limply.

'Er, yes.' She showed me into a small room. A red rope, hooked up ominously, ran from wall to wall.

'That's to support my body weight when I walk on you. You are here for the full treatment, aren't you?'

'Yes.' I promised myself a day saying 'No' to everything.

'So if you could take *all* your clothes off, please, and lie down on your back?'

She stressed 'all' in a way that was difficult to miss. I had only met Tracy that second and yet now I was supposed to undress, lie on the floor and let her walk all over me. Somehow I seemed to be down a cul-de-sac.

'I have to salute my teacher to ask for healing energy to work with you. That OK with you?'

'Yes, fine.'

She disappeared and a curiously incongruous chanting sound emerged from the next room. Well, if Divine powers wanted to be with her feet that was fine with me. I took off my clothes and lay down on my stomach. A rather unattractive plastic bottle of sesame oil stood on the floor next to a tin plate. The room was heated to about ninety-five degrees. Obviously, I was to be cooked.

She reappeared looking comically serious. Sesame oil began to get splashed all over me and rubbed in. So this is what it felt like to be basted. Then she started the massage. She ran her hand down in one incredibly long and firm stroke from my neck to my toes. And then again, and again. Where did she get such strength from? Had she slipped out been replaced by an Indian guru? Then I realised: it wasn't a hand, it was a foot. Weird.

It was quite a feat. Her toes dug in the tender spots like fingers and her heel seemed to have been designed for necks. Sometimes it was wonderful. Sometimes it hurt too much. 'Where were your feet trained?' I asked as she slid around on me.

'In India. But I prefer not to speak when I'm working. That OK with you?'

'Sure, yes.'

Nothing to do but lie there and enjoy it, then. I don't say that too often. Dear me, I'm getting smutty now. I do that if it gets embarrassing. When I eventually had to turn over I did feel vulnerable. I was lying naked, breasts in the air, on the floor with a woman I didn't know. She started to baste my top side.

I kept my eyes closed and thought of Robert Redford. He was never around when I wanted him. Just think, if he only knew the game I was playing today he could ring up and say, 'Would you marry me, Isabel?' and I could say 'Yes', just like that, without even hesitating.

She was now sliding her feet up and down from my neck to my toes on this side. It did feel good. When she got to my boobs she twisted her foot round and slid it down between them. It was very clever. She thirumal-ed the sides well and all those muscles down the side of the ribcage. And she put her toes in my tummy and reminded me of the stomach massages I was supposed to be giving myself. Thank goodness for the herbs. No unfortunate movement of gasses.

She toed the legs thoroughly and then sat me up to finish the neck and shoulders using her hands. She massaged my face and even rubbed the scalp vigorously. I think she got right through my scalp and activated parts of my brain. (Since this session, for instance, I have felt quite confident that I know how to spell antidisestablishmentarianism. The brain being more active . . . it's all relative.) She began to sing one note in a kind of semibreve followed by a semibreve rhythm.

I stood up and my body seemed to be working unusually well. She disappeared to make her parting prayers. Probably of thanksgiving. As my clothes slid back on I caught sight of myself in the mirror. My hair looked as if it had half a bottle of sesame oil in it. Well it did. I said my own thanksgiving prayer. 'Thank you, God, for my ridiculous purple cycling helmet.'

'You'll phone me if you want another session, will you?' she asked. I was glad she had worded it like that.

'Yes, I certainly will.'

On the way home, while weaving my way between buses and death on Oxford Street, a war broke out. I thought I had enjoyed the massage but my masculine and feminine sides had other thoughts. Mr Masculine was being his usual self: 'That's it. You get one more chance. One more. I don't care if it was two hours. Fifty pounds is a ridiculous amount of money and we don't have it. This ultimate massage quest is getting out of hand.'

It had got out of hand, actually. Ms Feminine was also upset. 'Why can't I be massaged by a man? Is that asking so much?'

I thought they were both very ungrateful. Mr Masculine was adamant. 'Look. Find a local sports masseur. Try the athletics track in Battersea Park. Stop all this silly fancy nonsense. Stop listening to all your crazy friends and listen to me.'

So this was my last chance. I cycled down Battersea Park Road and into the park. 'Good morning, peacocks,' I shouted merrily as I turned down a path marked 'No Cycling'. The peacocks shrieked at me. Obviously St Francis had a more subtle approach.

The athletics track is an alarming place to visit. If you even stroll past you are in danger of seeing seriously fit people running in a way that isn't humanly possible. It's one thing to slob out on the sofa watching Olympic athletes on TV while eating crisps. Entertainment is a good thing. But to see these people with your own eyes means there is no way to avoid admitting that they do actually exist. They run down the track and leave a vacuum in the air behind them. You can see the lines in space like in cartoons. And they smile, too. The day I went two blonde girls, each about eight foot high, were doing three-minute miles before breakfast.

'Are you here to join the athletics club?' A black guy spoke to me. He had come from the weights room. His chest looked like a diagram of the major muscle groups.

'No.' Great word. 'I just want to find a local sports masseur.'

'We recommend a guy called Terry. Lots of the runners go to him. Here's his card. Anything else I can do for you?'

I looked at his chest. 'Er, no.'

The very next day I met Terry Kingscote. Older than I expected, nearly sixty. A bit like your local butcher in appearance and in manner. 'Take off all your clothes and lie under the towel. I'll just wait outside while you undress.'

I didn't feel vulnerable at all. Just very comfortable. No 'plinky plinky' New Age music here.

'So, any particular areas of stiffness?' Finally someone who asked this question.

'Yes, my neck and my shoulders.'

'Right, OK.' And he started his day's work. He applied an oil with no perfume and began. Oh, good grief. I was finally in the hands of a professional.

'Been doing this long?'

'Yes. Six days a week for thirty years.'

'I see.' He pressed hard on all the stiff areas. He pummelled them. He squeezed them, he gave such a deep kneading every other massage experience was instantly forgotten. Even the stones that I had loved. Oh, faithless woman. I decided he had definitely been a butcher in a former life. I think they call this tenderising the meat.

'Yes!' shouted my inner masculine. 'Now *this* is a massage.'

'We like him,' the inner feminine agreed. Harmony? There had to be a first time.

He found the gristly bits and kept working on those. 'Why does it get so stiff?' I groaned.

'It's a build up of a natural protein in the body caused by stress and tension. You know when you eat meat some bits turn to gristle? That's what these bits are.'

I knew he was a butcher.

'I'm afraid a cannibal would leave most of your neck and shoulders on the plate.'

He kneaded and pummelled all down my back and legs and then said, 'Turn over and keep the towel covering you.' He slid the towel up and down tastefully. He was so wonderfully down to earth about the whole thing. I decided to keep the mind/body/spirit exercises separate. Here was a man who knew how to tenderise my body and leave my mind and spirit alone. I liked him very much.

Then he started on my feet. Pressing different points. 'Ow!'

'That's your eye muscles. Spend much time at the computer?'

'Hours every day. But you don't strike me as a reflexology type.'

'No. I'm not. My sister dragged me on to a course and I was dubious but I touched a point on a woman's foot last week and she nearly shot off the table. When I told her the point related to her right ovary she said that it was blocked and was due to be operated on the following week. So I've become interested.' He was so delightfully un-mystical about the whole thing. No hushed, understanding tones. I could see why the athletes down at the track would be happy coming here.

When he got to my stomach and sides he gathered me up as if he was about to separate the muscle from the rest of me. He gave my arms a good rubbing and then spent a delightfully long time on the back of the neck prodding the point where the muscles join the skull. I managed to speak to him, 'I think you are releasing tension that has been there about twenty years.'

'Yes,' he said chattily.

He stopped. My life is a tragedy. 'You're done. Would you like to keep the giblets?' Sometimes I'm sure my memory of what exactly is said to me after a massage is a little hazy. I think it's the shock of blood being able to flow freely round my body.

He left the room and I got dressed. 'Would you like to make another appointment?'

'Yes. Oh, yes. One a month for the rest of my life.' I had found him, the beginning of a beautiful relationship. Shame he's nearly sixty, married and with two adult children. Still, I'd achieved one thing. Soon I'd be able to irritate friends. 'Oh my masseur? He's just a local sports masseur. [Flicking my hair back casually] I've been going to him for ages.'

Phase Twelve: Saying 'Fuck' with Style

I suppose, over the years, I have acquired some pretty weird friends. This blasted girl Fiona, for example. I've known her for twenty years and I'm sure she used to be quite sane. It's very sad. I'd be willing to bet that if your friends ask if you'd like to spend the day with them they invite you shopping? Or maybe to the cinema? Or for a trip to the seaside? These are the kind of 'days out' that I suppose would count as 'normal'. They would all be considered acceptable by my ex-husband's family, which is a sure sign of 'normal'. But when Fiona rings me she wants to know if I'd like to join her for an 'Anger-Release Day'.

'But I'm not feeling angry.' I tried to plead sanity. 'I'm CODA'd, I'm irrigated, I'm manifesting my inner goddess, I'm reborn, I've even made peace with aspects of myself from former lifetimes . . . Surely I must be cooked for a while? I don't even have road rage; I ride a bike. I don't feel angry, honestly, not with anyone.'

'Oh, don't make me laugh. Everyone is angry with someone. Do you want me to tell you who you are angry with?'

'No. Definitely not.' She knows me far too well.

'Come on then. I would like your company. Tell you what, I'll pay for you.'

'Oh, OK.' Doesn't take much to persuade me.

She drove up in her car the following Saturday morning not looking angry at all. I wasn't too happy. It was 8 a.m.

'Where are we going?' I croaked, clutching my trendy American-style portable coffee mug.

'St John's Wood'. As good a place as any to be angry in. The workshop was in the crypt of a church. A few hugely stressed individuals stood outside smoking frantically. Inside was comfortably carpeted and full of huge cushions and herbal tea. People sat about chatting and a couple of the now familiar genus 'men with a well-developed feminine side' were meditating earnestly.

Short courses often start with dancing. They put on music in four-four time with a loud base so everyone leaps around like crazy acid-house junkies. This ensures that you are then ready to explain why you are there as long as you can sit down. It's what they call the 'warm up'. Today the guru leading decided to educate us first. She was French and chubby but elegant with a round, smiling face, dark hair and wise, dark eyes. She had a 'been-there, done-that and not only got the T-shirt but "used the experience for my learning, upliftment and growth"' look about her.

She started to talk to us about anger. Anger was the cause of so many illnesses and drained us of our energy. Anger that was not expressed caused cancer and all manner of terrible physical problems. Repressed anger caused depression. Anger that did not speak up ruined partnerships and if it was not correctly channelled could adversely affect children and the people who we love the most. By the time she had finished talking I was glad I had come. This could clear out my system more soundly than colonic irrigation, it seemed.

Then we went round the circle and people said what had brought them. A woman who kept shouting at her flatmates. Someone whose boyfriend had sent her along because she kept hitting him. A man who admitted shamefaced that he had been violent with his toddlers. The usual crowed of followers of this particular guru who just liked the way she worked. And then people who had been dragged along by friends, into which category, once again, I fell.

'I'm not feeling any particular anger at the moment,' I said. 'But I may have improved by the end of the day.' They smiled at me wearily. The way you do with people who say things that aren't funny.

Fiona was now in an' I want to kill my father/ex-boyfriend/ current boyfriend and all members of the male species' kind of mood. It sounded vaguely familiar and the women understood.

Then we had to work in pairs and play out different situations that would unleash some anger for us. A conversation in which the other person just said 'No' or 'You're wrong' or 'That's stupid' or any of the other common put-downs we human beings seem to love to inflict on each other.

There was one in which we had to play a parent or a young child and it was the job of the small child to try and get the parent's attention by saying 'Listen to me' and the parent's job to ignore the child by talking on the phone or just not answering. I realised, with some joy, that I had never had this experience. Having been raised by a mother and grandmother who both adored me, I may have been spoiled but I was never ignored. Nor had I ignored my daughter in this way. But for some in the room the situation was obviously all too familiar. They shouted, and were ignored.

The next exercise involved walking across the room and simply saying in a loud voice 'No, no, don't dare!' and making a strong gesture with the hand away from you like a policeman saying 'Stop'. A simple enough job. But it got me. I stepped out boldly and said 'No!' and with the first 'No' realised I had never really said this word before. I said 'No!' again and felt my power as if for the first time. I could say 'No!' It felt like a revelation. I had said 'Yes' to men so many times. Because I wanted to please them. Because I didn't want to lose them. Even the girl with the strong inner masculine had never felt safe to say 'No'. It was like scales falling from my eyes.

By the time I got to 'Don't dare!' I knew exactly to whom I was speaking and what old resentments had yet to be resolved. I had never dared to say 'Don't dare!' Wow, a woman that can say 'No!' What a concept.

Then back across the room. 'No! No! No! Don't dare!' Sounds daft, doesn't it? Like you could find better things to do with your Saturdays? But I was hooked already. For the first time in any life I was affirming that I had the right to say 'No' as well as 'Yes'. I could have gone on with that exercise for a couple of hours.

Then the next phrase to be spoken in full voice: 'Leave me alone'. Some of the mousy men in the room who had been barely audible in their 'No' now found a voice and shouted joyfully 'Leave me alone!' I guess they never had the courage to say that to whoever had made them mousy.

Then a third: 'Get off my back!' All the sat-on and down-trodden, into which category I also have fallen, were enjoying this. I suppose most of us have felt at some time that someone was sitting on us, stifling us, or even being critical in nasty, insidious ways. It felt good to shout 'Get off my back' with feeling. No one we were shouting at was there to feel attacked. It was just an exercise.

Then the next walk around: 'I am taking my power back'. Only this time we had a variation. While one person proclaimed this in full voice another was to walk beside them and utter improvised derision. 'Huh! You? Power? Don't make me laugh! You spineless cretin, you've never had any power anyway. You never will have.'

As I sat and listened to the ease with which we derided those who were reclaiming their power I was shocked. As I've been living alone with my daughter for many years I don't live with this any more. All my friends love me. If someone doesn't like me I simply don't spend time with them. I was horrified to hear what people said. People live with this abuse, criticism and rage? This is how we treat our loved ones? Alas for love. Why do couples do this stuff to each other?

'Does your husband really speak to you like that?' I asked one woman.

'All the time.'

'Why do you stay with him?'

'Because of the children.'

'Does he yell at the children like that?'

'Yes. But I couldn't go; I couldn't live without him.'

It's not often I'm lost for words.

The next walk, also to be followed by derision, was: 'I know my truth'.

I was back to my process now. I thought of times when I had been mocked and derided. I proclaimed, 'I know my truth' wishing I'd had the guts to say these things in my life. A man walked across the room taunting me: 'You're a joke' to which I said in a louder voice 'I know my truth' and ended with an improvised phrase of my own. 'So fuck off.' Never can resist playing to the audience.

At the end of this exercise we were given pieces of plastic piping about a foot long and cushions and invited to hit the cushions until we could hit them no longer.

Strange. I had said that morning that I was not feeling angry. All this going to church and doing seminars and stuff . . . I honestly thought I'd got rid of my outstanding resentments long ago.

Hitting cushions is huge fun. I remembered things that had been said to me. I once gave a man a poem I'd written. It was a love poem. He'd said 'Shakespeare does it better, doesn't he?' It was fifteen years until I wrote another. I remembered when I'd been deceived, let down, misunderstood. Yes, I could hit the pillow as well as anyone.

It's not that I'd want to hit anyone with plastic pipe in real life. Well, let's be honest here. I can think of a couple of people I'd quite like to hit. But I wouldn't choose to even if I had the chance. I used to have a wonderful fantasy about shooting a certain man and his lover. I had the location planned in my mind and everything. It would have been dusk under one of those lights that said 'Stage Door' in a theatre he was working at. It would be evening. The lighting would have been in yellow from an old lamp. Soft focus. Him first, then her. A gun with a silencer so not a lot of noise. Just thud, thud. And lots of blood. It would have been worth going to prison for the rest of my life. I think you could have said I was angry with this man . . . a little upset? Anyway, I decided against it in the end and now I wouldn't even want to hit him with a plastic pipe. Not in the flesh, anyway. But this hitting a cushion thing. You should try it some time.

People were shouting, too. The words 'bastard' and 'bitch' were being hollered regularly out of the crypt. The pedestrians passing by must have been most interested to know what form of church service was taking place. The good Lord did tell us to forgive people, after all, but he didn't get too specific about how to do it. According to our facilitator for the day, it is necessary to get rid of all this anger stuff before real forgiveness can be done. Somewhere a bell was ringing. Something was sounding familiar. But I didn't have to think about it. I just hit pillows some more.

When we were all totally exhausted she announced lunch. We moved from deep and personal conversation to the usual banalities. 'So, er, where abouts do you live?' – to a woman who has just confided that her husband beats her. It makes you wonder about the secrets the people on the next table in restaurants carry with them. The couple with the children looked happy enough. I wondered whether he calls her a 'brainless bitch' when they are at home. Or what terms of endearment she screams at him? 'I hate you, you drunken bastard. You're a nobody.'

If you'd seen us in the restaurant in St John's Wood you'd have seen a laughing happy group of friends. The kind of group I look at with envy if I'm lunching alone and wonder why everyone else seems to have huge groups of companions. So next time you see a very happy bunch of people, bear in mind that they may have just spent an hour beating the living daylights out of a bunch of innocent cushions.

We walked back with trepidation. What on earth could she have planned for the afternoon? I was surprised by what she was attempting. Drama. She asked for a volunteer. I sat still. A girl of about twenty-five got up and told her story. From the age of eleven she had been bullied and victimised in school. Gangs of girls had hit her, kicked her, taken her work, pushed her downstairs. At fourteen her mother had finally found out when she saw bite-marks on her daughter's arm. 'I never did anything to them.' She stood in front of us and questioned the room as if we could tell her why she had been bullied so intensely.

We couldn't tell her. But we could in some small way give her power back to her. She was asked to choose faces from the room to re-enact her persecutors. Four girls were chosen. A life-sized teddy bear was put on the floor to represent her. The girls stood around and kicked it. They shouted abuse. 'You're a cry-baby'; 'You're stupid'; 'Don't you dare tell or we'll get you'.

It was agony, even to watch it. She cried. Then the facilitator said to her, 'So what would you like to happen now?' She flew on to her feet screaming at them: 'What the hell do you think you are doing? Do you know how old I am? Why are you hurting me?'

The three make-believe bullies stood listening to her, dumbfounded.

'Don't you realise what you are doing? I was eleven when you started this, for God's sake! Why me? What did I do to you?

Look at these bruises.' She screamed and screamed at them until finally she started to laugh. 'I've wanted to say that to them for years.'

'Is that enough?'

'Yes. Thank you very much.'

'Everyone drink water,' said the Frenchwoman. Plastic cups were passed round. Always good for chewing on, a plastic cup.

'Anyone else?'

An American woman got up. She was in her thirties, but tiny.

'My mother used to hit me. We had terrible rows,' she said.

'OK, so pick someone to be your mother.'

She looked around; her eyes fell on me.

'Isabel.' Oh, good grief. Did I want to do this?

'So how old do you want to be?' I asked her.

'I'll be about fourteen.' So is there a God? What do you think? My daughter's age exactly.

'And what did you row about?' I asked.

'Oh, anything.'

'OK, I know the sort of thing.'

So I started an imitation of me at my absolute worst. Ratty and overtired. 'Are you ever going to pick up anything behind you or do any washing-up? I mean, I'm just sick of asking you!'

'And I'm sick of you nagging me!' she yelled back.

'Isn't it about time you made some contribution to this house if you want to be considered an adult? I do everything around here. Everything.'

'I don't ask you to clear up, do I?'

'Don't be ridiculous – someone has to wash the dishes, don't they?'

'Do you think I care?' she screamed.

'Well, you bloody should care.'

'Go fuck yourself.' My daughter never said this to me. Thank God or I may have hit her myself. But I knew the next line.

'Don't you speak to me like that. Who do you think you are speaking to?'

'I'm speaking to you, you bitch.'

It was weird. Like a terrible row with my daughter. The type we have about twice a year, only worse. It was horrible to hear myself screaming like this at a kid. Even if she was thirty-five and pretending. I felt ashamed.

'Hit her on the arm,' the facilitator whispered in my ear. I winced and I hit her.

'Fuck you,' she said. I hit her again.

'Don't you speak to me like that!' I screamed. I hit her again on the arm, quite hard. What did I want? Some horrendous submission? Tears?

'I hate you,' she screamed.

'I've had just about enough of you. You're impossible.'

I was about ready to burst into tears myself. This was acting out my worst nightmare.

'OK, that's enough.' The facilitator came to my rescue.

She turned and spoke softly to the thirty-five-year-old teenager. 'And what would you like to say to her now?'

I expected her anger. It was an anger workshop, after all. But I didn't get it. 'Mom, I'm sorry. I just want to say I've been angry at you for so long. I just didn't understand what it was like for you, with Dad gone and all that. It's true what you said – I never did anything for you – but I was a selfish kid and I didn't understand, and Mom?' she said to me.

'I know,' I said. 'I understand. I'm your Mom. I love you. I'm sorry.' She hugged me.

I sat down and thought about my daughter and my relationship with her. We hadn't rowed for months. I vowed silently to myself that next time she was rude or pressed my buttons I would walk out of the room. I had played this scene now. By the grace of God I never wanted to play it again. I'd come to the workshop to learn about anger but I hadn't expected this lesson. I was more shaken than the American woman.

'Water?' she said. I needed whiskey.

'Let's have a break,' said the facilitator, looking at me and putting on some dance music. Yes. I danced a silly waltz and remembered all the time I'd danced silly waltzes with my daughter. All the songs we'd sung together, all the games we'd played. I made my dance a thanksgiving for the beautiful young woman at home with her friends. I wanted to rush home and say, 'I'm sorry for the times I've yelled at you'. But she'd have raised her eyes heavenwards with a long-suffering look and sighed, 'Oh, Mother . . . Have you been doing one of those workshops again?'

The dance ended and the facilitator said, 'We've time for one more.' A mousy woman got up. She looked as if she'd been scared all her life. She had been. We looked at each other in the room for reassurance. It was what we had dreaded. Child abuse. She described the scene for us. The woman used the life-sized bear to represent her in her bed. Aged six.

A man bravely volunteered just to walk up to the bear and pull back the cover. She pleaded with him. 'You sick man. I was six years old. *Six years old*. I've been a victim all my life. Get away from her. Don't you dare touch her, you sad, twisted man.' She screamed at him. She wept for the lost innocence of that six-year-old. She finished screaming at him.

We sat in awestruck admiration of her work. Then we applauded. The courage that people display on these workshops is so inspiring. The human will to forgive, to forget, to move on – whatever the injury that has been done – never ceases to move me.

Then, just when I thought we were all done, we went back to hitting cushions. I wacked the cushion and wondered why I was hitting it now. Then I remembered a man I'd never met. Some-where in another dimension a man stood waiting for my forgiveness. Roger Woolger had said to first get rid of your anger and then have compassion. I thought of the scene of a starving woman and three children and I thumped the cushion till I was exhausted. Then I remembered my father. I wacked the cushion a bit for him. 'You have no idea how difficult it was for my mother. You bastard.' I didn't really feel that angry with him. But it felt good saying it anyway. I wacked the cushion another fifty times for good measure.

Then, blissfully, there was a meditation. She played wafty New Age music which was perfect for flight to the spirit world where an unknown man was still waiting. I stood in front of him and spoke – about forgiveness. 'I've been angry. I've been cruel to my daughter the way you were cruel to me. You didn't mean to hurt me. You didn't understand. You didn't understand anything but you were a desperate man and I've been a desperate woman. I am no better than you so yes, I can forgive you. Can you forgive me?' And somewhere in my meditation a voice said, 'Of course'.

As the meditation music finished I felt a little lighter.

The day ended and I saw Fiona smiling at me. She was trying not to say 'I told you so' but it was in her eyes. 'Oh well, all right, I admit it. I suppose the workshop was useful.'

I'd thought that morning that I didn't have any anger in me. Self-awareness? Just consult the sage of Battersea.

Phase Thirteen: The Hypnotist, the Genius and the Fat Man

One of the disadvantages of being on the Road to Enlightenment is that you get a lot of weird mail. If you do a seminar of any kind your name gets put on a central register labelled 'Gullible New Age-Type' and every guru in London then wants to invite you on to a course or two or three.

Another TV job came and went. I had made an entire programme about Freud and I still didn't know anything about him. I was feeling very backward. Should I now launch myself into reading *The Complete Works* of Siggy or could I have more fun checking what the post had to offer.

One morning a leaflet:

> Like learning music from Mozart, physics from Einstein or painting from Picasso, you can learn NLP from the creative genius who started it all, Richard Bandler.

Now, I've heard some claims in my time but this one has to win the prize for nutcase of the year. A grey-haired man, backlit in mystic yellow, with pock-marked skin and black-painted fingernails, stared at me off the leaflet. Two other slick dudes stood beside him. One was wearing a rather unattractive tie and was apparently Paul McKenna the 'TV hypnotist'. The third man just looked rather fat, but he did have a more tasteful tie.

I think I was supposed to have heard of Paul McKenna but I don't watch TV. I'm not in the least interested in television. Perhaps I'm in the wrong job? Of course, I have to pretend I watch a lot of TV. At one interview I was asked what my favourite daytime TV chat shows were. I couldn't even make up an answer to that one. And of course I'm not in the least impressed by someone having their own series – except when they are a hypnotist.

So here was an opportunity to learn something weird from a TV megastar, an egomaniac and a fat man. They offered 'A New World of Possibilities', and also claimed to be the largest and most successful NLP trainers in the UK with more than 400 'delegates' per training. Neurolinguistic Programming, to give the discipline its full name, is something that I'd often heard spoken of but knew nothing about. I know that Insight make some use of bits of it but I don't know when. I'd even once heard someone say proudly, 'Did you see that? I NLP'd him.' I looked at this person in dumbstruck ignorance. I could work out that 'neuro' means the brain, 'linguistic' means language and 'programming' means, er, programming. And hypnotism came into it somewhere. That's clear then, isn't it? On a course with 400 people I'd also stand a statistical chance of meeting an interesting man. Do interesting men study NLP? Is there any reason that they shouldn't? The trainers looked like wide-boys to me, grinning and offering new life. But, as ever, I was curious.

The course was in a conference centre in Tottenham Court Road. I arrived and was given a huge contract to sign were I had to promise not to set up NLP trainings myself. At the same time I was given a badge that said: 'NLP Practitioner Isabel Losada' and told that by the end of the week I would be a member of The

Society of Neurolinguistic Programming and I would be licensed. All I had to do to obtain this qualification was pay my money and stay in the room and I could convince any other gullible people like myself that I was trained to change people's lives. I could have a framed certificate on the wall to prove it.

I entered the room and scanned the 400 people in the two seconds it takes for a woman to spot if there is an interesting man within 200 yards. There was one but he was bald. I could check him out later. We all sat. The conference room, with no outside windows, was huge and dominated by two speakers which were blaring out some heavy rock in four-four time. The music man had obviously been told to put on something 'loud and upbeat'. Then riotous applause, led by the helpers at the back, and the fat man and the hypnotist walked on to the stage.

They began in self-congratulatory mode. The fat man told us how successful the courses were and we applauded each group who had travelled from across the sea to be here. 'Let us welcome those from Kuwait and the United Arab Republic.'

We applauded obediently.

'Let us welcome those from Germany.'

We peered round to look for them and clap. This went on. Italy, Spain, Monaco, the Netherlands, Denmark, Norway, Portugal, Israel, Turkey and Never Never Land. When we finally finished the hypnotist added: 'And is there anyone from Kensington, because I need a lift home?'

He's funny. Which was a relief because the fat man, who was doing most of the talking, wasn't. I sat there thinking unpleasant things about him. Paul McKenna is obviously brighter and more entertaining, so why was the fat man talking so much? You know how irritating it is when a speaker patronises his audience and it isn't appropriate to shout, 'Hey, that's not true!' This was the situation he was putting us in. At one point he grinned at us and said: 'On this course people will lose their fear of words.' Bloody cheek, I thought. I may be afraid of being bored to death by speakers of dubious skill but a fear of words I do not have.

'We don't teach theory,' he said. I'd rung a friend who knew about NLP and she'd said, 'They aim to give you an experience on a subconscious level. So they don't actually bother to teach you anything.' She'd said it would be a wasted week. I already thought she was right and there was a spring sticking into my bum from the conference-style chair. Then someone passed round manuals. They were 144 pages long and full of theory. Hadn't they just said that they weren't going to teach theory? I turned a page. It said, 'The manual is not the training'. That's OK then, I decided, I won't have to read it. I used it to cover the spring on my gammy chair. McKenna started to talk about communication.

'I hated geography. Perhaps it was because of the boring tosser who taught it to me.' Women in buttoned shirts shuffled uncomfortably. 'We use a lot of profanities here. They are very carefully thought about. We have meetings.'

They continued to tell us how brilliant their training was. 'All the other NLP organisations disapprove of us. They say NLP can't be taught in seven days. That's because people who do NLP are such nerds.' I wasn't sure that being christened a nerd on the first day was endearing me to the principles. Then they started on a double act of telling us how brilliant the 'genius who created it all' was. 'Bandler is the most skilled communicator I've ever seen.' They agreed with each other again. My bum longed for the coffee break.

It came and I wandered out, overtaken by a compulsion to consume biscuits with jam in the middle. Other nerds of all forms chatted and nodded enthusiastically to each other. A tall male version approached me grinning in a worryingly friendly fashion.

'I'm here to help my son,' he said.

'Oh really?' I feigned interest. 'How old is he?'

'Twenty-five.'

This conversation would need more unsolicited advice than even I was prepared to embark upon. And I was in no mood to listen sympathetically.

A very thin woman approached. She wore an empathetic smile. I didn't want empathy. I suddenly became a smoker: 'I'm just popping outside for a cigarette.' It wasn't true but it gave me satisfaction to lie to a total stranger. I wanted to spill my coffee on her too. I guess I wasn't in a very good mood. I smoked my invisible cigarette, tar factor extra high, and sulked back into the hall. I changed seats but found another still less comfortable than the last.

Suddenly there was a fanfare. Ecstatic applause from the helpers at the back and the egotist with the black fingernails appeared. He looked like a demonic mass-murderer who was about to produce a machine gun and mow us all down. He was on some other level of consciousness. Was he drugged, crazy, or possibly both? Then he spoke. A voice of deep resonance caressed our eardrums.

'If you connect pleasure with learning, people will do it more often,' he stated. I wondered why no one had thought of this at my daughter's school. A man in the front row was taking notes. Bandler walked up to him aggressively. 'Can you forget the number 379?' he asked. The man mumbled back in monosyllabic terror. 'No? Then how are you going to forget a whole workshop?' The notebook was placed obediently on the floor.

Then he started on what appeared to be a thirty-minute stand-up comedy routine. His first theme was that psychotherapy was a waste of time. 'Most therapists teach you to be depressed about your life. There isn't anything in psychotherapy that cheers you up. Most of it is bullshit. If someone has been in therapy for years and they are still not happy why don't they ask for a refund?'

No one could accuse Bandler of not speaking his mind. His

jokes were interspersed with stories on the theme of how stupid everyone else was and how clever he was. He was often right, it seemed.

'Take catatonics . . .' His passion held our attention. 'If you are a catatonic patient it means nobody can help you and nobody is going to try. I hit a catatonic patient who hadn't moved or spoken for ten years very hard on the little toe with a hammer. Twice. I made sure it hurt a lot. His nervous system still worked. I was walking around with the psychiatrist who had done nothing to help him. I was about to hit his toe a third time and suddenly the patient's hand moved and grabbed my arm and he shouted 'No!' in the most almighty rage. I stepped out of the way and let him vent on his psychiatrist. As the patient pinned the doctor to the floor I coached him on releasing his anger: 'Yes, yes, let your rage out.'

Bandler was acting the patient and the doctor simultaneously. He really hated any kind of mental institution, seeing them as a kind of prison from which everyone should be released. I was with him on this. It had always struck me that the idea of taking groups of people who suffered from delusions, putting them together and giving them drugs was hardly likely to help them function in what we call reality.

Once he had told a group of doctors that he had slipped some mind-altering drugs into their tea. The doctors all panicked and then started to act strangely. Of course, he hadn't really spiked all the doctors but it amused him greatly watching them. He later said that they shouldn't prescribe anything that they didn't know the effects of and preferably had tried themselves. He had made his point with style.

'Don't go to a psycho-the-rapist,' he said and stared at us like Jack Nicholson in *The Shining*. 'If you go and talk about the time you were first depressed and connect it to the time you were angry and then see how that has made you confused, you'll end up impotent.' Instead he put positive delusions into people.

'A patient said, "People come out of the television and follow me around".' I said, ' "Have you heard of the Playboy Channel?" '

I seemed to be laughing. I decided to give *The Complete Works of Freud* a miss. Then he finished a story and we had a moment's teaching.

I can pass it on to you with ease: 'How many of you talk to yourselves inside your head and make yourselves feel bad?'

We all raised our hands. 'Stop it.' He glared at us threateningly. 'And if you must speak to yourself like that do it with a really sexy voice.' He altered his register and suddenly Dietrich was in the room – 'You made an absolute mess of that,' he whispered with an intonation that said, 'You are a gorgeous sexy creature.' It made the negativity absurd. 'If you must be unpleasant, at least be sexy about it.'

The one-liners were constant. 'It's impossible to be disappointed unless you are actively involved in planning it'; 'Don't marry anyone who doesn't like you'. I wished I'd met this man years ago. Then he asked us, 'What colour are your lover's eyes?' I went to lunch in a very good mood. As long as the mad egotistical genius stayed on stage and not the fat man, I'd be happy.

After lunch the fat man and the skinny hypnotist were back. They were going to teach us how to hypnotise someone. Just like that. Paul McKenna stepped forward. 'Can I have a volunteer who would like to go into a trance?' My hand was in the air before he had finished his sentence. Not that I'm compliant at all.

'Yes, OK, you then.' It was day one and already I was on the stage. Applause. Do they imagine that I find it difficult being on a stage in front of 400 people? I tried to look nervous.

'So, have you ever been hypnotised before?'

'No. I'm not sure I believe in it.'

'Have you ever arrived at your destination when you've been driving with no recollection of the last half hour of the drive?'

'Yes.'

'Have you ever been so engrossed in a conversation that you've not been aware of the people around you but only of the person you are speaking with?'

'Yes.'

'Have you imagined yourself in any kind of situation and been able to see a picture of yourself?'

'Yes.'

'And you don't believe in hypnosis?'

'No.'

'Do you know what hypnosis is?'

'Er, not really no.'

'But you don't believe in it?'

'No.'

Laughter from the audience.

'This, ladies and gentlemen is the perspective you will most often meet from the general public. Thank you for demonstrating that to us.' Meet Isabel, the perfect nerd.

'So, would you like to go into a trance now?'

'Oh, yes.' I can wrong about hypnosis, can't I? It's good to be wrong. They told me so at CODA.

'OK, Isabel So if you could please feel your eyelids getting heavy and close your eyes.'

So I closed my eyes. Not because I felt compelled to but just because I was doing what the man said.

'Now take some deep breaths,' he said in a very deep, hypnotic voice. I started to giggle. If he thought he could hypnotise me using that 'I want to have sex now' voice he was wrong. I giggled some more. 'This sometimes happens when people are nervous about going into a trance,' he smiled. Bloody cheek. I wasn't nervous, I just thought he was funny. But he didn't ask me – he just told the audience I was nervous. I was indignant.

'So now laugh as much as you like.' One more giggle and I was cured.

'OK, so now as you breathe in and out you will start to enjoy feeling more and more relaxed.'

He was doing something clever. I've a feeling that he watched my breathing and matched his inflection to the rise and fall of my breath. Then he slowed down. Now please stay awake as you read this.

'So now . . .' he intoned melodiously . . . 'as you are becoming more and more relaxed you are probably wondering how deep a trance you are going to fall into . . .'

I listened to him.

'As you relax the muscles around your eyes and the muscles in your face, you are feeling the relaxation taking you over more and more deeply.'

I only heard his voice by now. It's not that I didn't know where I was; I just wasn't thinking about it. I wasn't thinking about anything. I was just listening to him.

'I'd like you to remember a time when you felt very happy and very excited.'

His voice had an excitement in it that seemed infectious. I remembered a time when I had been very successful in a stage show.

'And as you see a picture of yourself at that time I'd like you to step into the picture. See the things you saw, hear the things you heard and feel the things you felt.' I started to feel hot and happy and excited. What kind of a schmuck am I? This event happened years ago.

'Now, as you experience this happiness flooding over you I'd like you to take that feeling and double it.'

I grinned like a ridiculous Cheshire cat at the image inside my head and the feeling inside my body. 'Mmmm,' he intoned. 'That feels gooood, doesn't it?'

It felt very good. I liked this piece of a day ten years ago becoming the present and being turned up and intensified. I liked it very much. I wondered why I hadn't chosen a moment of passionate love-making. I was beginning to wish I had.

'Now, once more, I'd like you to double the intensity of this feeling.'

Mmm. Wow. Was he trying to make me explode?

'So now I'd like you to keep that feeling with you as I count down from five to one. When I get to one I'd like you to open your eyes. So, five, four, three, two, one.'

I obediently opened my eyes.

'How was that?'

I smiled at him. He said, 'That was a hypnotic trance.'

'But I could still hear you.'

'Yes. That shows you are not dead. Did you feel anything else?'

'I felt excited. I felt exhilarated. I felt entranced.'

'Entranced?' I'd lost my case.

'So if you'd like to take your seat in the audience again I'd like to talk a little about what a trance state is. A trance state, which can be lighter or deeper, is a loss of multiplicity in the foci of attention.'

In other words Mr Hypnotist was defining my 'altered state' as a trance. I felt interested but also cheated somehow. I'd rather hoped he'd be able to get rid of my conscious mind completely and give instructions directly to my subconscious, 'Your breasts are growing bigger. And now I'd like you to take the size they've reached and double it.'

Still, it was only Monday afternoon. The course was seven days.

The week started to blur. The mornings began with the three-hour stand-up comedy routine from the mad genius. One morning while I sat there drinking my coffee he started to imitate an American policeman drinking coffee.

'They fill themselves with caffeine and then they start to eat doughnuts. Now, as anyone who has studied chemical changes in the body knows, caffeine and sugar are a lethal combination. But that's what they put in their bodies all day long. More and more caffeine and more and more doughnuts. Then the phone rings and they get a rush of adrenaline. So with adrenaline surging through their system as well they go out and put fifty bullet-holes through someone who doesn't have a gun.'

It was weird listening to a nutcase telling us to be more aware of our bodies – only, he didn't use those words, of course. He'd say, 'There are other ways than drugs to alter your state of consciousness. And I should know. I've taken all the weird fucking shit that's out there. Once I've tried it and I know what it does I learn to do that to my brain myself, without the drug. It saves money.'

This was definitely one of the most interesting people I'd met on the planet. He railed on: 'The nervous system doesn't know the difference between a real and a vividly imagined experience.'

So that's why when I'd remembered an exciting moment on Monday I'd started to experience excitement. This might all seem very obvious but the fact is that we can all make ourselves miserable by remembering unhappy events in our lives time and time again. Why do we choose to do that? And if the nervous system really can't differentiate between real and imagined experiences it's no wonder I'd felt exhausted after the past-life workshop.

'You need to practise feeling good. Douse yourself with endorphins.' He went on stating the obvious that wasn't obvious. 'And when you get negative voices inside your head repeat this mantra, "Shut the fuck up".'

He talked for three hours each morning, by the end of which time my bladder felt like a football. But I didn't want to leave the room. It was so simple what he was saying – variations on 'learn how to feel great'. When we began to droop with hunger he'd say, 'I know you guys are hungry but that's OK because

I'm not hungry and we're doing it my way.' He was so obnoxious that I just wanted to sit and listen to him more.

In the afternoons the fat-and-thin duo took over and we got our chance to try hypnotising a partner into a 'resource state'. This was reproducing a state of feeling mega-happy by enabling them to recreate it. 'See what works for your partner.' They'd suggest that you list words likely to get a response and see when their face lit up. 'You can try money, men, women, job offers, chocolate.' When you see something that works for them you can say, 'Yes, let's work with that one.'

This was the opposite of the past-life work. I noticed the timbre of my partner's voice when she said 'sticky banana-toffee pudding'. As she kept her eyes closed I talked her through it. 'Now I'd like you to see the banana and the toffee melted over it. Now I'd like you to pick up a spoon and select which side of the pudding you'd like to eat first. Now I'd like you to lift the spoon up to your mouth . . .'

Just call me Pavlov from now on. I know how to make anyone salivate with no food for miles around.

By Thursday morning I was rushing in so that I could be in the front row for the morning comedy sessions. No one of power and position was spared Bandler's vitriol. Anyone from the church was especially hated. 'When I moved to a new area the Catholic priest came to my house one too many times. I had a sign put up next to his crumbling church. Stop the renovation – end the tyranny.' But Bandler did explain that it is very important to study religion 'so you can understand why everyone is screwed up'. He has a small dog. 'I've taught it a special trick: to fly at the genital area and bite, so when the Jehovah's Witnesses come round . . . Funny, I don't seem to get visits from them any more.'

He also had a particular way of dealing with feminists. 'I was asked to replace a female friend of mine to talk to a group of women's rights activists. One hundred and seventy-five women who were all really "right". I greeted them with "Hey, babes, how ya doin?"'

We sat and imagined the respónse this opening line would have created, the chemical body changes that would have been produced.

'I went on, "It's such a shame Sally couldn't be here; I think it's a time of the month problem. You know how fragile women are".'

He said it all with a straight face. There was something great about the thought of these women trying desperately not to ignite with rage and tell him he was the best example of a chauvinist bastard they had ever met and how could he dare to speak to them like that, etc., etc.

Are you bristling? You see, his aim was not to trash feminism but rather to point out that you can't afford to be reactive. He was not suggesting that anyone should allow prejudice and bigotry; but feminism is supposed to be about liberation – if he could 'enslave' them and press every button they had just with a 'Hey, babes' greeting, how free were they? If he patronised them and they just smiled at him, then he had no power over them. But I guess you have to be a good speaker to pull this one off.

He was as bad with his attacks on men.

'Take football, for instance. They run around a field after a spherical object and get dirty and bang their heads together and get hurt and then they say, "It doesn't get any better than this". I say to them, "You've been dating the wrong girls".'

And not just football. Those people who ski down mountains and jump of ledges at ninety degree angles say it gives them a huge adrenaline high. 'You can tell that they haven't done too much work on their sex life because it's possible to get a better experience than they are having without leaving the bedroom.'

I perceptively deduced that he probably isn't a sportsman. But maybe it was possible to enjoy sport and have that much fun in the bedroom. I was certainly paying attention. He went on to give a tip on how to get what you want. 'If you see someone you like the look of, don't hesitate – go right up and speak to them.'

When lunchtime came, a bald man approached me, the one I had picked out in the first two minutes as being the most interesting man in the room.

'Would you like to have lunch with me?'

I smiled at him. He was obviously considering me to try out some of Bandler's theories about skiing. I was happy to have lunch with him.

'So, you don't look much like a nerd . . .' I began. (Is this what they call a backhanded compliment?) 'How come you're here?'

'You are less like a nerd than any woman I've ever seen.' He said. (Ouch, the compliment direct.)

'My name's Mark. I'm here for my work – I'm a trainer, and this course seemed like a radical introduction to NLP. They teach in seven days what most people take months to learn. I was curious.' Ah ha! Curiosity. Now there is a quality I like in a man.

'So who do you train?' I had never met a bald facilitator before.

'Next week I'm teaching conflict resolution at the Ministry of Defence.'

I laughed.

'No really. And the week after I'm teaching assertiveness to teachers. Vegetarian food OK for you?'

I toyed with the idea of saying 'Yes, as long as it doesn't contain wheat or dairy or fruit or vegetables.' But perhaps I didn't want to put him off just yet.

Three nerds joined us for lunch so we just sat and listened to their various opinions about the course. Whenever anyone said that they thought Bandler was offensive I was reduced to helpless giggles. I didn't want to explain that it was deliberate, or they might feel better. I could have launched into 'It's about self-awareness you see . . .' but it was such a joy feeling smug and watching their indignation. Anyway, surely by Sunday they'd have understood? Mark said nothing either, he just listened. No unsolicited advice anywhere. When we got back to the centre he'd saved a place for me. Suddenly I was being looked after. This was an experience I hadn't had for so long I felt like saying. 'A place saved for me? I'm sorry there must be some mistake.'

That afternoon the fat man was to educate us about how to change people's states in everyday life. He began, 'I don't usually mind having injections. However, I was a little concerned on the last occasion when I could see by looking at the nurse that she was not in a fit state to put a needle in anyone's arm. She was running a stress level that was so high she was actually shaking.' There are times when knowing how to change someone's state is useful. The first thing he had to do was acknowledge how she was feeling, match her state and then change it. I warmed to him as he told his story.

He went on: ' "You look very busy," I said, and I didn't go anywhere near her with my arm. I had to cheer her up first. "You look like a nurse who really likes to do a good job?" "Yes, that's right," she said. "And," I said, looking her straight in the eyes, "You look like a nurse who really wants her patients to feel good, don't you?" She smiles. "Yes, I do." "I tell you what, I'll sit down here and look the other way so I can relax and then you can relax too and give me the injection just when you're ready, OK?" She looked at me, sat down and relaxed. I rolled up my sleeve very slowly while I kept smiling at her. When she had given the injection she admitted, "I usually get very nervous when I have to give injections because I know I'm going to do it badly and give the patient a bruise." I'd avoided the bruise. So, you see, all this stuff can be useful.'

The main technique he was using was what they call 'hypnotic suggestion'. When he says 'You like your patients to feel good' he is literally telling her what she thinks. A subtle form of mind control, if you like. It's a scary thought, but we hypnotise each other in this way all the time. This is what you do when you say to people, 'You're looking tired' and they had been feeling OK until you told them they weren't.

Of course, this is especially important with children. If you say, 'You're really good at maths, aren't you?' they believe that they are. If you say, 'Everyone in our family is hopeless at maths' then you know what their results will be. If your child really struggles at maths and has a teacher who makes matters worse, you need to be clever. 'You're really getting better at maths, aren't you, and even though you used to find it hard – now you are really starting to enjoy it.'

If you happen to have a teenager you have to be very subtle. On Friday morning, the daughter rushed out of the house returning five minutes later. Instead of greeting her with the usual weary line of, 'What have you forgotten?' I remembered to say, 'Ah, you've remembered something. Well done.' She beamed at me. 'Yes, I remembered this book.'

And then there is self-hypnotic suggestion. I do this to myself as follows: 'I'm just no good at getting up in the mornings. I'm an evenings person and if I don't have eight hours' sleep I feel dreadful. I just love my bed and I have the best pillows in the whole world. When the alarm rings in the morning I never have any desire to move.' Then half an hour later if I'm late leaving the house, I'm complaining to myself, 'You're hopeless, why can't you get up earlier?'

One of the ways of talking someone through a negative belief is to put it into the past. So if you were 'coaching' me on this you'd say, 'So, you used to have a problem getting up in the mornings, then? And how will it feel when you don't have that problem any more?' Then you get me into a wonderfully positive state thinking about how I'd feel if I woke up like a cereal commercial and leaped out of bed. I'd have more hours in the day to vex my teenager. Apparently, if you get to be really good at this 're-framing' then the next time the situation occurs the problem simply isn't there any more.

Mark and I tried this with a girl who was nervous about getting in the lift. She'd been attending the course. You'd have thought that as she knew how this particular magic worked it would lose its power. Not so. 'I can't get into lifts.' She looked frozen in terror.

'It's a good thing you've come on this course, then, to over-come things that used to bother you,' I said, half joking.

'How will it be when you aren't bothered any more?' Mark asked with a smile.

'I'll just step into the lift. Like this,' she said. And stepped into the lift. We looked at her in surprise and stepped in swiftly after her. Now, if I'd said at this moment, 'So you get panic attacks in lifts then?' we'd have had an interesting situation on our hands. It was tempting, but I managed to resist it.

Mark said, 'The mirrors in here make it feel very spacious don't they?'

'Yes,' she said hesitantly. Mark looked at me with a twinkle in his eye. I went on applying what we had learned that very day. 'So it's great that in the past you didn't like lifts and now you're OK about them. Look at you, you're in a lift and you're talking to us and you're feeling good.' The lift arrived at the third floor. We stepped out.

'So you are happy about lifts now, aren't you?' said Mark. She looked at us in dumfounded amazement.

'That's the first time I've been in a lift in five years,' she said. 'I used to break out into a sweat but I was fine, wasn't I?'

I seized the moment. 'Would you like to go down again?' Mark and I stepped back into the lift. 'Just so you have proved to yourself that you are happy in lifts now.' It was important to word it very positively and to avoid the use of the phrase 'don't have a fear of lifts' – simply because that line would contain the words 'fear of lifts'. The part of the fearful person that is like a small child needs to hear the phrase 'happy with lifts'.

When we got down to the basement we got back in the lift again. By this time she was smiling. 'Perhaps I could have lunch in here tomorrow?' We discussed opening a small hot-dog bar in there. It seemed amazing that these mind tricks were so simple to apply.

'We've got to go now. Any more fears that you'd like to overcome? Buses, for example?' She looked exhilarated, like someone who had just done a bungee jump.

Mark and I strolled off in a state of stupefaction. I had never cured anyone of a phobia before. 'Coffee?' he asked.

'Always,' I said, turning swiftly into a coffee shop.

'It can't have been a very bad fear of lifts.' We talked ourselves down like true self-effacing Brits. 'Perhaps we succeeded because we were so laid back about it?' he asked.

'Yes, I thought you were joking at first. Didn't she hear him teach us how to do that today? Yet she seemed to swallow every line.'

But we had done something memorable. 'The fear on her face, Mark, before she first stepped in was real. I felt it.'

'I suppose we just changed her state. Or maybe it was nothing to do with us and it was just a fear that she was ready to get rid of.'

We decided that was probably the safest conclusion to draw.

'So, where are you travelling to?' I asked.

'I live in Devon but I'm just staying at a friend's empty flat tonight. It's miles away.'

'Would you like to spend the evening with me then? I'm going to a party tonight and my friend was complaining that there aren't enough men coming. I'm sure she'd be delighted if I brought you along.'

He hesitated for one second. 'I'd love to.'

Here was a development I hadn't expected: a man to take to a party. He was good at spontaneity and he was curious. And he was bald. But Patrick Stewart's bald too and he still gets to captain the *Starship Enterprise*.

We went to the party and he listened politely to everyone. Then we came home and I showed him the spare room. He was bashful and quite charming. Friday morning was another joyful three hours of comedy interspersed with a minimum amount of teaching. Unless it was all teaching – I was unsure by this stage. The one-liners went on.

'If you want to be patronised you have to participate fully'; 'What's the use of a limitation?'; 'If you don't have confidence maybe it's because you don't have competence . . . take a course'. Then he's into another story.

'These two psycho-the-rapists who were very highly respected, but not by me, brought me a patient who for several years had a paralysis in one leg that they knew was psychosomatic but that they could not cure. She also had seizures if anyone chewed gum near her.' He explained how he put her into a trance state and did the same with her therapists. Then he found the decision she'd made that had caused her habits and showed her that she didn't need them any more and half an hour later she was free. She'd been suffering for years.

'It had been so easy I was furious. I looked at the two jerks who were supposed to be her doctors and I felt angry. So I took the two problems she'd had and I gave the paralysis to one psychotherapist and the fear of gum chewing to the other.'

As he brought them all back to consciousness he started to chew gum and one of the therapists 'went apeshit'. The other one found that his leg didn't seem to be working properly. They assumed this was some short-term 'gift' Bandler had given them as an exercise in empathy. They underestimated the level of his anger. When they came to him a week later and asked him to remove whatever he had done, he told them to cure themselves. They were professionals, after all.

This probably sounds highly unbelievable and made up but seeing how much personal power the man had I didn't doubt the story for a second. We laughed when we listened to him because of the way he imitated the therapists but when Mark and I chatted about this story over lunch we realised it wasn't so funny. We wondered whether he could really be that nasty or whether it was made up. Perhaps I'd finally been trapped by a story I found offensive or perhaps he meant every word. That afternoon I was to experience an example of his anger for myself.

He was working in a one-to-one process with a man a couple of rows behind me, talking him through a guided meditation. There was a point when he said, 'And every pleasure you experience you will know a new level of sensitivity. You will learn to slow down time so that you can enjoy every moment of sexual pleasure.' This sounded good. I made a whooping noise of support and appreciation of the work – but I had interrupted. He was furious and glowered at me. 'This isn't your process. Your name is not John. What, are you gay or something?' Woosh, I felt an electric wash of negative energy over me. There was no opportunity to reply. But I sensed the power of the man and that the energy he so often used for good he could use maliciously if he chose to. It seemed to me that he was not a man to get on the wrong side of.

I put up an invisible stainless-steel barrier against his suggestion pretty quick. I know how much I love men so I don't doubt which way my sexuality swings but if I had been a weaker person I could have been confused by his suggestion, laid on me as it was with 1,000 megavolts of energy. After all, I had meant no harm. I had intended, in fact, to support him and appreciate his work, to acknowledge that the abilities he was offering to John he was offering to us all. I thought of other people; I thought of the two psychiatrists. They had also done their best but he'd had no compassion for them. I left the room in a less joyful state as I wondered whether he may have misused his power.

Over lunch another delegate nerd argued that he had only had that power because I'd allowed him to have it. I said that my concern was that I'd had to protect myself. It was the negative energy he threw over me. 'I was sitting next to her,' said Mark, 'and I felt it too.' The mad genius had said, 'Some people think I'm the devil. I'm not but he does work for me sometimes.' I'd laughed. But what is evil if not the misuse of power?

But I still wanted to go back. I was learning a huge amount and I'd laughed more this week than I ever remembered laughing before. I'd have gone for the whole week just to hear him say, 'About learning: the secret of lifelong learning is to stop comparing yourself to other people and only compete with yourself. Ask yourself how you can double your ability to learn every year and pay attention to your own process. What do you want to know about? Then when you've decided what you want to know, don't read a book. Go and find out about it.'

On Friday afternoon the hypnotist and the fat man taught us about visual cues. This is a method of watching people very carefully when you are trying to learn what they know. If you find someone who is good at something, anything, ask them how they do it, exactly, and then you watch them extremely carefully while they tell you. The reason for this is that they may not know themselves if they are making pictures in their head or whether they hear a voice or run an internal dialogue. This was man-watching carried to a fascinating extreme and then made useful. I realised I've never really looked at anyone. I could barely answer the question about the colour of my last lover's eyes.

On Saturday morning they brought in snakes and spiders and asked for volunteers who were terrified of them. I have always loved snakes and spiders and greatly envied the person who was going to get to play with the tarantulas. A woman was invited on to the stage. They brought in a glass case to the back of the hall, a considerable distance away, and she started to scream. The spider-keeper and his case retreated. I remembered Roger Woolger's explanation of these irrational fears as imprints from former lifetimes where spiders were poisonous. It seemed a good explanation in the face of this hysteria.

McKenna relaxed her and talked to her just the same way he had done with me. 'Do you remember the first time you were frightened of spiders?' She told us the story in detail. Every time she saw a spider she played the original film over in her mind, so knew it well. 'Do you see that you made a choice then that you no longer need?'

A pause. 'I'm not sure.'

McKenna wasn't phased. 'You are now ready to make a new choice. Is that right?' 'Yes.' Then he talked her into a positive state by getting her to remember a time when she'd felt powerful. We had learned that fear is a chemical state in the body. If you produce a chemical state that relates to happiness and empowerment then the fear can't be produced. He asked her to open her eyes and asked her how great the fear was on a scale of one to ten. She graded it at six. Then he asked her to make it greater and turn the fear up to eight.

She smiled at him. 'I'm not sure if I can do that,' she said. McKenna said, 'Can we bring in the spider now then? Her name's Octavia, by the way.'

'Sure.' The man with the tarantula appeared again. Halfway across the room she said, 'That's close enough, thank you.'

'So can you take the fear up to eight now?'

'Sure.'

'Now can you take it down to five?' She nodded. 'Can you take it down to three?' To two? Can we bring Octavia over then?'

'OK.'

Then he started to dazzle her with zoological details – weight, size, natural living environment – and explained that when she held her, she would have to take care because the spider was fragile and she must not drop her or it could damage her. Maybe this was true, maybe it wasn't. But it had the effect of making the volunteer so inquisitive and so watchful that her focus had gone entirely from her fear. The process had taken about twenty minutes and she had the spider walking over her hand. It was about six inches across. We stood up and applauded.

Now, you are probably wondering if this person had been planted. I don't think so and I am a sceptic too. I spoke to her afterwards and there was no doubt in my mind that she was an average punter just as I was. If you are afraid of spiders or snakes you may think, 'He wouldn't cure me that easily'. You may be right and you may not be. You remember that phrase they use in Insight, 'There are those who think they can and there are those who think they can't, and they're right.'

But back to the story. Saturday afternoon we all fast became phobia therapists. One person had been asked to think of a fear or phobia. I had a partner who was terrified of public speaking. I asked him to close his eyes and remember the time when he'd first become frightened. His first experience of public speaking had been in a job interview before a panel of judges; he'd been ill-prepared and humiliated. Then I asked him to think of a time when he had felt happy and empowered. It turned out he was a rap singer. He could sing in public – he just couldn't speak. I had him access the state of the second experience and then asked him to see himself speaking at his brother's forthcoming wedding from that place. He began to laugh and said, 'It seems silly now that I was so afraid.' I wished the wedding was now.

It was so easy. Apparently when you have that dreadful feeling of fear turning over and over in your stomach you can take the fear out and turn it over. Then you place it back in your stomach so it rotates the other way and then it becomes excitement and strength. I know it sounds crazy. Try it.

Saturday night Mark took me to dinner with some friends of his. I drank too much wine and was loud but they laughed and he still wanted to come home with me. There is no putting off some people. Sunday morning they presented us with our certificates. We had a ceremony where we had to take the envelopes the certificates came in and put them on our heads like a Bishop's mitre. Bandler had us repeat an oath: 'I promise not to become a dick-head and act like a superior mother-fucker but to go out into the world and make people feel happy for no reason at all.'

We finished at about 2 p.m. As we strolled through Hyde Park in the sunshine we discussed the week and decided that it had been good. It's easy to see why the other NLP organisations hate it. They hardly taught any theory but they tried to demonstrate the underlying principles. Bandler had written much of the theory himself but he still had a struggle to teach people the benefits of NLP but without producing nerds who latched on to the minutiae of how NLP works without applying the greater principles of freedom in their lives. The person who had told me I would have a wasted week had been wrong. I'd learned how keen I was to continue my quest on how to be more happy more of the time. And I'd learned new ways to achieve it. Mark had said how interested he'd been to see how open we all are to suggestion and that he'd be able to use some of the ways to induce relaxation in his work. Just when we were getting to the positive use of language, he suddenly altered his tone of voice: 'I was wondering whether you'd like to go out with me?'

'Er, er, er . . .' I looked at him. He was bald (as I mentioned) and there was another thing. He was a northener. He had a funny way of pronouncing words like bath and path. 'Where were you born?' I asked. He obviously wondered what difference this could make.

'Scotland.'

'So you aren't a northerner by birth then?'

'Scotland's north isn't it?'

'Oh no, that's quite different.' A southern girl has to have some principals. And after all, I'd married a Yorkshireman once and I wasn't going to put myself in any danger of that happening again.

'I see. I was born in Scotland and brought up in Derby.'

'I see. [Sigh] How long would this going-out thing be for?'

'Till August.'

'Why August?'

'Because one day in August you are going to be on a beach in Devon drinking an exceptionally good red wine.'

'I am?' I think this is what they call hypnotic suggestion. 'And what else is involved?'

'A promise of faithfulness on my part and a requirement of the same on yours.'

'I see.' What, no more Americans? 'I'll let you know. If that's OK?'

'Sure.'

We walked on to Paddington. I waved as a shiny scalp disappeared. A hand waved above it. Immediately I started to argue with myself. How could I go out with a northerner? I mean, he didn't have the running abilities of my Olympic-athlete ex. Or the singing abilities of another ex. He didn't have the sparkling conversation of my married writer friend, the ruthlessness of my gay friend or the joy of the last American who didn't want me. And he wasn't Louis de Bernières. Worse still he didn't have all these qualities rolled into one.

Ms Feminine even seemed to be arguing with herself now instead of arguing with the masculine side. 'I'm not happy that his train has gone. He's so kind and so gentle.'

'But am I excited?' I asked.

Mr Masculine: 'Look, he lives on the same side of the Atlantic. That constitutes some considerable progress.'

'Yes, but I like American accents and American attitudes and American freedom. I like French accents, Spanish accents, any Mediterranean accents – Irish, Scots and Welsh accents! I like all accents in the world apart from some northern accents.'

Mr Masculine lost his temper. 'Isabel, I've heard you use some ridiculous reasons for not dating someone but pronunciation of the word "bath" has never been one of them. You don't deserve to be happy with someone else. Why don't you just go on working on being happy on your own for the rest of your life? You are ridiculous!'

He didn't even use a sexy voice. She started to whine. 'Who says we're not going out with him? I like him. Why can't we go out with him?'

'Because she . . '. he said, referring to me in an aggressive tone, 'hasn't let go of the last ridiculous American.'

'But he rejected her,' she whined.

'I know. But that hasn't stopped her loving him. Isn't she ridiculous?'

I walked to a coffee bar feeling a headache coming on. So much for my NLP course. I was in a state of confusion. Then I remembered the mad genius's advice for dealing with inner voices and edited the profanities. I tried to be polite with them: 'Would you both please shut up?'

Silence.

So I'm still thinking. I know for certain that the American who turned me down is very special. He said no before he even got to know me. I know I could love him in a way that he doesn't yet understand. And, you see, like many foolish women I say 'yet' because I'm open to the possibility that he will understand one day. Maybe one day I'll get a phonecall and a voice I love will say, 'OK, so what's all this I'm missing?' And if I'm not married maybe I'll be able to show him. But if he's going to go on not ringing me and dating other people what am I supposed to do? Wait? I don't think so. I'm not suggesting that my American is perfect – far from it – I just never got a chance to love him anyway. But he was exciting, challenging, funny and always a step ahead of me. The bitter truth was this man was now happily dating one of my friends. New paragraph, right?

So if I go out with someone instead of waiting for what I'd really like I may become human. Mark was offering a chance to love him, and offering to love me too. Even though I told him it is against all my principles to date northerners. 'A hardworking northern lad is prepared to date an avaricious southerner? You don't realise what a break with my principles I'm making.' He smiled patiently.

Then he made a clever move. He asked my daughter's permission to date her mother. Of course, she laughed and said he'd better ask me. But he got her approval all the same. I was touched. So I think I'll go out with him and see what happens. Is it possible to be happy while dating someone? Here is an interesting twist in the Road. Instead of meeting the prince in the last chapter and riding off down Battersea Park Road in a white Mini I have to live real life. I have to meet a real man before the end of the story and get to find out whether my quest for blissful happiness is made easier or harder. After all, even in fairytales we never get any details of how 'happily ever after' works. How exactly is that achieved? Will I be happy dating him? Will I want to stay with him or leave him and can I be happy either way? Am I about to discover why none of the gurus ever dated?

Phase Fourteen: Angels, Fairies and Bald Northerners

This could be the chapter where you decide I've lost it. Life trundled on and I got some work doing 'proposal research'. This is a form of employment in TV where you spend weeks working on ideas for programmes that never get made. Some bright spark at Channel 4 had the idea for yet another medical series. They had asked this independent company to compile a series of programmes each of which had to have a brand new medical treatment for a life-threatening illness that was dramatic and visual. One of my 'friends' at the company looked round for some schmuck to undertake this task. My phone rang. 'They all have to be real cases and real diseases,' he tittered, and, 'I'm afraid the money isn't all that good . . .'

Meanwhile I was in a turmoil of confusion about this new man. He had a habit of inviting my daughter and me for glorious weekends in North Devon: climbing, surfing and walking through breathtaking countryside. I decided that he definitely wasn't for me, but I did seem to be spending time with him. I decided that I was definitely not dating him, but I did seem to be sharing his bed. So I thought maybe we should spend more than an occasional weekend together and that this might help me make a decision one way or the other. I had a convenient birthday and I waited for him to go all smoochy after a celebration dinner. Ms Feminine posed in the candle-light.

'So, what would you like?' He gazed indulgently.

'Anything?' I purred, Mr Masculine watching in disgust.

He fixed his eyes on me, looking every bit like a trainer of the MOD. 'Anything.'

'There is this workshop . . .'

A look of dumbfounded amazement crossed his face. I don't think it was the answer he expected. 'Yes?'

'It's on the Isle of Man.'

'That's nice. I've never been to the Isle of Man. What's the workshop on?'

'Angels.'

The Manx airline flies twice a day. It's one of those little planes where you walk up real metal steps to board. It always reminds me of Marilyn Monroe and JFK or of important world politicians about to fly off to negotiate some momentous world-peace deal. Maybe in my next lifetime.

We decided to go early and explore the island. They have real Thomas the Tank Engine trains and grown-ups travel on them to go to work every day. A man who looked like the Fat Controller changed a signal by pulling a lever, Percy the Green Engine and four third-class carriages chugged in, and we jumped on. Amid the romance of a train that goes 'Choo-choo, choo-choo, Wooo! Whooo!' everyone forgets how smelly they are. I was soon feeling sick and wondering how much damage was being done to the ozone layer by burning all that fossil fuel.

Mark was sitting looking joyful, making fun of the city girl. Endless opportunity for wit. 'Those animals are called cows,' he commented. I grumbled about the smell until we arrived in Purt Chiarn, pronounced Port Erin.

It was a seaside town. Come to think of it, pretty well all the towns on the Isle of Man are seaside towns. There was a sandy beach and a postcard bay surrounded by water-colour drawing-book hills and one of those little tea shops that you only find on an official promenade. We crashed in with our suitcases, perhaps looking a little like visitors from London, to ask for B&B directions. 'We're looking for something with a pink candlewick bedspread,' I demanded happily. A seaside postcard lady who was surely dedicated to a life of eating only home-made chips gave us an address and served us hot chocolate.

The sun shone as it should and I was just beginning to feel affectionate towards the bald man sitting opposite me when he said, 'The number-plates are interesting. Look! They've obviously changed the notation on them in the last ten years. On the older ones there is a number followed by the word Man whereas the new ones have the initials NM with a prefix letter followed by a number.' I wondered how to respond to this information. He went on, 'Or sometimes they are using a number of letters and another number on a yellow background.'

I took a deep breath. 'Shall we go now?'

We found the required bedspread in a seafront room and then wandered out to explore. I had been told to expect hundreds of hunks in black leather. I'd seen the motorbike races and I suppose somewhere in the back of my mind I had wondered whether there would be a seafront of oversized Americans on Harley Davidsons. But as luck would have it we had fallen on the weekend of the push-bike races. As we strolled through the town a man with a megaphone was saying, 'And now the under tens.' Little boys in lycra T-shirts were lining up their bikes to cycle around the block and try to win three pounds. Not a piece of cow-skin in sight.

I am far too cowardly for competitive sports. It's the losing I can't cope with. All those crestfallen little cyclists. 'I want them all to win.' I looked at them with my heart fit to explode. 'They're enjoying themselves,' a hard-hearted local said reassuringly as they pedalled off with fathers shouting, 'Go on, Johnny.' It was utterly compelling. Flags waved and victorious boys stood on plinths to have photos taken for first, second and third places. I wanted to give medals to all those not on the plinth and rush up to them all and say, 'You did well too' and give them all three pounds. Obviously I have been too much influenced by strange New Age ideas to be able to cope in the harsh reality of seafront bike-races. The age groups went up and we were still standing there when they reached the 'veterans'. This elderly group turned out to be forty and over. I stomped off, counting on my fingers how many years I had left before becoming a 'veteran'.

We walked along the shore and watched the sun go down. I started my 'robbing the beach of stones' trick. I decided to collect a rounded piece of white quartz to give one piece each to the participants of the seminar. Mark waited patiently. 'They fine you for taking the stones away, you know.'

I'd decided I definitely liked him and then, just as the sun dipped into the water, he said, 'When my kitchen has been decorated I'm going to have all matching oven-to-table ware.' I decided I was definitely leaving him. Soon. Then he'd irritate me by knowing the names of all the seabirds and being able to tell me all about the tides and the moon and the effects of the wind on the sea swell. All this seemed like a mystical magic to me. I could have told him in great detail of the opening and closing times of Starbucks on the King's Road.

The next day, Mark wanted to take the train up the 'mountain'. There was the steam-train and then the electric-train. Mmm. I decided not to wonder whether he took more interest in travelling on trains than I might have hoped. He was so sweet, so undemanding, so kind. He'd say: 'What would you like to do this afternoon, sweetheart?' and just when I was thinking, 'This man is so lovely, why would I ever want to be without him?' he'd say, 'Look at the varnish on that wood. It could have done with a bit more sanding down . . . I expect what they've done is they've just put it on layer after layer instead of giving it a good sanding between each coat.'

Could I take any more of this? 'And I expect it's polyurethane instead of real varnish. It doesn't have any real lustre, does it?'

'No, dear,' I'd answer, fleetingly considering the romance of flinging myself under *Percy the Green Engine*.

We reached the top of Snaefell mountain from which you can see England, Scotland, Ireland and Wales. I decided to treat Mark to my rendering of the song 'On a Clear Day, You can See Forever'. This was me doing irony, you see, because the day we went you could see mist in four directions. But the sheep were pretty and they did good tea and jam doughnuts in the café. We struck up a conversation with a lone bachelor who informed us that the night before he'd been up the mountain for the annual party of railway enthusiasts. There were two hundred of them on the island, all with cameras, snapping away at the engines. This is true, I'm afraid. I warned Mark that if he expressed any more disapproval of polyurethane I would sign him up as an enthusiast.

To reap my revenge that night I took us on a trip to visit a friend who I had been in the Girl Guides with. I had been a Kingfisher Patrol leader, which of course I'd loved because it was a perfect justification to give barrel-loads of unsolicited advice. I'm sure you'll not be surprised to know that, even at an early age, I showed a formidable talent for bossiness and as a result managed to spend time that should have been spent on school homework putting up tents. The six girls unfortunate enough to have fallen under my 'care' have never forgotten me but, being of a forgiving nature, this one wanted to give us tea and show us her Manx cat. It's really true that they have cats without tails. It looked very odd, as if it shouldn't have been able to balance, but kind of cute. 'It's a genetic defect,' my friend Miki said as we bored Mark silly reminiscing about reef knots and triangular bandages. He even managed to look interested when we looked through her wedding photos. It was most impressive.

That night we took a horse-drawn tram back to our B&B. He was so easy to spend the day with. And, as you were no doubt wondering, easy to spend the night with too. I was glad we were about to go on a course. Maybe I could discover that our guardian angels were incompatible?

It is usually wise to approach workshop accommodation with caution. On one workshop I took, no one slept at all the first night because the bedrooms were so cold. So it was with some surprise that we entered the Brightlife Institute in Andreas on the north of the island. The Centre for Retreats and Business Courses was a five-star hotel and more. We were shown into a luxurious bedroom that was larger than my entire flat on the Battersea Park Road.

They had registered me as Mark's wife and when I said that my second name was Losada I became Mrs Losada. 'There is no Mrs Losada,' I tried to explain. Now it looked as if I was married to someone else and having an affair. The housekeeper smiled understandingly. 'No, really – there is no Mr Losada either. I'm single. I'm not having an affair.' I swam in deeper and deeper.

'We don't mind if you are having an affair, dear,' she whispered quietly.

'No, I'm sure you don't. But I'm not.'

'That's all right then, isn't it?' she winked. There must be a way to avoid this situation.

Mark and I went to greet the other participants for happy-hour with trepidation. You'll not be surprised by now to hear that it was ten women and four men, four locals from the island and the rest of us from all over Britain. I spoke to one of the men, an overweight *Sun*-reader-type who looked most out of place. I enquired as to what he did for a living (not that I ever ask that question, as you'll remember) and it turned out that he was a gardener, which pleased me greatly. He informed us, over the first glass of wine, that the course was actually called 'Working with Angels, Fairies, Muses, and Nature Spirits'. Mark was almost ready to leave. But then William Bloom arrived. I don't know what I expected from someone running a course about fairies but this man wasn't it.

We sat at table for the haute cuisine three-course dinner and I quizzed William, who teaches internationally, has had about ten books published and is in constant demand as a speaker, on his original discipline. 'Did you study fairies as an academic?' I asked, dead-pan serious.

'My father was a Freudian psychiatrist and my mother was a New York journalist. I did my degree at the London School of Economics in international politics and took a PhD in political psychology before lecturing in psychological problems in inter-national relations.'

'Ah.' And this man was about to teach us about the spirit world? Mark was confused already. Jolly good. I ordered another helping of meringue and summer fruit pudding.

When dinner was finally over it was the first meeting of the fairy circle. Only he didn't call it that – I did. After the usual compulsory intros William explained what would happen.

'The course is twenty per cent me talking and eighty per cent experiential. The aims of the course are to help you clarify what the world of angels, muses and nature spirits is all about, secondly to help you experience the world of spirits, and thirdly to enable you to tap into that awareness whenever you want to.'

'How did you first find out about the spirit world?' asked an earnest-looking long-haired lady of about sixty. William launched into his introduction.

'I've always been sensitive to atmospheres and, like many people, since childhood I had from time to time sensed that everything was alive – not only animals, trees and plants but even landscape and rocks. Everything seemed to have a vibrant quality and I was interested beyond my academic pursuits to explore this. When I was twenty-five I came across an old manuscript from the thirteen hundreds about a man who spent six months making an invocation to meet his guardian angel. I moved to Morocco and lived in the mountains to repeat his experiment. I built a chapel and every day I prayed: "I'm sorry to be a wanker but please can I meet my guardian angel." On the last day I waited in great earnestness, praying like crazy, and nothing happened. I felt a complete twat.' We all laughed. Everyone liked him already. He went on. 'I went back to my bed exhausted and wept. When I woke I felt pulled to go back to my prayers and then I felt a huge presence of love enfolding me. It was absolutely real, so much so that I couldn't doubt it or dismiss it as my imagination or a projection of my desire. It was real. And ever since that day the peak experiences I'd had of feeling and seeing the throb and beauty in everything, are with me all the time.'

'All the time?' asked a sceptical male yoga teacher.

'Unless I'm drunk or stressed or in a bad mood. Most of the time I'm none of these. Honestly.'

He was completely credible. 'Just a little theory tonight . . .' he began and produced a flip chart. 'There is an electromagnetic field around the human body.' He drew one round a stick figure. 'When something enters your energy field you can feel it. You don't have to see anything or be clairvoyant to know that something is there. You just have to be sensitive and aware enough to notice. Ninety-nine per cent of people sense things. You know if your partner comes home in a bad mood before you see them – you can feel it. People are often desperate to see spirits but what you are seeing is an energy field anyway.'

Then we began the first process, a meditation to get us 'into our bodies'. Everyone sat comfortably, some on cushions or the floor, some on chairs. We closed our eyes.

'Now, I'd like you to imagine a deer curled up comfortably on the ground with its nose touching its tail.' I thought of a fawn, safe in a corner of a forest, beside its mother and father, resting on leaves, twigs and the mossy earth. I imagined having four legs and living inside that speckled skin. 'Breathe into your lower stomach,' William intoned. 'And now I'd like you to become a curled-up cat, sleeping safely.' My old ginger tom, a bedfellow for fifteen years, had given me lots of demonstration of this one. I know what it feels like to have paws and to smell of warm fur. 'Breathe soft breaths to the area below your navel. Allow yourself to be in the same happy relationship to your own body that this cat is. Look into your body with love and appreciation.' I felt happy and contented and a little stuffed with too much summer pudding. This 'getting into the body thing' always feels so good. I guess that's why they call it coming to your senses.

Then we had to choose a partner and walk towards them so that we could sense their energy field. This isn't hard even for a city girl like me to do. In London I am quite familiar with someone sending good or bad vibes across a room. I can sense when someone is having a good leer, and I've often felt 'look at me' vibes and glanced across a room to see a smiling stranger. Vibes are real, that's for sure.

Anyway, I happened to be picked by a City whizzkid who, having achieved everything including the red Porsche by the age of twenty-six, had got bored with it all and was now exploring the mystical with equal passion. He stood and looked at me and we moved together across the room. His energy field was as clear to me as if it had been coloured in pink. I suppose, according to those who claim to be able to see auras, it probably was coloured in pink. I couldn't see it but I could sense it. Just like the energy that was handed to me in the shape of a ball by Monsieur t'ai chi.

Once we had sensed the energy we then had to play. I had to send invisible energy out of the top of my head, over in a circle and into his energy field, then down through what would have been his roots if he'd been a tree, then back into my roots, up through me and out of my head again towards him. This felt great fun. It was sending him good vibes, but consciously. Then William asked us to reverse the loop so he was sending his energy to me and I swear I did feel a subtle energy, a something. Then the last bit of this exercise was to open our hearts.

'Open-heart surgery on a Friday evening?' I enquired.

'No.' William attempted a smile.

This was the heart 'chakra' that we were to open. You know the spot. It's the bit behind your breast bone that aches when someone you love leaves or when you really miss a lover or are longing for their presence. You know that ache, don't you? That's your heart chakra. It's possible to open that spot to give and to receive more love. This is a good thing to try when you are making love and (unsolicited advice coming up) if you find that you don't want to open your heart then you are making love to the wrong person or at the wrong time. Not that I have ever done that, of course. But I'm digressing again.

I was just anticipating the evening whiskey when William announced that we were going down to the beach to 'extend the exercise'. The Brightlife Institute provided a minibus, complete with a collection of rugs for sitting on the beach. They had thought of everything.

I wafted along the beach in a state of bliss. Then, Bang! A shot. 'Mark! They're killing something!' I cried like a crazy, distressed New Age hippie.

'Yes, dear – clay plates,' he smirked. 'Fancy shooting some one weekend?'

'Oh, yes please!' I bounced. There we have it, in two seconds, the inconsistency of womankind. Let's hope that clay plates don't have souls because if they do it seems I am very willing to release them to their next incarnation.

I stared at the beauty of the bay, the sea and the sky, and just when I was beginning to go quiet Mark said, 'So, the lighthouse at the north end of the island flashes four times with two-second intervals between the flashes and then there is a two-second interval before the pattern repeats. Tell me, do you know the difference between a flash and an occult?'

'You can't join a flash?'

He laughed politely, as if I'd said something funny. 'No an occult.'

'Enlighten me.'

'A flash is a second or less and if a light is occulting then it is over a second.'

I plucked up my courage. 'Why are you telling me this?'

'It's interesting.' Two oyster-catchers flew by. I wondered whether they have such problems choosing a mate.

Then William gathered us into our fairy circle. We stood in silence for a couple of minutes to take in the atmosphere of the beach and then he said, 'Now we are going to repeat the earlier exercise where we exchanged energy, only this time our partner will be the sea. Many of us are moved by the beauty of the sea . . .' he sounded very matter-of-fact about it all, 'but all most people do is look at it. They are unaware that they can deepen the relation-ship and experience the sea kinæsthetically'. I suppose swimming, surfing or sailing is one way but this was a safe on-land method that could be experienced in all weathers with no danger.

I sat on the beach cross-legged looking every inch the Buddha. I stared at the sea and the sea stared back. It made nice wave noises to me. I thought of my energy and imagined it expanding to embrace the horizon. I visualised energy coming from out of my crown, looping around and coming back to me through my feet. Then I reversed the loop. I opened my soul in every way I knew how to receive the power and gentleness of the tide.

I have always found the sea reassuring since my days of living in Brighton with my grandmother. Even as a noisy stage-school child I hadn't failed to notice that whether or not I got the part I wanted in *The Sound of Music* the sea was still the same. And later, whether or not the boys in the senior school drama department failed to notice my doting passion, the sea was still there doing its eternal thing. I loved it. And it felt good to be reminded of that and to feel that I could take in energy from the sea in a more concentrated form. Are you are thinking, 'That's your imagination, Isabel'? But who knows where imagination begins and ends? Dr Roger Woolger taught us to be wary of the phrase 'just your imagination'.

I sat and communed and felt the presence of the sea in every part of me. What the sea has that I don't have is an eternal perspective. And once again it seemed to me that everything was as it should be and even if it wasn't, even when there is suffering, in some way that I don't understand, that is OK too. I took Mark's hand and we walked up the beach.

Saturday morning started with one of those tables of everything you ever wanted for breakfast and smiling staff asking what you'd liked cooked. I ordered filter coffee, wondering how my colon was standing up to the onslaught. The threadworms, no doubt re-born by now, would be enjoying their stay at the Brightlife Institute.

We were to begin the day's work with a little more theory. A history lesson in the universal experience of a parallel world inhabited by spiritual creatures. The great mythologist Joseph Campbell pointed out that when the anthropological research from around the world began to be gathered in the eighteenth and nineteenth centuries what had been thought of as a culturally isolated incident of spirits was in fact a worldwide phenomenon.

Despite this abundance of evidence and experience, mainstream psychology believes that all their experiences are the creation of the biological brain, so any discussion of the angel worlds suggests that the speaker is in severe need of well-qualified psychiatric treatment. (That's OK, you knew that about me anyway.)

It is yet another example of the arrogance of Western culture, William asserted reasonably, that we dismiss the thousands of classical, mystical and tribal cultures who believe in spirits as deluded with psychological imaginings. I suppose most people must think it's all made up but personally I don't have a problem believing in the unseen world. Angels are spoken of in the Old Testament, the Koran, and the Eastern religions, and people in local churches all around the world stand up every Sunday and say in the Christian creed: 'I believe in God, the maker of heaven and earth and of all things visible and invisible.'

But as to getting to know the invisible world, that is another question. I was just beginning to think that all this was very unlikely when, from somewhere behind me, the gardener spoke: 'I didn't want to tell anyone, but working outside there is something there, some kind of presence, but I never want to talk about this to anyone in case they bring the men in the white coats to take me away.'

William instantly had some similar stories to reassure him. He opened a book and quoted the explorer Sir Francis Smythe who said that on climbing Everest he felt accompanied by a presence on the final stages of his journey. He read:

In its company I could not feel lonely, neither could I come to any harm. It was always there to sustain me on my solitary climb up the snow-covered slabs.

Then he quoted the Irish Poet George Russell:

The Golden World of Invisible beings is all around us . . .
beauty is open to all and none are shut out from it who will
turn and seek it.

Then he told a story of his own. I didn't doubt him for a second.
'Some friends were camping in a remote forested area. About 3
a.m. they were woken by a voice telling them to get out of their
sleeping bags and move their tent. It was so clear that, despite
the effort, they did just that. Towards dawn, a huge fir tree fell
and crashed on to the exact spot where their tent had previously
been.'

Of course you may not believe this. But I bet you've heard
similar accounts of supernatural experiences before. How many
stories like that would it take to convince us completely?

But the next bit is hard to believe. One of the staff appeared to
bring us morning coffee and served strawberries dipped in
chocolate. Now, I know I've stretched your credibility before
but has anyone, on any course of any kind, served chocolate-
covered strawberries?

William chatted on. He admitted that – his experience in
Morocco aside – when he started to take workshops like this
one he really didn't know much. He learned from the people
who arrived.

'I noticed that they all divided naturally into groups. The first
group were the healers: medical doctors, teachers, social workers, faith healers and therapists. The next group were artists:
architects, musicians, designers, actors and creative people in
general. Computer programmers and engineers also appeared
in this group. Then there was a group who work with rituals:
priests, nuns, white witches, shamanic students and even free-
masons and ritual occultists.'

I thought that I'd like to spend a day listening to the conversation in that group.

'Then there was a group of people who work with plants and

landscape: farmers, gardeners and horticulturists. Finally there were business people: office workers, lawyers, entrepreneurs, publicists and marketing professionals.'

The people who came to William's seminars, from all these groups, were people who noticed that some invisible and subconscious help was available. As an actress I am familiar with the concept of Shakespeare's muse of inspiration, but somehow I had ended up in a room with a man who claimed to understand how to contact it. I was listening very carefully.

I expected a mystery but the teaching can be summed up in one word: pause. All these people had somehow discovered the benefit of pausing for a few minutes before beginning an activity to tune in to the 'spirit' of the task.

One of the women, an artist, spoke up. 'That's exactly what I do. I pause for a while. I'm attuning to "something else". Call it the spirit of the painting if you like. It's like a muse. It doesn't tell me what to do or how to do it but it is somehow inspiring me. I seem to know better how to flow with the painting. I become more present'.

A spirit can also be seen as a blueprint for the perfect patterning in all aspects of life. I was taking notes furiously by this stage. William explained in terms that went way over my head how it is that contemporary science has trouble understanding how the energy particles and waves bind together to become coherent atoms. The missing substance is the deva or spirit of the atom which holds an energy pattern of how the atom should be. Like Jung's archetypes (apparently). Have I lost you yet? Spirit holds the blueprint and magnetically attracts the best possible outcome. Let's change the example. We all 'imagine' that there could be such a thing as perfect justice. The law courts rarely approach it but the spirit of justice is there, more than just a concept but a spiritual reality, an energy form that provides the pattern of how things could be. There is a pattern for perfect democracy, a form of parliamentary debate, which perhaps just sometimes, maybe not often, parliament approaches. There is a spirit that does the same for the different elements of a ceremony. In the Catholic and Orthodox traditions William noted a 'profound magic' takes place within the ritual.

'Some mystics have described the Eucharist as the supreme ceremony of Western culture,' he added, explaining that being a part of these rituals over and over again gives the time and space to sit quietly within them and contemplate their energies and atmospheres.

Then we had a process to do. We had to close our eyes and focus on our bodies and think of the breath until we felt calm and still and then simply tune in to the atmosphere in the room. In the silence of our own heads and hearts we were to think of the 'invisible world'. I remembered a line in my favourite film, *Truly, Madly, Deeply* when, walking through a park, a young Spanish student says to Juliet Stevenson, 'The Spirits are everywhere, they are with us now'. I wondered if this could possibly be true. And I said 'hello' to them in my head just in case they were there. And I thanked them in my head just in case they could hear me.

The word 'picnic' always makes me want to jump up and down and say 'Yippee' and it's even better when someone else has filled picnic baskets with all manner of wondrous goodies. We were to be taken off on a mystery tour. Our little van, with a couple of cars provided by the Brightlife Institute, drove into the secret depths of the island and we found ourselves in Ballaglass Glen, which has to be one of the most beautiful and unspoiled pieces of countryside that I've ever seen. The task here was simple: to enjoy ourselves, paying attention to the atmosphere and spirits that lived in the place. If there is such a thing as a spirit, there obviously were spirits here because it was so idyllic that they'd have been daft not to have taken up residence.

I sat on a rock by a waterfall and looked at the water playing. Could it be that there was more than I could see? The surrounding trees were alight with a glow that was 'visible' even to me. William had told us that the nature spirits had been anthropomorphised as fairies and elves not because any little beings flit about with pink dresses and wings but because that is how the spirit of flowers feel. The energies around roots of trees have an earthy feel so man has imagined them as gnomes. There are no little men living in the woods, but that kind of energy pattern is there. As I wandered from the waterfall to the woodland and from an overturned rotting tree to a green anemone freshly grown through the undergrowth, I listened with my whole being and not just with my ears. I even sat opposite a tree and repeated again the exchange-of-energy exercise that I had shared with the City banker and the sea. A tree is so independent. Roots that stretch far down into the darkness and arms that stretch up to the light. Maybe I could just meditate on the trees in Battersea Park on a regular basis, absorb their vibes and give them some of mine. But then again I quite like those trees. It would be a shame to see beautiful London plane that has been there for fifty years keel over with stress and exhaustion.

Meanwhile some of the arty folk were sitting and sketching. Don't you hate people who can recreate all the beauty of a landscape on a piece of paper with a few brushes of a lead pencil? We had two such people. I stared at their sketches in awe and thought of the inadequacy of words.

Then it was back into the van and off to the next mystery location. This time we drove to one of the highest spots on the island to find a circle of stones, one of the meeting places of the old parliament. From this high point we could see most of the island. It was a perfect spot for quietness and calm, which is what William was trying to bring about. He had reckoned without me. After we had gobbled up our excellent picnic and lay down to rest I felt a bouncy mood coming on.

'I know a game!' I shouted. 'You take a blade of grass and when someone's sleeping you poke it up their nostrils to make them sneeze. It's really fun.' I darted about with my blade of grass. William watched, unsure whether to laugh or shoot me. He glanced at Mark imploringly. 'Isabel! Come and lie down!' Mark tried to speak firmly. I was busy disturbing someone. 'Isabel!' Finally inspiration came to him and he threw a glass of water over me. I let out a loud wailing sound. 'That's just typical of boys,' I shouted, 'they have no sense of proportion.' I took my rug and stomped off to lie down at an indignant distance from them. They had achieved exactly what they wanted and could now sleep in peace.

An hour or so later we woke. The wind was blowing a sweet, warm air over the mountain. William spoke. 'This is a sacred place because it was from here that the island was overseen by its protectors. All ancient towns and cities have a spirit who looks after them, an overseeing presence. I'd like you think of the size of the spirit of this island and tune into that energy. If while you do this you think of something that you could do for the spirit, then just notice that.'

We sat and looked out. I imagined what it would be like to be this spirit and to somehow be there to inspire and breathe life into everything in that place. There are 70,000 people living on the Isle of Man and in some mysterious way, according to William, the angels and spirits were involved in their day-to-day concerns. Again the words of the Nicene creed came into my head: 'I believe in God, the maker of heaven and earth and of all things visible and invisible . . .' I never heard a sermon preached on this topic. Maybe the priests who have explored this area found it too intangible to approach. There is not much doctrine on angels. Thank God. We sat in silence for a while doing that being thing. And then we all went home to tea.

Saturday evening we split up and Mark and I both joined the group heading back to the beach. It was my idea to sit at the water's edge and meditate. Now you think I'm going to say that I got wet, don't you? What makes you think that I'd admit it? I'm hopeless at meditation, as I told you. I've only got to close my eyes and take two deep breaths and I'm asleep. The fact that I'm sitting straight-backed with the wind blowing in my face seems to make no difference. How am I supposed to make any progress in the path of deep meditation if my subconscious is going to keep seeing opportunities for deep sleep? 'Awareness? Ugh!' It says, and before I know it, I'm snoring.

When I woke I saw a ring of people had gathered around Mark. He is something like a world champion in stone-skimming and can make a solid object bounce on the surface of the sea more times than is physically possible. People were counting, . . . 'eight, nine, ten . . .' and then braking into rapturous applause. All the women on the course (and the men too) were in love with Mark by now. But he still seemed to want to be with me. There is no accounting for some people's taste.

Then, as we were driving back in the van, Mark woke me from my reverie by suddenly saying, 'Look!'

'What is it?' I asked, alarmed.

'Oh no, nothing. I thought for a moment I'd seen sequential number-plates.'

Sunday morning we had a slide-show. I love slide-shows. Click, whirr . . . 'And here we see . . .' Like reading but without the effort of turning over the pages. Better still we had William Bloom in person giving us yet more technical, historic and universal information about angels. 'This artist has depicted her sensation of this spirit using a double helix,' he taught us as if he was lecturing in science. 'And this image shows a canopy like a jellyfish with a body like a vortex. Painting an invisible feeling gives artists a challenge but it is interesting to see similar patterns emerging regardless of time and culture.' When the paintings were over he showed us some flowers and trees and I was so attuned to invisible energy I could sense the patterns that were not painted in.

Coffee arrived and with it many glorious boxes of pastel crayons. William took us through a wonderful meditation on our own guardian angels and then invited us to draw our impressions in some form. 'Draw yourself, as a stick-pin figure if necessary, then draw your energy field and then draw in your angel.' I picked up a red crayon and drew an outline of myself. I left the inside white. I guess I feel pretty blank most of the time. Then I took bright colours and drew my energy field. Loads of pink with red, blue, yellow, green, orange, purple. At least my energy seemed to be fairly brightly coloured. Then I undertook to draw my angel. I started just with colours above my head, brighter still than the colour of my aura. I drew a coil in the middle so the form had a distinct centre and then many bright colours emerging from it. I pondered how much to join the colours in my angel to those of my energy field and then, smiling, I took yellow and joined the two together. Stand aside, Picasso, Losada is here.

I love drawing because I feel no obligation to be good at it. The second sketch was of our homes and we had to draw a spirit of the home inside the house. I drew some room outlines placing nothing in the house except little green bubbles of energy for the plants and round balls of red energy for my daughter, the lodger and myself. Then with a pinky-red I took in the angel. I had the colour cover my daughter entirely. I'm not sure quite why but it felt good that way. Also I felt happy covering my lodger's energy with the angel, but when I got to my room I had it hover in the corner of the room looking at me, my energy on one side and the angelic energy on the other. I don't know why I didn't cover myself with angelic energy too. Maybe I was worried that I might have to change and enjoy cooking or something. Then we showed our pictures to each other and chatted about them for ages like excited junior-school kids. It's funny how much a bunch of adults can enjoy themselves given half a chance. I wish I'd had William as a teacher when I was at school.

Then it was the closing process. We sat for the last time in our fairy circle. One of the women said, 'I've learned that instead of just looking I can be a part of life. I've never been able to do that. It's been an amazing experience.'

The City banker said that the weekend had contributed to his discovery that he was gifted as a healer. 'I'm just learning to trust angelic presences and they can do so much to help. I've been part of healings that you couldn't contemplate. I feel very grateful.'

Not everyone spoke and a miracle happened – I kept quiet.

Mark spoke up. He said, 'The sea and outside has felt like home to me for as long as I can remember. Whenever I'm outside I feel something and maybe it's the harmonics you were speaking of. I know I'm always touched and I feel better afterwards. Ballaglass Glen and the beach . . . they feel like home to me.' There was a moment of silence where people took in his words and then we applauded.

I skimmed William's book later and found the line, 'If someone has a sense of respect and wonder, who cares if they believe in angels?'

It was no surprise that William liked Mark.

I wasn't doing so well. When everyone had finally left the room William smiled at me. 'Mark and I were thinking of going for a walk this afternoon – he's very special, isn't he?'

'Yes, he is, but I'm in confusion,' I confided, 'I can't decide whether I want to be with him or not. It's as if we vibrate on a different frequency.'

'Have you talked to him about this?'

'I can't,' I said pathetically. 'I have no reason to criticise him. He is as he is. It's me I know, so it doesn't seem fair.'

'It doesn't seem fair to me that you tell me more of your doubt than you tell him.'

'No.'

He and Mark strolled off together after lunch. I decided I liked Roger Woolger better – how annoying it was of William to tell me something that I didn't want to hear. I'd liked him very much till then but the last thing I needed was someone else being right. Ugh. This meant I had to once again contemplate the possibility that I was in the wrong.

Later that day I attempted the 'talking to Mark' thing.

'Er, I really don't know if I'll stay with you. It just doesn't feel right to me in so many ways. I can't talk to you. I don't like to say anything nasty to you ever. I'm so confused.' I wailed pathetically. Gosh, such maturity. I think they call it 'emotional intelligence', don't they? I'm in junior school.

'That's OK, he smiled. 'I don't mind if you're confused.'

'Doesn't it mean I'm using you if I'm not sure I want to stay with you?'

'I'm not sure either, so can I use you too?'

He's so lovely. What am I to do with a lovely friend who I don't want to be with, who has an interest in sequential number-plates and who I always look forward to seeing? It's not supposed to be like this in books, is it?

I went and banged on William's door that night when he had already gone to bed and was enjoying a little privacy after the day was over. I bounced in like someone who had not just attended a course that trained sensitivity and started to chat in a loud voice, thrusting books into his hands for him to sign.

'I spoke to Mark,' I said.

'Good.' He was obviously wondering what on earth I was doing in his bedroom. 'Could you sign this one too?' I chatted on while he looked at me in disbelieving amazement.

'Er, I'd like to go to sleep now.' How unreasonable of him. Just when I wanted to sit and talk for half the night.

'Oh, yes, of course.' I scurried from the room thinking, 'Now he hates me.' It had been such a lovely week; why had I gone and ruined a potential friendship by barging into his room at whatever hour it was? How could I be capable of such complete insensitivity? And if I was capable of it after a week of becoming aware of atmospheres and the subtle spiritual nature of living things what hope was there for me in the future? I sat down on the outside steps and looked at the stars.

I glanced down at the book. He'd written, 'Wishing you love and grace, William.' I thought, 'Mmm, he probably thinks I need them.' Then I spotted four Xs. I'm hopeless, but William had enough grace to love me anyway.

Epilogue: Standing in the Middle of the Road

'So – what have you learned?' I hear you ask dubiously.

I can see some Tibetan Lama smiling and letting me know that if I think I've learned anything then I'm suffering from a delusion and I would have been better not to have made any attempt to move down the Road at all. He would grin and say something like: 'Better to sit and mediate on the grass than to walk the path of illusion.'

So here are some of my illusions, she says cheerfully.

First there is the magic spell taught by Insight which has become a lynchpin of my batty belief system. You know the one – all together now: 'Use everything for your learning, upliftment and growth.' I really do apply this principle. So when something shitty happens, as well as saying 'Oh, Shit' I think, 'What can I learn from this one?' So this idea may be a delusion but it's an eminently practical one, don't you think? And worse still, I like to imagine that I'm constantly growing into a more wonderful individual as a result of this. My ego is especially fond of this idea. In the real world perhaps I'm just becoming more deluded. And I have noticed that all this is completely egocentric but I can hardly answer the question about whether I've learned anything without taking the already deep waters of self-indulgence in this book to whole new fathoms. So jump in. You can always apply all this to yourself and then we can be unashamedly self-indulgent together.

Regarding this 'being a better person . . .' There is actually one idea that may have helped slightly and that has been the realisation that what we say about others is a sure clue to what we need to work on in ourselves. Two comments I've heard recently from friends; 'My mother is so judgemental!'; 'My boyfriend is completely intolerant'. You see how it works? Who, in these conversations, is being judgemental and intolerant? Firstly the speaker and secondly, to a greater degree, me. I notice now that all criticism of others reflects immediately back on to ourselves.

You see, I can be noisy and opinionated and judgemental and selfish and warm and kind and gentle and sensitive. That's who I am and I can love and accept myself in spite of all the bad things. This I have to learn if I am to love others – no matter what. There are other problems we have with our lives but it's loving and being loved that we really care about, isn't it? It's strange when people ask, 'What's life all about?' Isn't it simple? Isn't it all about love?

And what about happiness? Am I happy, you ask. Completely, abundantly, joyfully, stupidly? To have tears streaming down my face and know that is OK? That feeling misunderstood, or abandoned or whatever it is I feel, is OK? And to be at peace with the pain and the suffering? To know that I'm doing my best and you are too and that whatever it is that is difficult or whatever it is that is joyful, that this too will pass? To celebrate everything? Yes, this is happiness. It isn't what we usually mean by happiness. The other kind, based on relationships, money and career success, may be a lot more fun but it can vanish overnight. Which would you prefer?

Life is exciting. We can all offer something and there is so much out there to do and to learn. You really don't need much money; just to throw away the TV and get creative. If it really isn't too late to do all those things we've always wanted to do, what then? See if I can make a bowl on a pottery wheel without spinning the top off. Take a year-long tantric sex course. Read *Memories, Dreams and Reflections*. Find a way to visit the rainforest while there still is some. Have my very own compost bin. Make bread. Own a dog. Play Prince Charming in panto at Christmas. Travel around South America. Work as a volunteer with Mother Teresa's nuns for six months. Ride a camel. Paint a big picture with primary colours. Study politics, history, geography, biology, geology, theology, psychology . . . well, no, maybe not psychology. But reflexology – there is a discipline I could love. And I've just found somewhere in Britain that teaches astral travel. You know those 'out of body experiences' people have when they die? You can now learn this while you are still alive. Can you believe that?

We have a limited number of heartbeats left. So whatever it is that I want to do, I guess I have to do it now. And what should we be doing? Whatever brings joy to us and joy to those around us. There is so much inspiration available. Look at the lives of Helen Keller, of Christopher Reeve, of Mandela. Pick your own favourites.

But enough of that. Perhaps you'd like to know the end of the romance part of the story? My American rang this morning. He said, 'Isabel, I've made a terrible mistake. It has to be you. [Enter orchestra] It has to be you – I wandered around and finally found it has to be you.' He has realised that, without me, his life will always be incomplete.

I wish I was a fiction writer.

From being born again I'm supposed to have learned that I can be with a man I want who wants me. But I still can't say that without smiling.

I love the bald northerner with an interest in sequential number-plates but somehow there has always been a but-somehow.

August came, the month when I was required to make a decision. We sat on the beach one night and drank red wine, just as he had hypnotised me into knowing we would. He said all the right things: 'I love you. I want to move in with you.' And I sat like a ridiculous female and cried. But instead of kissing him and handing him the key like I was supposed to, I just went on looking pathetic. He sat and looked at me. I didn't want him to move in. I didn't want to spend my life with him.

I mumbled, 'Can't I just see you like we have been doing?'

'No. I want more.' Suddenly the script was sounding familiar from too many episodes of soap-operas.

I was silent. Sometimes it happens.

He looked out to sea and said, 'Well, OK. I'll drop you at the station in the morning.'

'And put me in the spare room tonight?' Good grief.

'I think so. I think it will be good for us both to be alone anyway. The real journey is with ourselves.' Was there an echo or was there a nun on the beach somewhere?

'Will you call me?' I asked.

'Maybe.'

'Can I call you?'

'Of course. Whenever you'd like to.' We smiled at each other slightly stupidly. A strange kind of happy ending.

The morning came and, good as his word, he dropped me at the station.

Perhaps you think I'm hopeless? Dysfunctional beyond redemption and that all my attempts at improving have been dreadful failures? Perhaps you think I should have stayed with the bald northerner as he was foolish enough to want me. But I made my choice, didn't I? Or rather he did, because I didn't have the guts. And good for him. He wanted all or nothing. Strange thing, that. Traditionally it's the man who is supposed to be against commitment. But I would have married the last crazy American; I wanted to learn how to love him, so I don't think I have a problem with commitment as long as I think it's to the right person. Damned elusive, the right people, aren't they? So I've got the opportunity to experience my relationship with myself. Blast it.

Today is another day. It's a Tuesday. My teenage daughter smiled at me. A ginger cat has moved into my house uninvited and this morning he is looking rather elegant sitting on the squashed flowers in the window-box. The postman brought letters with hand-written envelopes. The sky is a horrible shade of grey and I'm sure it's going to rain any minute. I stroll out into the middle of the Battersea Park Road and I'm absurdly happy for no reason at all.

I wanted to learn how to radiate cheerful optimism whatever is going on in my life. I seem to be doing it. And I wanted to be thoroughly nauseating – I think I'm close, don't you?

Further Enlightenment

In case you want to try any of these, here is the info!

Phase One

Lots more happens in the Insight Seminar that I didn't tell you about, because I didn't want to spoil the experience for you if you go along . . .

Insight Seminars
37 Spring Street
London W2 IJA
Tel: 020 7706 2021
E-mail: london@insight-seminars.org
Website: www.insight-seminars.org

Insight Worldwide
2101 Wilshire Boulevard
Los Angeles
California 90403
USA
Tel: 001 310 453 3212

Insight Australia
59 Christie Street
St Leonards
NSW 2065
Australia

(Postal Address)
PO Box 405
St Leonards
NSW 1590
Australia
Tel: 00 612 9439 1488
Fax: 00 612 9439 1785
E-mail: mail@insightseminars.com.au
Website: www.insightseminars.com.au

Books

'Life 101' Everything we wish we had learned about life in school – but didn't

Do It!; A Guide to Living Your Dreams both by John Roger and Peter McWilliams, published by Thorsons

Phase Two

T'ai chi of various kinds is taught all over Britain. It's good to try a few different teachers until you find one that is right for you. Remember, t'ai chi is a way of being, not just exercise, so look for someone you feel you can respect and learn from. Information can usually be found at your local health-food shop, sports centre or library.

Books

Teach Yourself T'ai Chi by Robert Parry, published by Hodder and Stoughton

The T'ai Chi Manual by Robert Parry, published by Piatkus Books

Phase Three

If you would like to visit one of the beautiful convents or monasteries in the country there is a guide book called the *Anglican Religious Communities Yearbook* published by Cantebury Press. For information on Roman Catholic communities contact the National Religious Vocations Centre and ask them about retreats (to ensure they don't think you want to become a nun or monk). Tel: 020 74991541 or E-mail: NATRVC@aol.com

Or for more information about visiting convents you could read *New Habits* by Isabel Losada (excellent author), published by Hodder and Stoughton, You can have a copy delivered to your door if you look on the Internet at amazon.co.uk

Phase Four

Astrologers! Plenty of those around. Do the research carefully and find someone who really knows the subject. If you'd like to visit the same one I did he is Richard Norris and can be reached in London on 020 7586 2730.

Books

The Instant Astrologer by Felix Lyle and Bryan Aspland, published by Piatkus Books. *Jonathan Cainer's Guide to the Zodiac* by Jonathan Cainer, published by Piatkus Books. *Aspects in Astrology* by Sue Tompkins, published by Element Books.

Phase Five

If you are female and feeling brave:

Celebration of Woman, The Goddess c/o Paritosh Peachy
Croydon Hall
Rodhuish
Minehead
Somerset TA24 6QT
Tel: 01984 642200/Fax: 01984 640052
E-mail: paritosh@croydonhall.co.uk
Website: www.croydonhall.co.uk
Celebration of Woman, The Goddess in America
Rajyo Markman
PO Box 304
Corte Madera
California 94976
Tel: 001 415 479 9744
E-mail: rajyom@aol.com

Phase Six

Skydancing Tantric Sex UK. Experimental workshops in the tantric art and practice of sacred sexuality.

Co-ordinator: Robert Osborn
183 Godstow Road
Oxford OX2 8PG
Tel: 01865 428374
E-mail: robert-osborn@supranet.com

Books

The Art of Sexual Ecstasy by Margo Anand, published by Jeremy P Tarcher

The Art of Sexual Magic by Margo Anand, published by Piatkus Books

The Art of Everyday Ecstasy by Margo Anand, published by Piatkus Books

Phase Seven

Co-Dependents Anonymous (To discover the location of local meetings, which take place all over the UK)

The Ashburnham Community Centre
Tetcott Road, London SW110 OSH
Tel: 020 7376 8191

Books

Co-Dependency by David Stafford and Liz Hodgkinson, published by Piatkus Books

Teach Yourself to Meditate by Eric Harrison, published by Piatkus Books

Phase Eight

Colonic irrigation is offered in many alternative heath clinics. In the London area, if you'd like to visit the same one I did, she is Linzi Deayn and can be contacted on tel: 0956 502342.
For information about local practitioners contact the Association of Colonic Hydrotherapists on tel: 01202 717727.

Books

Tissue Cleansing Through Bowel Management (catchy little title!) by Dr Bernard Jenson, published by Avery Publishing Group
The Principles of Colonic Irrigation by Jillie Collings, published by Harper San Francisco

Phase Nine

For a list of re-birthing practitioners or trainings around the UK, Europe and the USA you can contact Diana Roberts on Tel: 020 7834 6641 Fax: 020 7834 6641

Books

Re-Birthing in the New Age; Celebration of Breath both by Sondra Ray, published by Celestial Arts
Rebirthing by Deike Begg, published by Thorsons

Phase Ten

Information about Dr Roger Woolger's workshops can be obtained from:
Woolger Training International
Briarwood

Long Wittenham
Oxon OX14 4QW
Tel: 01865 407996
E-mail: Woolger.uk@talk21.com

Woolger Training West
6226 Willow Lane
Boulder
Colorado 80301
USA
Tel: 001 303 527 1509
E-mail: woolger@earthnet.net

Books and Tapes
Other Lives, Other Selves by Dr Roger Woolger, published by
    Thorsons
Eternal Return (tape set) published by Sounds True (Colorado)
Many Lives, Many Masters by Dr Brian Weiss, published by
    Piatkus Books
The Tibetan Book of Living and Dying by Sogyal Rinpoche,
    published by Harper San Francisco

Phase Eleven

If you'd like to be rolfed (there is certainly more to this discipline
than I experienced) you could contact the Hale Clinic in London
and they should be able to give you a list of practitioners
nationally. Tel: 020 7631 0156.

If you would like a list of trained kahuna practitioners ring
01869 347276.

If you'd like to get stoned you can ring the British School of
Complementary Therapy at 140 Harley Street, London W1N
1AH or call them on 020 7224 2393

If you'd like a foot massage you can contact Natureworks at

16 Balderton Street, London W1 or call them and ask for chavutti thirumal on 020 7355 4036.

If you'd like to meet Terry Kingscote (neuro-muscular masseur) you can ring him care of Total Look on 020 7351 1123.

Better still if you have a husband, wife, or partner of any kind, go on a massage course with them immediately.

Phase Twelve

The co-ordinator for the anger workshop is Ruth Morris, Tel: 020 8445 7515. Soizic Ayme comes to England about five times a year to take workshops.

Or, if you are feeling angry, you could also call Insight (see Phase One).

Phase Thirteen

For NLP workshops with Richard Bandler McKenna Breen Tel: 020 7704 6604 Fax: 020 7704 1676.
E-mail: happening@mckenna-breen.com

Phase Fourteen

For angel workshops with William Bloom contact him care of:

Holistic Partnerships
10 The Murreys
Ashtead
Surrey KT21 2LU
Tel: 01372 272400
E-mail: welcome@holisticpartnerships.com

William takes regular couses of many kinds all over Britain. For other courses at the Brightlife Institute on the Isle of Man

call them up and ask for a catalogue then pick what takes your fancy (Dr Roger Woolger also takes his Past-Life workshops there) Tel: 01624 880318 Fax: 01624 880967.
E-mail: brightlife@enterprise.net

Books

Working with Angels, Fairies and Nature Spirits by William Bloom, published by Piatkus Books

Finally, a word of warning: in my quest to learn something I put a lot of research into who to go to and who not to go to. There are a lot of well-meaning people out there with dubious ideas. It may be unnecessary unsolicited advice, but please be wise and take care of yourself.

A NOTE ON THE AUTHOR

Isabel Losada, actress, singer, dancer and television producer, lives in Battersea with her long-suffering teenage daughter.